THE IMAGINATIVE WORLD OF
ALEXANDER POPE

THE IMAGINATIVE WORLD OF ALEXANDER POPE

LEOPOLD DAMROSCH, JR.

University of California Press
Berkeley · Los Angeles · London

University of California Press
Berkeley and Los Angeles, California

University of California Press, Ltd.
London, England

© 1987 by
The Regents of the University of California

Library of Congress Cataloging-in-Publication Data
Damrosch, Leopold.
 The imaginative world of Alexander Pope.

 Includes index.
  1. Pope, Alexander, 1688–1744—Criticism and
interpretation.   I. Title.
PR3634.D36 1987   821'.5   86–25080
ISBN 0-520-05975-1 (alk. paper)

Printed in the United States of America

1 2 3 4 5 6 7 8 9

Contents

Acknowledgments

I am grateful to the members of a graduate seminar at the University of Maryland who helped me think through the materials in this book, and to four readers whose advice contributed greatly to revision: Stephen Greenblatt, Frederick Keener, Earl Miner, and my wife, Joyce Van Dyke. I also owe a debt of gratitude to an anonymous reader for the press, whose detailed critique alerted me to many points that needed improvement or obliteration. Perhaps opposition is true friendship, as Blake said.

A Note on References

Pope's poems are cited by line number from the Twickenham edition, abbreviated *TE: The Poems of Alexander Pope*, ed. John Butt et al., 11 vols. (London: Methuen, 1939–1969). Quotations from the letters, abbreviated *Corr.*, are taken from *The Correspondence of Alexander Pope*, ed. George Sherburn, 5 vols. (Oxford: Clarendon, 1956). Quotations from the *Dunciad*, except when otherwise indicated, are from the final four-book version of 1743. The short titles *Epistle* and *Satire*, followed by an identifying Roman numeral, refer to Pope's imitations of Horace. *Epilogues* I and II refer to the two parts of the *Epilogue to the Satires*. Poems by readily available major poets like Dryden and Swift are cited by line numbers only; for other writers fuller references are given. For the sake of consistency, I use italics for all titles of poems, whether short or long.

Rashly perhaps, I have ventured to modernize Pope's capital letters and italics. Without doubt they had significance for him, though (like his contemporaries) he used them more sparingly as time went on. But they tend to distance the poems from modern readers, who are accustomed after all to reading Shakespeare and Milton in modern typography, and I have sought to eliminate them as an unnecessary barrier. (Pat Rogers says in his edition of Swift's poems, "The modes of emphasis thus attained are not recapturable simply by following the identical typographical conventions.") I have also expanded endings in accordance with modern practice (*stooped* rather than *stoop'd*) and have occasionally modernized spelling when the distinction seemed irrelevant (*money* for *mony* and *bias* for *byas*, but not *satire* for *satyr*, since Pope's spelling preserves an etymological assumption and a pronunciation).

INTRODUCTION

Reconstructing Pope's World

Alexander Pope, the greatest English poet of the eighteenth century, died in 1744, almost two and a half centuries ago. Reading Pope is necessarily an act of imaginative recovery, not so much of details (Sappho is Lady Mary, Timon isn't Chandos) as of a world. My theme is the *Lebenswelt* that Pope creates in his writings, in its reciprocal relation with the world that he shared with his contemporaries, but above all in its own phenomenological fullness. I am particularly interested in the ways in which Pope's imaginative world attempts to encompass an increasingly recalcitrant external world. Reluctantly but certainly it participates in the relinquishing of traditional symbolic categories that marks the birth of the modern age. We are accustomed to think of Pope as a committed "Ancient" and of Defoe, who gets a couple of jabs in the *Dunciad,* as a "Modern," but just as Defoe is the first modern novelist, there is a sense in which Pope is the first modern poet.

Let it be told, Pope proclaims in the *Epistle to Arbuthnot,*

> that not in fancy's maze he wandered long,
> But stooped to truth, and moralized his song.
> (340–41)

"The term," says Pope's friend and editor Warburton, glossing *stooped,* "is from falconry; and the allusion is to one of those untamed birds of spirit, which sometimes wantons at large in airy circles before it regards, or *stoops to,* its prey."[1]

---

1. William Warburton's edition of Pope's *Works* (1751), IV, 39. For Pope's apparent source in Denham see *TE* IV, 120n.

Whether or not Warburton is right about the allusion, Pope certainly intends a paradox in descending to truth, which is normally thought of as exalted. In a ringing platonizing manifesto Sidney proclaimed that nature's world "is brazen, the poets only deliver a golden."[2] By Pope's time the golden world was looking all too unreal, and he saw no choice but to stoop to the brazen. "Urged by thee," he tells his friend Bolingbroke at the end of the *Essay on Man,* "I turned the tuneful art / From sounds to things, from fancy to the heart" (IV. 391–92).

Like most people in his time Pope thought of reality as objective and stable; he and Swift constantly derided alternative ways of seeing as insane. But of course there is also a sense in which his world was profoundly subjective. So were the worlds of his contemporaries, and so are those constructed by modern interpreters, even if they have begun to replace the Augustan World Picture with more exciting generalizations like Power and Desire. The rich pictorial descriptions in his poems are in part attempts to give language the determinate veracity of visual images. But no one today believes in such veracity. As the philosopher Nelson Goodman has said, the picture theory of language has been replaced by the language theory of pictures. Each artist, and of course each writer too, uses conventional devices to represent a particular version of reality: "None tells us *the* way the world is, but each of them tells us *a* way the world is."[3]

In historical hindsight Pope's assertions of objective order look like a defensive campaign against modern subjectivity and ad hoc value systems. Hindsight, however, should not blind us to the earnestness of the effort; it would be a massive distortion to pose an "official" Pope who defends order against a "real" Pope who subverts it. But I shall argue that the order Pope seeks is less fully achieved than he

2. Philip Sidney, *An Apology for Poetry,* in *English Critical Essays,* ed. Edmund D. Jones, World's Classics (London: Oxford University Press, 1947), p. 7.
3. "The Way the World Is," in Goodman, *Problems and Projects* (Indianapolis: Bobbs-Merrill, 1972), p. 31.

hoped, or than many of his modern interpreters believe. And I shall argue further that his notions of order were grounded far more in social experience than in metaphysics, in contrast to those of Milton before him or Coleridge after him. In some ways this places Pope more in the novelistic tradition than in the poetic; Gray and Collins are far more "Miltonic," and more congenial to the Romantics, than Pope is. But Pope still *wants* a metaphysical order to guarantee the social order, and his writing is peculiarly open to the inherent conflicts in both.

Ever since the Romantics, it has been a commonplace that the poet stands outside his society, aware that it may need poets for its spokesmen, but that it does not want them. From Blake and Coleridge down to Yeats and Lowell, the poet has constantly tried to speak for his fellows, but perceived his career as a diminution and exclusion, in which his talent could not conform itself to the way of the world. At one extreme, in Baudelaire for instance, this failure of connection defines the poet as a being of a different species, the albatross whose mighty wings impede him from ordinary walking: *"Ses ailes de géant l'empêchent de marcher."* At another extreme, as in Stevens, the professional and the poetic lives are severed by a kind of voluntary schizophrenia, and the poems occupy a realm far different from the ordinary evenings that call them forth.

The roots of this attitude can be discerned by the middle of the eighteenth century, at a time when many people began to feel that the old Renaissance harmonies—of self, of society, of symbolic meaning—were no longer persuasive. Gray and Collins, in the 1740s, are famous for the uneasiness with which they viewed their own modest achievement, in contrast with the literally inimitable monuments of the past.[4] Pope, very differently, has been treated by scholars as the last Renaissance poet, if not indeed the last Roman one: a mag-

4. See esp. Walter Jackson Bate, *The Burden of the Past and the English Poet* (Cambridge, Mass.: Harvard University Press, 1970), and John E. Sitter, *Literary Loneliness in Mid Eighteenth-Century England* (Ithaca: Cornell University Press, 1982).

isterial spokesman for his culture even as he stood apart from its vulgar failures (bad poetry, manners, politics, and financial innovations). Swift too, languishing in bitter exile in Dublin, has been elevated to centrality in his art if not his life; he and Pope stand unchallenged as the twin stars of the eighteenth-century firmament.

The present book has a double purpose. One is to continue an investigation, already begun on other fronts, of the problems of representing experience at the beginning of the modern age, when traditional religious, philosophical, and aesthetic systems were breaking down.[5] The second purpose is to consider Pope not as the still center around which an Augustan Age revolved, but as an early instance of the modern poet, who claims to speak for his culture but lacks a secure institutional or cultural basis for doing so.

All art is vicarious, of course, but it often succeeds in concealing its vicariousness; even while he writes for a "fit audience though few," Milton speaks as if from the center of a true culture. Wordsworth with his quasi-religious posture manages something similar, and Dryden as laureate takes for granted his right to do so. Pope frequently admits that he fails, and the honesty of that recognition seems strikingly modern. He began by thinking of himself as the English Virgil, and modern scholars of the eighteenth century have amply examined—indeed have celebrated—the symbolic claims that he makes in early poems such as *Windsor-Forest*. In mid-career, however, Pope dropped this exalted plan, and apart

---

5. When I first began to think about this project a decade ago, I imagined a single book with an introductory chapter on Pope, several chapters on the novelists and other writers, and a final chapter on Blake. A trial version of the Blake chapter soon developed a life of its own and became *Symbol and Truth in Blake's Myth* (1980). The exploration of poetic and religious symbolism which that book entailed then influenced my reflections on the novelists, which were extended backward to Puritan narratives and became *God's Plot and Man's Stories: Studies in the Fictional Imagination from Milton to Fielding* (1985). Meanwhile I began to work at last on the chapter on Pope, and this raised so many questions that it too has evolved into a book. I hope to complete my investigation of the period between Pope and Blake in a final book, tentatively entitled *Fictions of Reality in the Age of Hume and Johnson*.

from the ambitious *Essay on Man* he "stooped to truth" there-
after in a series of satires that are bitterly critical of his culture
and remarkably explicit about his own marginal and insecure
relation to it. Even as he tries to describe his world literally
and accurately—the new ideal of "truth" eschews Renaissance symbols and tropes—he finds himself alienated from
the world he wants to describe. Aspiring to be a spokesman
for his culture, he cannot keep from betraying the fact that
he is excluded from that culture. There is a further paradox:
marginal though he felt himself to be, Pope seemed to many
contemporaries (Johnson for instance) to be the very type of
privilege and security. So what is at issue is Pope's ambiguous
self-image, which seems characteristic of many modern writers: in some ways he was indeed central and privileged, in
others alienated and thwarted.

Similar kinds of uneasiness are apparent if one focuses on
the history of ideas rather than the history of culture. Instead
of the late-Renaissance *concordia discors* which scholars used
to promote, one may well be struck by an unsettling frag-
mentation of the "intellectual world," as Locke calls it in the
final words of the *Essay:*

> A man can employ his thoughts about nothing, but either the
> contemplation of *things* themselves, for the discovery of truth;
> or about the things in his own power, which are his own *ac-
> tions,* for the attainment of his own ends; or the *signs* the mind
> makes use of both in the one and the other, and the right
> ordering of them, for its clearer information. All which three
> . . . being *toto coelo* different, they seemed to me to be the three
> great provinces of the intellectual world, wholly separate and
> distinct one from another.[6]

Pope is not much bothered about epistemology, and tends to
take the world of things for granted, but he is certainly wor-
ried about the relation of moral action to the world of things,
and like the rest of his contemporaries he puzzles over the
authority and reliability of signs.

To clarify the aims and scope of my undertaking, let me

6. John Locke, *An Essay concerning Human Understanding,* IV.xxi.5.

try to situate it in the context of modern Pope studies. Ever since the 1940s these have followed two parallel tracks, criticism exploring the fictiveness of art, and scholarship establishing its basis in historical fact. William K. Wimsatt, writing in the heyday of the New Criticism, called the English Augustans "laughing poets of a heightened unreality" and defined their achievement as "the art of teasing unreality with the redeeming force of wit." Stooping to truth, from this point of view, is an unfortunate falling away. Wimsatt deplores the lines about turning from fancy to the heart ("The pity is that he was more or less telling the truth"), derides Gay's town eclogues for their circumstantial detail ("I believe his *Trivia* is a poem highly prized by historians of the city"), and declares his admiration for "the Augustan repertory of pregnant junctures, metaphoric insinuations, covert symbols, hinted puns, sly rhymes, cheating jingles and riddles."[7]

The New Critical interest in artifice is very different from the postmodern: it emphasizes coherence above all things, and harmonizes easily with the 1950s scholarly campaign to establish Pope's affinity with tradition. Wimsatt himself makes the connection in the final lines of his essay: "Augustan poetry was a retirement from areas of 'nature' that were beginning to look sterile, a spirited rearguard action in the retreat of Renaissance humanism before the march of science" (p. 164). Many a modern academic has continued to fight that lost battle. If I sometimes confront the older critics in an adversarial way, it is because their influence still pervades eighteenth-century studies, and because their fundamental assumptions need examination.

In a classic 1949 essay, "Wit and Poetry and Pope," Maynard Mack celebrated Pope as a poetic master in New Critical terms; the following year Mack published his edition of the *Essay on Man*, which demonstrates Pope's deep immersion in Renaissance ideas and might almost make one think (as Reu-

7. "The Augustan Mode in English Poetry," first published in 1953, quoted from Wimsatt, *Hateful Contraries: Studies in Literature and Criticism* (Lexington: University of Kentucky Press, 1966), pp. 158, 154, 156, 152.

ben Brower remarked) that *Paradise Lost* was written by Pope.[8]
When he stooped to truth, Pope wrote in telling detail about
scores of his contemporaries, and Mack's later work has
splendidly illuminated them. But Pope's achievement is still
said to be based in an idealized realm of classical and Biblical
harmony:

> Pope's poetry, like the book he was accustomed to call Scrip-
> ture, begins with a garden and ends with a city. To be sure,
> the city in Revelation is a holy city, whereas the city in the
> *Dunciad* of 1743 is a version of Augustan London. Yet both are
> in an important sense visionary, and beyond the *Dunciad*'s city
> looms another that is more abiding: the eternal City of man's
> recurring dream of the civilized community, only one of whose
> names is Rome.[9]

Among recent scholars who continue to see Pope as the noblest Roman of them all, some have been explicit in their
nostalgia for a lost ideal: "Form is the glory of Augustan art,
and many of us—though the drab or jarring monuments of
our own less gracious times suggest that we are a diminishing
fellowship—continue to find it congenial."[10]

Mack himself, as recently as 1985, has identified in Pope's
poetry "a kind of luxuriant flowering of certain Renaissance
traditions and values in the face of the crescent edge that was
to prove to be Romanticism." One might not easily suspect
that he is talking here about the *Dunciad*. More largely, Mack
has continued to idealize Pope's garden-grotto, and to use it
as an occasion for his own meditations, with a solemn nostalgia that demands to be heard in its full amplitude:

8. "Wit and Poetry and Pope: Some Observations on His Imagery" is
reprinted in *Eighteenth-Century English Literature: Modern Essays in Criticism*,
ed. James L. Clifford (New York: Oxford University Press, 1959), pp. 21–41;
The Essay on Man is vol. III-i of the Twickenham edition. Brower, "Form and
Defect of Form in Eighteenth-Century Poetry: A Memorandum," in *Eighteenth-Century Studies in Honor of Donald F. Hyde*, ed. W. H. Bond (New York:
Grolier Club, 1970), p. 366.

9. *The Garden and the City: Retirement and Politics in the Later Poetry of Pope,
1731–1743* (Toronto: University of Toronto Press, 1969), p. 3.

10. Martin C. Battestin, *The Providence of Wit: Aspects of Form in Augustan
Literature and the Arts* (Oxford: Clarendon, 1974), p. vii.

Was it simply that it reminded him of the famous caves, often furnished with a nymph or nymphs, of which he had read in such favorite poets as Ovid and Homer? Can the murmur of its waters have helped induce in him, as the sound of water is often said to do, states of trance or meditation, like those we hear of in the testimony of other poets, when one is laid asleep in body to become a living soul, or sinks so deep in hearing music that you are the music while the music lasts? Did he pause to consider that a teasing symbolism might lurk in making the main walkway between the river and his garden a sort of dark underworld passage, where, as in the *Aeneid* he knew so well and the *Odyssey* he was soon to translate, the lost wanderer looking for his home must forgo the familiar world to consult a world of shadows and a blind seer named Teiresias or a prophet-father named Anchises? Could one only gain, or regain, the lost Garden, after passing through a darkness filled like life itself with "an undistinguishable Mixture of Realities and Imagery." . . . Which—if any—of these connections or intentions the poet actually entertained, we have no way of guessing. Perhaps none.[11]

Against the glowing world of traditional eighteenth-century literary scholarship, one might wish to set a distinguished historian's summary (published only a year after "Wit and Poetry and Pope"): "There was an edge to life in the eighteenth century which is hard for us to recapture. In every class there is the same taut neurotic quality—the fantastic gambling and drinking, the riots, brutality and violence, and everywhere and always a constant sense of death."[12] This is the scary world of *Roderick Random*, the disturbing social reality that assailed Pope at every turn and elicited reproofs like Swift's: "You advise me right, not to trouble myself about the world. But oppression tortures me" (*Corr.* III, 492).

While traditional eighteenth-century scholarship has continued to ponder the old questions—Pope's indebtedness to

---

11. Maynard Mack, *Alexander Pope: A Life* (New York: Norton, 1985), pp. 473, 365. "An undistinguishable Mixture of Realities and Imagery" is a comment made by a visitor to Pope's garden.

12. J. H. Plumb, *England in the Eighteenth Century* (Harmondsworth: Penguin, 1950), p. 95.

Horace or Lucretius, his deviations from Homer, the unity of
An Essay on Criticism, the classical tropes that universalize
Hervey or Walpole—the time seems ripe for the New Historicism to invade this field, and signs of it have begun to appear. But the New Historicism would be no better than the
old if it merely extrapolated vast cultural syntheses from a
few passages in Althusser or Foucault or E. P. Thompson, or
if it formulated the whole experience of the past in terms of
power and subversion. Marxism, which claims a greater theoretical consistency, is not necessarily a reliable guide: Thompson himself has criticized "definitions which can be swiftly
reached within theoretical practice and without the fatigue of
historical investigation."[13] And it is a rare scholar (I am not
one) who can master social history deeply enough to prove
that literary texts are direct expressions of institutional structures. What the New Historicism teaches at its best is a scholarly skepticism and humility, recognizing that the life of the
past is densely complicated by factors which are almost impossible to recover today, and that what went unsaid was
often as significant as what was said.

Here we must consider the latest trend in literary studies,
the investigation of ideology in literature. With this I am entirely sympathetic, if ideology is defined loosely as the socially conditioned framework through which one experiences
and understands one's world, the whole mass of assumptions, sometimes acknowledged and sometimes unper-
ceived, that frame a person's existence. I would dissent however from a sociological definition of ideology as "ideas
serving as weapons for social interests," since the implications of *weapon* are needlessly aggressive (though of course
ideas sometimes are weapons). I shall not accuse Pope of false
consciousness, "thought that is alienated from the real social
being of the thinker,"[14] since I do not feel qualified to define

13. "Eighteenth-Century English Society: Class Struggle without Class?"
Social History, 3 (1978), 147.
14. Peter L. Berger and Thomas Luckmann, *The Social Construction of Reality* (New York: Doubleday, Anchor, 1967), p. 6.

Pope's "real" social being and to determine which aspects of his thought are "alienated" from it. And I see no point in taking an accusatory stance toward someone who was born three centuries ago. There is something incongruous in fiery Marxist accusations issued by comfortable academics who are building careers in departments of literature. Not all contradictions are confined to past ideologies.

In the same year as Mack's biography, Laura Brown published a brisk polemic that discovers, in poem after poem, "a tension that signals the central ideological problems of Pope's poetry." The problems in each case resolve into the same thing, the commodification of life, which emergent capitalism is supposed to have imposed, and the attendant growth of imperialism. "As a consistent advocate of the beliefs and ambitions of the capitalist landlords and of an imperialist consensus, Pope must be scrutinized, doubted and demystified." There may be a sense in which Pope spoke the language of the commercial interests he thought he was criticizing, but I believe that the tensions in his poems derive from many sources—psychological and intellectual as well as ideological or political—and that Brown's critique is unacceptably reductive. A tendentious exposition of selected passages of imagery is simply not enough to demonstrate that "Augustan" ideology is "an ideal constructed from the superimposition of an abstract and neo-classical system of aesthetic valuation upon a concrete programme for mercantile capitalist economic expansion."[15]

My own view is that, as many sociologists argue, a society harbors multiple ideologies rather than a monolithic one, and that an individual may be partly inside and partly outside of any of them.[16] I am drawn to Alfred Schutz's account of "multiple realities," grounded in a phenomenological sociology of knowledge rather than in Marxism.[17] And I want to insist

15. *Alexander Pope* (Oxford: Blackwell, 1985), pp. 69, 3, 124.

16. See Peter L. Berger, *Invitation to Sociology: A Humanistic Perspective* (New York: Doubleday, Anchor, 1963), pp. 111 ff.

17. *Collected Papers*, I, *The Problem of Social Reality* (The Hague: Nijhoff, 1967), pp. 207–33.

upon the warning against reductive analysts offered by the great Marxist critic Lucien Goldmann:

> Since they considered the work as merely the reflection of social reality, they were much more successful the more they dealt with minor creative works, which reproduce reality with the least amount of re-ordering; furthermore, even in the most appropriate instances, they break up the content of the work into fragments, concentrating on highlighting whatever is a direct reproduction of reality and disregarding everything which has to do with imaginative creation.[18]

Current literary fashion seems to be tending to a total contextualism, in which any text, "literary" or otherwise, is to be interpreted in exactly the same way. To disapprove of this trend is not merely a sign of reactionary literary values. Many historians are skeptical of it. In a recent essay addressed to this issue, John Patrick Diggins argues persuasively that texts create their own contexts: "The texts' 'meaning' may have as much to do with the internal demands of mind as the external pressures of the cultural or political environment."[19] Carl Schorske, in his distinguished study of Viennese culture, says similarly, "Historians had been too long content to use the artifacts of high culture as mere illustrative reflections of political or social developments, or to relativize them to ideology."[20] It would be ironic if literary scholars were to treat literature in ways that historians deplore as reductive.

If one descends from the heady abstractions of theory, moreover, one has to recognize the extreme difficulty of any attempt to recover the past. It is a function of our own historical limitations, not of accidental failures of diligence or imagination, that such reconstructions must always remain

18. "'Genetic Structuralism' in the Sociology of Literature," tr. Petra Morrison, in *Sociology of Literature and Drama,* ed. Elizabeth Burns and Tom Burns (Harmondsworth: Penguin, 1973), p. 120.

19. "The Oyster and the Pearl: The Problem of Contextualism in Intellectual History," *History and Theory,* 23 (1984), 153. See also, in the same issue, Dominick LaCapra, "Is Everyone a *Mentalité* Case? Transference and the 'Culture' Concept," 296–311.

20. *Fin-de-Siècle Vienna: Politics and Culture* (New York: Knopf, 1980), p. xxi.

tentative and incomplete. Pope's *Epistle to Augustus* (*Epistle* II.i) deploys a series of sustained ironies that depend upon the disparity between George II, christened George Augustus, and the Roman emperor. But for Pope and his readers George II was simply the king, a living presence whom no amount of research can now recreate. For us, both Caesar Augustus and George Augustus are remote and "literary" figures. When Margaret Thatcher and Ronald Reagan have faded into a distant past, they will have become what George Augustus is now.

And of course these considerations are not limited to politics. "Belinda dressing," Warton remarks, "is painted in as pompous a manner as Achilles arming." An eighteenth-century lady at her dressing table has a "period" quality today that could not have existed for Pope's readers in 1712, or even for Warton in 1756. *The Rape of the Lock*, Warton continues, is "the best satire extant" and "contains the truest and liveliest picture of modern life."[21] Or as Johnson more comprehensively expresses it:

> The subject of the poem is an event below the common incidents of common life; nothing real is introduced that is not seen so often as to be no longer regarded, yet the whole detail of a female day is here brought before us invested with so much art of decoration that, though nothing is disguised, everything is striking, and we feel all the appetite of curiosity for that from which we have a thousand times turned fastidiously away.[22]

For us Belinda's ceremonious toilette is filtered through temporal and cultural remoteness, tinged perhaps with the glowing images of Fragonard and Watteau (though recent feminist writers have had a good deal to say about that). Warton and Johnson needed Homeric devices to make them pay attention to so commonplace a subject; today, when Pope's world and

21. Joseph Warton, *An Essay on the Writings and Genius of Pope* (1756), I, 224, 246.

22. Samuel Johnson, *Life of Pope*, in *Lives of the English Poets*, ed. G. B. Hill (Oxford: Clarendon, 1905), III, 234.

Homer's have both receded into the past and are both "literary" in the same sense, the gulf between Belinda and Achilles has narrowed.

Whatever scholarship may recover of eighteenth-century contexts, we are left with the partly real, partly fictive world generated by the poems themselves. As literary criticism moves away from formalism, which always finds a way to find form, we see more clearly that eighteenth-century literature exhibits, in the words of a recent commentator, "conflict between smaller balance and larger disorder."[23] It is still a rare Pope scholar who will admit that modern interpretations of (for instance) the *Essay on Man* "are a good deal more coherent, more consistent, more fully integrated than the poem itself."[24] Such a recognition is salutary, indeed essential, if we are to appreciate the energies and conflicts in Pope's writing. As is well known, Pope composed his poems by a process of *bricolage*, assembling couplets and larger fragments into ever-revised wholes. The wholes thus assembled are quite openly built upon gaps and paradoxes, as in Swift's ironic critique of his own satire: "Whatever philosopher or projector can find out an art to solder and patch up the flaws and imperfections of nature, will deserve much better of mankind, and teach us a more useful science, than that so much in present esteem, of widening and exposing them."[25] The goal was to use art to get beyond art. "In the cunning, truth itself's a lie" (*To Cobham*, 127). But only in the dishonestly cunning. The role of the satirist, like that of the philosopher whose robes he sometimes dons, is to strip bare the lie and show the truth beneath.

I shall argue in the end that any order Pope achieved was more rhetorical than structural, and that his growing sense of an unstable world was complicated by a desire to affirm

23. Peter Hughes, "Restructuring Literary History: Implications for the Eighteenth Century," *New Literary History*, 8 (1977), 265.

24. Miriam Leranbaum, *Alexander Pope's "Opus Magnum,"* 1729–1744 (Oxford: Clarendon, 1977), p. 38.

25. Jonathan Swift, *A Tale of a Tub*, "A Digression concerning Madness," in *Gulliver's Travels and Other Writings*, ed. Louis A. Landa (Boston: Houghton Mifflin, 1960), p. 333.

stability. Martin Price long ago stressed "the dialectical excess as much as the balance and moderation of the Augustans."[26] His study was a valuable corrective to idealizations of order, but it produced a strangely Blakean Pope, urging transcendence where Pope stressed limitation, and borrowing Blake's term *selfhood*, which is the hypertrophy of reason or limitation, to gloss Pope's *pride*, which in Blakean terms is really healthy energy and desire. I shall argue that whatever may have been true for the Romantics, dialectic was not a viable mode of reconciliation for Pope: he had too deep a commitment to a hierarchy whose permanent structures admitted of no dialectical progression. Experience kept on disappointing and thwarting him, of course, and his attempts to cope with that partly understood perplexity are at the center of my study.

Rather than proceeding poem by poem as most writers on Pope do,[27] committing themselves thereby to a set of inherited questions and expectations, I offer a thematic study. Any adequate account of the poems, as Pope's admirers have always known, must take account of his emotional attachments, physical constitution, religion, politics, and even personal finances. My aim is to show that these matters are not detachable "background," but pervade his imaginative world. A thematic approach does run the risk of distorting chronology and ignoring differences at various stages of a long career. I have tried at every point to take account of such differences. But I believe there is also much to be said for an attempt to see the poet whole. My subject is the Pope who is distributed throughout his writings, in a way that was entirely apparent to his contemporaries. Henry Brooke wrote to him in 1739,

> There is one great and consistent genius evident through the whole of your works, but that genius seems smaller by being

26. *To the Palace of Wisdom: Studies in Order and Energy from Dryden to Blake* (New York: Doubleday, Anchor, 1965), p. vii.

27. This is the procedure even in two valuable surveys that examine Pope's personality in his poems: Frederick M. Keener, *An Essay on Pope* (New York: Columbia University Press, 1974), and Dustin H. Griffin, *Alexander Pope: The Poet in the Poems* (Princeton: Princeton University Press, 1978).

divided, by being looked upon only in parts, and that deception makes greatly against you; you are truly but one man
through many volumes, and yet the eye can attend you but in
one single view; each distinct performance is as the performance of a separate author, and no one being large enough to
contain you in your full dimensions, though perfectly drawn,
you appear too much in miniature.

(Corr. IV, 199)

Pope's letters are indispensable, though of course carefully
calculated for effect, and also concealing vast gaps: writing to
Caryll he mentions Cobham as "a friend, whom I've known
ten years without writing three letters to, and shall probably
never write another to, yet esteem as much as any friend he
has" (*Corr.* III, 474). In addition I draw, more than most critics,
upon the writings of Pope's contemporaries. Commentators
like Spence, Warburton, Warton, and Johnson can tell us
much about the assumptions of eighteenth-century readers;
the first two were closely associated with Pope personally,
and Johnson still seems to me the most acute and thought-
provoking of Pope's critics. The poets too are invaluable, and
not just in the "source" passages that get into the Twickenham footnotes. Gay, Swift, Young, Addison, Lady Mary, Tickell, Parnell, Hughes, Harte, Broome, Fenton, and the rest
help to throw light on Pope's preoccupations and poetic
choices. They are every bit as valuable, in providing a context
for the poems, as are much-studied masterpieces such as the
Aeneid and *Paradise Lost.* I quote especially often from Pope's
close friend Swift, whose poems are still not as well known
as they deserve to be, and in their muscular bluntness form
an interesting complement to Pope's. But in this age of revised canons, it is worth adding that the canon remains much
as it was. Introducing his fascinating study of Grub Street,
Pat Rogers remarks, "Ten years' research convinced me that
the gap in talent between, say, Pope and Leonard Welsted
was underestimated rather than overstated in the received
wisdom about the subject."[28] Pope really is enormously more

28. *Hacks and Dunces: Pope, Swift and Grub Street* (London: Methuen, 1980),
p. 15.

skillful and interesting than Hughes and Lyttelton and Mallet, all of whom were his friends and therefore, by definition, not dunces.

Pope wrote sarcastically of commentators on Homer, "Their remarks are rather philosophical, historical, geographical, allegorical, or in short rather any thing than critical and poetical."[29] Some modern scholars are in danger of emulating Pope's Bentley:

> Turn what they will to verse, their toil is vain,
> Critics like me shall make it prose again.
> (*Dunciad* IV.213–14)

Pope's interest in gardens is usually treated in historicist or iconographic terms, but from his letters one gets a strong sense of sheer pleasure in shade, color, soft air, and ease. So also with his poetry: it does promote ideas, but it comes to rest in the unforgettable phrase, the perfect cadence. In exploring the world that Pope creates, I want above all to be true to the energy and vividness with which he *embodies* its complex life:

> The spider's touch, how exquisitely fine!
> Feels at each thread, and lives along the line.
> (*Essay on Man* I.217–18)

It is that gift that gives continued existence to Pope's imaginative world, when those of able writers like Addison and Gay—let alone Mallet and Lyttelton and Hughes—are forever lost.

---

29. Footnote to the opening lines of the *Iliad*, TE VII, 82.

PART ONE

EXPERIENCE

1

The Shaping of a Self-Image

More than any poet before him, Pope makes his personality and experience central to his poems. He does not celebrate or deplore his uniqueness like a post-Romantic poet; he could not have written Lowell's "Shed skin will never find another wearer," or even Blake's "O why was I born with a different face?"[1] Yet Pope does manage to tell a great deal about himself. There is far more subjectivity in Wordsworth's *Prelude*, but far less personal detail: we learn very little about Wordsworth's parents, his friends, his way of working, even his physical appearance. Pope increasingly presents such matters, and his career as a poet can be justly described as "his gradual discovery that he was his own best subject."[2] This is not simply a matter of egotism. Pope becomes his own subject because he is, in the philosophical sense, *the* subject. Nothing else seems adequate to hold together the kaleidoscopic details of lived experience.

Ever since the Romantics there has been a tendency to suppose that each person strives to express a unique and innate disposition. As a psychologist has optimistically put it, "It is within the nature of the individual to actualize himself and become whatever he is meant to be."[3] That insinuat-

1. Robert Lowell, "Soft Wood," in Lowell, *Selected Poems* (New York: Farrar, Straus and Giroux, 1977), p. 131; Blake, poem in a letter to Thomas Butts, 16 Aug. 1803, in *The Complete Poetry and Prose of William Blake*, ed. David V. Erdman (Berkeley: University of California Press, 1982), p. 733.
2. Dustin H. Griffin, *Alexander Pope: The Poet in the Poems* (Princeton: Princeton University Press, 1978), p. 100.
3. Clark E. Moustakas, "True Experience and the Self," in *The Self: Explorations in Personal Growth*, ed. Moustakas (New York: Harper, 1974), p. 8.

ing "meant to be" is an inheritance from Rousseau's secular-ization of Calvinism, and would have made no sense at all to Pope. Like many people in the eighteenth century—Addison or Hume or Gibbon or Franklin—he consciously put together a self, with much planning and revision, that might answer to his own hopes as well as to the expectations of others. The effort could not, of course, be wholly successful, and some very interesting energies and contradictions are revealed at the points of slippage. But it would be wrong to grant the contradictions a privileged status, to imagine that they are more authentic than the harmonious structure he worked so hard to build. In fact, the self Pope invented was above all a social self: he was an outsider who longed to be an insider, and a man of sharp passions who sought to define himself by communal standards of order and control.

There are two crucial facts in Pope's development: his early sense of privilege and potential achievement, and his physi-cal disabilities. He was the much-loved child of elderly par-ents, born when his mother was forty-six and his father forty-two (there was a considerably older half-sister), and as Leslie Stephen says, "From the earliest period he seems to have been a domestic idol."[4] In later childhood, however, Pope contracted tuberculosis of the spine, which halted his growth at four feet six inches and condemned him to hunchbacked deformity and illness. In the poems, references to his condi-tion are carefully wry:

> Weak though I am of limb, and short of sight,
> Far from a lynx, and not a giant quite.
>
> (*Epistle* I.i.49–50)

The old dramatist Wycherley referred affectionately to Pope's "little, tender, and crazy carcase" (*Corr.* I, 55), and years later Pope himself wrote more grimly of "the wretched carcase I am annexed to" (*Corr.* III, 444). In a letter written in his early twenties he suggested ironically that two diminutive men having lately died, "I may now without vanity esteem myself

4. *Alexander Pope* (New York: Harper, 1902), p. 2.

the least thing like a man in England" (*Corr.* I, 89). That is to say, he is not the thing least like a man, but the least thing that one could still call a man.

As the term *annexed* suggests, Pope seems more than most people to have thought of his body as an object distinct from himself. Even in jest, he tended to describe it as an inept artifact: "As to my health, I'm in a very odd course for the pain in my side: I mean a course of brickbats and tiles, which they apply to me piping hot, morning and night; and sure it is very satisfactory to one who loves architecture at his heart, to be built round in his very bed. My body may properly at this time be called a human structure" (*Corr.* II, 17). In more serious moods he explicitly invokes a dualism of soul and body, as when he writes to Bathurst:

> Let me tell you my life in thought and imagination is as much superior to my life in action and reality as the best soul can be to the vilest body. I find the latter grows yearly so much worse and more declining that I believe I shall soon scruple to carry it about to others; it will become almost a carcase, and as unpleasing as those which they say the spirits now and then use for vehicles to frighten folks.
>
> (*Corr.* III, 156)

Pope goes on to say that his condition makes him a poor guest who would do better to stay at home, and he adds significantly, "I begin to resolve upon the whole rather to turn myself back again into myself" (p. 157).

Beyond the disgust and shame Pope felt at his weak and misshapen "carcase," he had to endure the constant pressure of more or less serious ailments—"this long disease, my life" as he called it in the *Epistle to Arbuthnot* (132).[5] His letters are full of remarks like "I have been in almost roaring pain, with a violent rheumatism in my shoulder" (*Corr.* III, 176) and "I am now getting out of a violent fit of the headache" (p. 177).

5. Pope's medical history is interestingly surveyed by Marjorie Nicolson and G. S. Rousseau, *"This Long Disease, My Life": Alexander Pope and the Sciences* (Princeton: Princeton University Press, 1968), pp. 7–82. See also Maynard Mack, *Alexander Pope: A Life* (New York: Norton, 1985), pp. 153–58.

The drastic medical methods of the time were hardly palliative: "A constant course of evacuations and plasters and phlebotomy and blisters, etc., etc., etc." (p. 190). It is this very topic that elicited Swift's famous comment about life as a ridiculous tragedy: "From your own letters as well as one I just had from Mr. Gay, I have by no means a good account of your health. The common saying of life being a farce is true in every sense but the most important one, for it is a ridiculous tragedy, which is the worst kind of composition" (*Corr.* III, 190). In his letters to Swift, Pope often expressed envy of the simple ability to ride and walk energetically. Spence once saw him at Oxford when a coach mishap had forced him to walk three miles, "quite fatigued to death, with a thin face lengthened at least two inches beyond its usual appearance" (*Corr.* III, 493). At another time Pope wrote that he could not visit Swift in Ireland because the doctors advised that seasickness would kill him (*Corr.* IV, 179).

Such a man, as Mack has eloquently shown, was compelled "to extract ornament from inconvenience of a rather painful kind—to find, or make, some ground for pride in all too visible defects."[6] Since the defects were indeed so visible, ordinary vanities were effectively ruled out. There is an unforgettable moment in *Villette* when Lucy Snowe sees a group of strangers approaching and suddenly realizes that it is a reflection in a mirror: "For the first, and perhaps only time in my life, I enjoyed the 'giftie' of seeing myself as others see me. . . . It brought a jar of discord, a pang of regret; it was not flattering, yet, after all, I ought to be thankful; it might have been worse."[7] If Pope could have known the Burns line, he would have applied it differently: it was his goal *always* to see himself as others saw him. One can easily imagine the pain with which he included an admirer's consolation in *Poems on Several Occasions* (1717):

6. Maynard Mack, *The Garden and the City: Retirement and Politics in the Later Poetry of Pope, 1731–1743* (Toronto: University of Toronto Press, 1969), p. 61.

7. Charlotte Brontë, *Villette*, ed. Margaret Lane (London: Dent, Everyman's Library, 1957), ch. 20, p. 189.

Thy wit in vain the feeble critic gnaws,
While the hard metal breaks the serpent's jaws.
Grieve not, my friend, that spite and brutal rage
At once thy person and thy muse engage;
Our virtues only from our selves can flow,
Health, strength, and beauty to blind chance we owe.
But heav'n indulgent to thy nobler part,
In thy fair mind expressed the nicest art:
Nature too busy to regard the whole,
Forgets the body, to adorn the soul.[8]

Nature, whose goodness Pope always celebrated, was some-how careless of his person, and made it necessary to regard him almost as a disembodied mind or soul.

Pope's poetry is intensely public, in that not just the poet himself, but other people as well, are consistently presented as seen from outside. This is true even of moments of apparent privacy, like Belinda's toilette. Not only is Belinda expressly arming herself for social combat, but she is assisted by a "priestess" maid, watched over by attentive sylphs, and continuously aware of her external image, as represented by the mirror. So also the scores of memorable "characters" in Pope's poems, whether in the *Ethic Epistles* or the *Dunciad*, act on a public stage. It gives one a start, therefore, in reading Pope's letters to come upon a rare passage such as this: "No lone house in Wales with a rookery is more contemplative than Hampton Court; I walk'd there the other day by the moon, and met no creature of any quality but the King, who was giving audience, all alone, to the birds under the garden wall" (*Corr.* I, 470). One sees the king, and by implication the poet who looks on, as enclosed in a privacy for which there is no place in Pope's resolutely public verse.

Pope's life on the printed page was of special importance not just because it allowed him to present an ideal poetic self, but also because his despised physical self could be acknowledged in witty verse, admitting exalted comparisons while declining vulgar flattery:

8. Bevil Higgons, *To Mr. Pope*, in *Pope's Own Miscellany*, ed. Norman Ault (London: Nonesuch, 1935), p. 81.

> There are, who to my person pay their court,
> I cough like Horace, and though lean, am short,
> Ammon's great son one shoulder had too high,
> Such Ovid's nose, and "Sir! you have an eye—"
> Go on, obliging creatures, make me see
> All that disgraced my betters, met in me.
>
> (*To Arbuthnot*, 115–20)

Pope permitted, encouraged, and sometimes commissioned an extraordinary number of portraits of himself, usually nobly classical in aspect.[9] But none of these showed his bodily shape. In 1797 Warton used a Jonathan Richardson portrait as frontispiece to his edition of Pope's *Works* (see fig. 1), but also reproduced a drawing by William Hoare (fig. 2) with the comment,

> This is the only portrait that was ever drawn of Mr. Pope at full length. It was done without his knowledge, as he was deeply engaged in conversation with Mr. Allen in the gallery at Prior Park, by Mr. Hoare, who sat at the other end of the gallery. Pope would never have forgiven the painter had he known it—he was too sensible of the deformity of his person to allow the whole of it to be represented.[10]

Poetry, not painting, was the medium in which defect could be turned to advantage.

As a young boy, Pope was precociously bookish. His sister told Spence, "I believe nobody ever studied so hard as my brother did in his youth. He did nothing but write and read."[11] He himself represents his vocation as a spontaneous impulse: "I lisped in numbers, for the numbers came" (*To Arbuthnot*, 128). This is not, however, the familiar story of a child's escape into a private world. Rather, Pope seems from

---

9. See William K. Wimsatt, Jr., *The Portraits of Alexander Pope* (New Haven: Yale University Press, 1965).

10. *The Works of Alexander Pope*, ed. Joseph Warton (1797), I, ix. A reproduction of the original sketch, and of another by William Kent showing a seated Pope playing cards, may be seen in David B. Morris, *Alexander Pope: The Genius of Sense* (Cambridge, Mass.: Harvard University Press, 1984), p. 261. It is also reproduced in Mack, *Alexander Pope*, p. 154.

11. Joseph Spence, *Observations, Anecdotes, and Characters of Books and Men*, ed. James M. Osborn (Oxford: Clarendon, 1966), I, 13.

ALEXANDER POPE ESQ.

Engraved by J Holloway, from a Picture painted by J Richardson,

in the possession of Benj.ⁿ Way Esq.ʳ

Published January 1ˢᵗ 1797 by Cadell and Davies Strand London.

1.   Engraving after a portrait by Jonathan Richardson, frontispiece
to the first volume of Warton's edition of Pope's *Works* (1797). By
permission of the Folger Shakespeare Library.

To front Page IX [A 5] of Vol.I.

Published June 1 1797. by Cadell & Davies Strand.

2. Engraving after a drawing by William Hoare, in the first volume of Warton's edition of Pope's *Works* (1797). By permission of the Folger Shakespeare Library.

the very beginning to have written for judgment and approval. "When Mr. Pope was yet a child, his father, though no poet, would set him to make English verses. He was pretty difficult to please, and would often send the boy back to new turn them. When they were to his mind, he took great pleasure in them, and would say, 'These are good rhymes.'"[12] Before long Pope was seeking, and winning, the approval of a number of distinguished gentlemen of middle years; it is notable that he seems not to have had friends of his own age. The "voracity of fame" that Johnson speaks of was established from a very early age.[13] In a way Pope always looked forward to the posthumous reputation in which he would become his book, and his peculiarities would be entirely literary. One function of his imitations of Horace is to merge the living man into the literary persona.[14]

Horace was a model in particular for a "politeness" that kept literature firmly in its social place, in a literary pose of being superior to literary posing. Thus Warton praises *The Rape of the Lock:*

> Pope here appears in the light of a man of gallantry, and of a thorough knowledge of the world; and indeed, he had nothing, in his carriage and deportment, of that affected singularity, which has induced some men of genius to despise, and depart from, the established rules of politeness and civil life. For all poets have not practiced the sober and rational advice of Boileau.
>
> > Que les vers ne soient pas votre éternel emploi:
> > Cultivez vos amis, soyez homme de soi.
> > C'est peu d'être agréable et charmant dans un livre;
> > Il faut savoir encore, et converser, et vivre.[15]

12. William Warburton in his edition of Pope's *Works* (1751), IV, 18.

13. Samuel Johnson, *Life of Pope*, in *Lives of the English Poets*, ed. G. B. Hill (Oxford: Clarendon, 1905), III, 136.

14. As Frederick M. Keener suggests in *An Essay on Pope* (New York: Columbia University Press, 1974), p. 145. See also Maynard Mack, "Pope: The Shape of the Man in His Work," *Yale Review*, 67 (1978), 496–98, and Howard D. Weinbrot, "Masked Men and Satire and Pope: Toward a Historical Basis for the Eighteenth-Century Persona," *Eighteenth-Century Studies*, 16 (1983), 265–89.

15. Joseph Warton, *An Essay on the Writings and Genius of Pope* (1756), I, 246–47. Boileau is quoted from *L'Art Poétique*, Chant IV.

(Don't let verses be your everlasting occupation; cultivate your friends, be your own man. It's nothing much to be pleasant and charming in a book; one must also know how to converse and live.)

In just this way Pope seeks to represent a self that is grounded upon lived experience, while the poems in turn serve to establish, if not actually to create, the self and the experience.

Horace, indeed, is more explicit than Pope about shaping life to his needs. *Et mihi res, non me rebus, submittere conor:* "I would bend the world to myself, not myself to the world."[16] Pope's adaptation of this line suggests yielding rather than control:

> Back to my native moderation slide,
> And win my way by yielding to the tide.
> *(Epistle* I.i.33–34)

Or to put it more precisely, the language speaks of yielding while the couplet structure asserts control. Horace says in another poem that he intends to leave lyric poetry to school-boys, *sed verae numerosque modosque ediscere vitae:* "but to master the rhythms and measures of a genuine life."[17] Pope greatly expands this, emphasizing smoothness and boundaries where Horace had emphasized rhythm and genuineness:

> To rules of poetry no more confined,
> I learn to smooth and harmonize my mind,
> Teach ev'ry thought within its bounds to roll,
> And keep the equal measure of the soul.
> *(Epistle* II.ii.202–5)

Whereas thinkers after Rousseau might seek to liberate the true self from social restraints, Pope sought a socially grounded perspective from which to *judge* the self, with a goal of establishing character rather than freeing personality.

---

16. *Epistle* I.i.19, in Horace, *Satires, Epistles and Ars Poetica,* trans. H. Rushton Fairclough, Loeb Classical Library (London: Heinemann, 1929), p. 253. Fairclough's text gives *subiungere* for Pope's *submittere (TE,* IV, 280).

17. *Epistle* II.ii.144; Fairclough, p. 437.

In a triplet added to the second edition (1717) of *The Temple of Fame*, he praised

> wise Aurelius, in whose well-taught mind,
> With boundless pow'r unbounded virtue joined,
> His own strict judge, and patron of mankind.
>
> (165–67)

Personal, social, and artistic decorums become virtually synonymous, as in Pope's reflections on Homer's style:

> There is a graceful and dignified simplicity, as well as a bald and sordid one, which differ as much from each other as the air of a plain man from that of a sloven: 'Tis one thing to be tricked up, and another not to be dressed at all. Simplicity is the mean between ostentation and rusticity.
>
> (*TE* VII, 18)

When Pope was a youth, as he recalls in the *Epistle to Arbuthnot*, "Granville the polite, / And knowing Walsh, would tell me I could write" (135–36). The criterion of politeness is important: poetic art is meant to be inseparable from a way of living.

It has often been noticed that Pope's imitations convey much more of the poet's personality than the Horatian originals do.[18] In adopting this pose Pope wants to suggest that he has nothing to hide, so that art can freely coincide with life. "Methinks when I write to you," he tells Congreve, "I am making a confession, I have got (I can't tell how) such a custom of throwing my self out upon paper without reserve" (*Corr.* I, 274). Or in a Horatian poem,

> I love to pour out all myself, as plain
> As downright Shippen, or as old Montaigne.
> In them, as certain to be loved as seen,
> The soul stood forth, nor kept a thought within;
> In me what spots (for spots I have) appear,
> Will prove at least the medium must be clear.
>
> (*Satire* II.i.51–56)

---

18. See, for instance, G. K. Hunter, "The 'Romanticism' of Pope's Horace," *Essays in Criticism*, 10 (1960), 390–414.

Confession, of course, requires the revelation of what is hidden, and this is explicit in the Horatian original. Words are shut up in poetic feet (*pedibus . . . claudere verba*), with the paradoxical result that when secrets are entrusted to books (*arcana . . . credebat libris*) a poet's whole life is open to view as if painted on a tablet.[19] André Dacier, commenting on this passage in the seventeenth century, emphasized the sacred obligation of votive tablets to tell the whole truth, and their openness to public view.[20] Pope reveals few secrets, but if the "all myself" of which he speaks is not really his whole self, that is not because he is deliberately hiding things. Rather, he seeks to become and to live the self embodied in the poems, "as certain to be loved as seen," telling himself the same story he tells his friends and his readers.

That Pope became a fierce and controversial satirist is the most obvious fact of his career, and we shall return to it in Chapter 4. But for Pope himself it was an anomalous fact: either a misrepresentation by people who did not know him, or an unwanted role forced upon him by a sick culture that required satiric surgery. His self-presentation was altogether different from what his modern admirers, Louis I. Bredvold for instance, have sometimes chosen to emphasize. Bredvold dismissively quotes Addison on a habit of cheerfulness:

> The reader cannot but remark how perfectly this celebration of cheerfulness betrays Addison's limitations, his complacency, his lack of penetration. This is, indeed, the "serene, peaceful state, of being a fool among knaves." There is an abysmal division between men of this cast of mind and the satirists.[21]

Whatever may have been true of Swift, cheerfulness was Pope's ideal too. "Keep good humor still whate'er we lose," Clarissa counsels Belinda in *The Rape of the Lock* (V.30), and

---

19. *Satire* II.i.28–34, in Fairclough's edition, pp. 128–29.

20. See Frank Stack, *Pope and Horace: Studies in Imitation* (Cambridge: Cambridge University Press, 1985), p. 40.

21. "The Gloom of the Tory Satirists," in *Eighteenth-Century English Literature: Modern Essays in Criticism*, ed. James L. Clifford (New York: Oxford University Press, 1959), pp. 17–18. The quoted passage is from the "Digression concerning Madness" in Swift's *Tale of a Tub*.

like other irritable persons Pope longed to possess this quality. "I look upon myself," Johnson told an amazed Boswell, "as a good humoured fellow."[22] Even at his most Juvenalian, Pope never sustains for long Juvenal's tone of exasperation swelling to rage;[23] he prefers Horace's blend of moral indignation with playful irony. Above all, like many of his contemporaries, Pope admires the Horatian image of privileged refuge from a corrupt culture, in a haven of civilized friendship that has been described as "the mundane visited by a spirit of delight."[24]

Whatever his defects of temperament—in one letter Pope wryly describes himself as "a philosophical companion, half sour and half sick" (*Corr.* II, 457)—he placed loyal friendship at the very center of his ideal life. His friends in turn knew how much he wanted praise for this; the earl of Oxford (son of the great prime minister) wrote in 1724, "I will allow nobody to esteem, to value, or love you more than I do, and I do so from the conviction that you are the best poet, the truest friend, and the best natured man, these are characters that are extremely amiable but very seldom fall to the share of one man to possess in such a degree as you do" (*Corr.* II, 261). Pope made a great point of exchanging portraits in what has been well described as "one of the sacraments of friendship,"[25] and his poems express outrage at betrayals of it. As with friendship, so with sonship: whereas a novelist like Defoe might fictionalize the rebellion of children against parents, Pope enacted the ideal of filial piety so faithfully that Johnson declared, "Life has, among its soothing and quiet comforts, few things better to give than such a son."[26]

In every way Pope sought to live out an ideal of conduct

22. James Boswell, *Life of Samuel Johnson,* ed. G. B. Hill, rev. L. F. Powell (Oxford: Clarendon, 1934), II, 362 (18 Apr. 1775).

23. On Pope's increasing sense of affinity with Juvenal and Persius see Howard D. Weinbrot, *Alexander Pope and the Traditions of Formal Verse Satire* (Princeton: Princeton University Press, 1982).

24. M. J. McGann, "The Three Worlds of Horace's Satires," in *Horace,* ed. C. D. N. Costa (London: Routledge, 1973), p. 60.

25. Morris R. Brownell, *Alexander Pope and the Arts of Georgian England* (Oxford: Clarendon, 1978), p. 37.

26. *Lives,* III, 154.

that was constantly recommended in the eighteenth century, by Hume for example in his chapter "Of Benevolence":

> We may observe that in displaying the praises of any humane, beneficent man there is one circumstance which never fails to be amply insisted on—namely, the happiness and satisfaction derived to society from his intercourse and good offices. To his parents, we are apt to say, he endears himself by his pious attachment and duteous care. . . . The ties of friendship approach, in a fond observance of each obliging office, to those of love and inclination.[27]

The easy mingling of classical and social ideals is apparent in a letter written by Granville (the polite) to a friend who hoped to meet Wycherley:

> I can give you no Falernum that has out-lived twenty consulships, but I can promise you a bottle of good old claret that has seen two reigns: Horatian wit will not be wanting when you two meet. He shall bring with him, if you will, a young poet, newly inspired, in the neighbourhood of Cooper's-Hill, whom he and Walsh have taken under their wing; his name is Pope; he is not above seventeen or eighteen years of age, and promises miracles: if he goes on as he has begun, in the pastoral way, as Virgil first tried his strength, we may hope to see English poetry vie with the Roman, and this swan of Windsor sing as sweetly as the Mantuan.[28]

The Horatian allusions are as significant here as the Virgilian: it is not just that Pope may progress from pastoral to epic, but also that he will do so in the company of kindred spirits who sustain "Horatian wit" with old claret.

In 1717, when he was not yet thirty, Pope published a collected edition of his poems and wrote to his friend Caryll,

> My poetical affairs drawing toward a fair period, I hope the day will shortly come when I may honestly say

---

27. David Hume, *An Inquiry concerning the Principles of Morals* (1751), ed. Charles W. Hendel (Indianapolis: Bobbs-Merrill, Library of the Liberal Arts, 1957), II.ii, p. 11.

28. Lansdowne's *Works* (1732), I, 436–37, quoted by George Sherburn, *The Early Career of Alexander Pope* (Oxford: Clarendon, 1934), p. 52.

Nunc versus et caetera ludicra pono,
Quid *verum* atque *decens*, curo et rogo et omnis in hoc sum.

That *caetera ludicra* is very comprehensive: it includes visiting, masquerading, play-haunting, sauntering, and indeed almost includes all that the world calls living.

(*Corr.* I, 464)

Two decades later Pope translated Horace's lines thus:

Farewell then verse, and love, and every toy,
The rhymes and rattles of the man or boy:
What right, what true, what fit, we justly call,
Let this be all my care—for this is all.

(*Epistle* I.i.17–20)

Among other things, Horatian retirement means a license to abjure poetry, or to write only such poems as speak from retired tranquillity. Pope's movement in the 1730s from a Horatian to a Juvenalian rhetoric may reflect temperamental impulses, but it also reflects a bitter recognition that the outside world will not leave him at peace in his voluntary isolation. Like his friend Bolingbroke in political exile, Pope came to embrace Seneca's Stoic ideal of being useful to one's country even if hindered from full participation, rather than Horace's Epicurean ideal of cultivated retirement.[29]

Instead of conflating retirement with poetry, we might do well to observe a distinction between the two. Sherburn says of the first decade at Twickenham, "It is astonishing how in this period the poetic impulse diminished."[30] But Pope found it not in the least astonishing, for as he wrote to a fellow poet, Judith Cowper, after he had been at Twickenham for several years,

'Tis great folly to sacrifice one's self, one's time, one's quiet (the very life of life itself) to forms, complaisances, and amusements, which do not inwardly please me, and only please a sort of people who regard me no farther than a mere instrument of their present idleness or vanity. To say truth, the lives

29. See Stack, *Pope and Horace*, pp. 53–55.
30. *Early Career*, p. 270.

of those we call great and happy are divided between those two states; and in each of them, we poetical fiddlers make but part of their pleasure, or of their equipage. And the misery is, we in our turns are so vain (at least I have been so) as to choose to pipe without being paid, and so silly [as] to be pleased with piping to those who understand music less than ourselves.

(*Corr.* II, 194–95)

Feeling that poetry is an unrewarded and unappreciated trade, Pope chooses to go out of business except on his own terms, or at least pretends that he does. At any rate poetry no longer seems the irresistible mistress that it had in earlier days; Mack surmises at this period "some degree of imaginative exhaustion, depression, or distraction."[31]

Pope had celebrated "study, exercise, and ease" at the end of *Windsor-Forest* (240), and his poem to Jervas the painter proposes an ideal of the "sister-arts" as leisure rather than work:

> How oft in pleasing tasks we wear the day,
> While summer suns roll unperceived away.
> (*Epistle to Mr. Jervas*, 17–18)

It is worth emphasizing that unlike Swift or Johnson, Pope never had to hold a regular job, and that he was talking like this even in his teens.

> If you have any curiosity to know in what manner I live, or rather lose a life, in the country, Martial will inform you in one line.
>
> Prandeo, poto, cano, ludo, lego, caeno, quiesco.
>
> Every day with me is literally another tomorrow; for it is exactly the same with yesterday: it has the same business, which is poetry; and the same pleasure, which is idleness. A man might indeed pass his time much better, but I question if any man could pass it much easier.
>
> (*Corr.* I, 42)

---

31. *Alexander Pope*, p. 347.

Eighteenth-century novels are filled with exemplars of retired tranquillity that contrast with the bustle of modern life: Mr. Wilson in *Joseph Andrews*, Squire Allworthy in *Tom Jones*, Mr. Dennison in *Humphry Clinker*. The Roman model serves as a retreat from the present into a timeless georgic world, with British produce substituted for Italian:

> From yon old walnut tree a show'r shall fall,
> And grapes, long-ling'ring on my only wall.
>   (*Satire* II.ii.145–46)

Gay writes affectionately of Burlington's garden,

> Where Pope unloads the bough within his reach,
> Of purple grape, blue plum, or blushing peach.[32]

This is not quite the unfallen world of Marvell's *Garden*, where "the nectarine and curious peach / Into my hands themselves do reach," but it is a domesticated nature whose treasures are easily plucked by the diminutive Pope.

In addition to furnishing comfort and convenience, retirement offered a further hope of coming to terms with the self.

> Soon as I enter at my country door,
> My mind resumes the thread it dropped before;
> Thoughts, which at Hyde Park Corner I forgot,
> Meet and rejoin me, in the pensive grot.
> There all alone, and compliments apart,
> I ask these sober questions of my heart.
>   (*Epistle* II.ii.206–11)

For a temperament as socially alert as Pope's, there was always the danger of losing oneself in the activity of others, with a kind of ventriloquial mimicry. So he wrote to Broome,

Hurry, noise, and the observances of the world, take away the power of just thinking or natural acting. A man that lives so much in the world does but translate other men; he is nothing of his own. Our customs, our tempers, our enjoyments, our distastes are not so properly effects of our natural constitution,

---

32. John Gay, *An Epistle to the Earl of Burlington*, 3–4.

as distempers catched by contagion. Many would live happily
without any ill ones, if they lived by themselves.

(*Corr.* II, 302)

It is no contradiction of these sentiments that Pope was
frequently in the thick of things, "always so employed and
so dissipated by other people's affairs, as well as my own,
that I live in a hurry of thought, and too often in a hurry of
person" (*Corr.* II, 429). "I met our friend Pope in town,"
Bathurst wrote to Swift; "he is as sure to be there in a bustle,
as a porpoise in a storm" (*Corr.* IV, 88n). Seductive though
the town might be, it was inimical to poetry or encouraged
the wrong kinds: "How shall I rhyme in this eternal roar?"
(*Epistle* II.ii.114). And beyond poetry lay the goal of self-
knowledge and self-acceptance, viewed in "the clear, still
mirror of retreat" (*Epilogue* II.78).

Above all, the Horatian ideal signifies the ability to hold
oneself under control, protecting vulnerable points. "Let us
be fixed, and our own masters still," Pope appeals to Swift
(*Satire* II.ii.180). To be fixed in a world of flux means recon-
ciling—or eluding—conflicting impulses, as in "The Design"
of *An Essay on Man*, where Pope speaks of "steering betwixt
the extremes of doctrines seemingly opposite" (*TE* III–i, 7).
Pope allows the couplet form to generate its own logic, pair-
ing concepts and modes of behavior in patterns whose syntax
is irresistible. As early as the *Essay on Criticism*, written when
he was about twenty, he was trying on a self-image of balanced judiciousness:

> Careless of censure, nor too fond of fame,
> Still pleased to praise, yet not afraid to blame,
> Averse alike to flatter, or offend,
> Not free from faults, nor yet too vain to mend.
> (741–44)

Pope must have recalled the second of those lines in his characterization of the duplicitous Addison, "Willing to wound,
and yet afraid to strike" (*To Arbuthnot*, 203).

Ultimately this structural pattern goes back to John Denham's much-imitated couplet in *Cooper's Hill* that compares poetry to the Thames:

> Though deep, yet clear; though gentle, yet not dull;
> Strong without rage, without o'erflowing full.
> (191–92)

Almost invariably the pattern works to suggest that true energy is compatible with moderation, and that apparent contraries actually collaborate. Thus Pope's friend Garth praises "the man who's honest, open, and a friend":

> Forgiving others, to himself severe;
> Though earnest, easy; civil, yet sincere.[33]

In Pope's own poems Bolingbroke is "correct with spirit, eloquent with ease" (*Essay on Man* IV.381), and Jervas's paintings are "soft without weakness, without glaring gay" (*Epistle to Mr. Jervas*, 66). It was easy for Pope's young admirer (some said sycophant) Walter Harte to apply the Jervas encomium to Pope's own poems: "Soft without weakness, without labour fair."[34]

In Pope's conception, restraint actually intensifies energy:

> The wingèd courser, like a gen'rous horse,
> Shows most true mettle when you check his course.
> (*Essay on Criticism*, 86–87)

For a man of Pope's generation, in an era much disturbed by social and political strife, moderation seemed a challenging ideal rather than an endorsement of conventionality. "I find by dear experience," Pope wrote to Caryll about their embattled position as Catholics, "we live in an age, where it is criminal to be moderate" (*Corr.* I, 238). David Morris calls attention to a remark later in the same letter, "I will venture to say, no man ever rose to any degree of perfection in writing, but through obstinacy and an inveterate resolution against the

---

33. Samuel Garth, *Claremont*, in *The Works of Celebrated Authors: Volume the First* (1750), p. 348.
34. *To Mr. Pope*, in Harte's *Poems on Several Occasions* (1727), p. 101.

stream of mankind."[35] As Pope's ethical writings increasingly declare, most people live in extremes, and moderation represents a painful struggle against irrational social behavior. When Horace Walpole wrote that Pope "had twisted and twirled and rhymed and harmonized" his five acres of land,[36] he cleverly recognized the analogy between Pope's couplet art and his life.

Beneath all the praise of retirement, there lurks a fear that the dream of order is only a dream, that gardening is but a compulsive way of passing time, and that the Homeric contrast between grace and slovenliness operates in Pope's disfavor. So he quite poignantly addresses Bolingbroke:

> You laugh, half beau half sloven if I stand,
> My wig all powder, and all snuff my band. . . .
> But when no prelate's lawn with hair-shirt lined
> Is half so incoherent as my mind,
> When (each opinion with the next at strife,
> One ebb and flow of follies all my life)
> I plant, root up, I build, and then confound,
> Turn round to square, and square again to round. . . .
> Is this my guide, philosopher, and friend?
> This, he who loves me, and who ought to mend?
> (*Epistle* I.i.161–78)

Here outer and inner selves are all too congruent: disarray of dress reflects disarray of mind. Round forms may symbolize perfection and square ones rectitude, but they have become interchangeable emblems without real meaning. And Bolingbroke, intellectual hero as well as adored friend, is carelessly indifferent to Pope's inward suffering. Pope is imitating Horace closely here, but that only underscores the fact that the Roman model is not infallibly consoling. As he wrote many years earlier to Judith Cowper, "'Tis time enough to like, or affect to like, the country, when one is out of love with all but oneself, and therefore studies to become agreeable or easy to oneself. Retiring into oneself is generally the *pis-aller* of man-

---

35. *Alexander Pope*, p. 320.
36. Quoted by Mack, *The Garden and the City*, p. 26.

kind" (*Corr.* II, 141). When a bishop remarked to Johnson that Horace appeared in his writings to have been "a cheerful contented man," Johnson replied, "We have no reason to believe that, my Lord. Are we to think Pope was happy, because he says so in his writings? We see in his writings what he wished the state of his mind to appear."[37]

Pondering the whole expanse of Pope's life, one is struck above all by the painful inevitability of loss, in the spirit of Elizabeth Bishop's bleak villanelle that reiterates the line "The art of losing isn't hard to master." Just as Pope's body and his career are structures to be carefully built up, so is friendship, and when the persons vanish the structure must collapse.

> Nothing, says Seneca, is so melancholy a circumstance in human life, or so soon reconciles us to the thought of our own death, as the reflection and prospect of one friend after another dropping round us! Who would stand alone, the sole remaining ruin, the last tottering column of all the fabric of friendship; once so large, seemingly so strong, and yet so suddenly sunk and buried?
>
> (*Corr.* II, 253)

"The loss of a friend," Pope says in a letter when Atterbury had departed into political exile, "is the loss of life" (*Corr.* II, 180). His correspondence with Swift is filled with grief at separation, and he wrote somberly to Orrery in Ireland,

> I cannot but resume the subject of our friend, the Dean; it is what I do ten times every day of my life; his memory is dearer to me than any living friend's, and as melancholy as if he were dead. I seldom hear from him, and I seldom write to him: it tears out too much of my heart; and when I've said all I can, 'tis nothing, 'tis impotence, 'tis one short sigh! Pray my Lord see him as often as you can, love him you must. I almost wish I had never seen him.
>
> (*Corr.* III, 502)

More disturbing even than the loss of close friends was the loss of the self that the friendships defined. For as Pope wrote to Swift late in life, "You ask me if I have got any supply of

37. Boswell, *Life of Johnson*, III, 251 (9 Apr. 1778).

new friends to make up for those that are gone? I think that impossible, for not our friends only, but so much of our selves is gone by the mere flux and course of years, that were the same friends to be restored to us, we could not be restored to our selves, to enjoy them" (*Corr.* IV, 50). In one of the most moving passages in his work, Pope summarizes these themes with a deft allusion to Milton's sonnet "How soon hath time, the subtle thief of youth":

> Years foll'wing years, steal something every day,
> At last they steal us from our selves away;
> In one our frolics, one amusements end,
> In one a mistress drops, in one a friend:
> This subtle thief of life, this paltry time,
> What will it leave me, if it snatch my rhyme?
> If ev'ry wheel of that unwearied mill
> That turned ten thousand verses, now stands still.
>
> (*Epistle* II.ii.72–79)

For all of his protestations of retired ease among friends and flowers, it is Pope's rhyme that defines him, and when it leaves him he will cease to be. Without question rhyming is compulsive and exhausting, an unwearied mill. But it represents a vocation that cannot be denied, and one reason for its attraction is that it offers liberation from self-absorption. As Barbara Lewalski notes, the Miltonic allusion points up "the distance between Milton's earnest, youthful, religious anxieties about unfulfilled God-given talents and responsibilities, and the mature, urbane Pope's insistence that he has a right if he chooses to enjoy life without rhyming all the time and in unfavorable circumstances."[38] It is well to be reminded that Pope did not perceive himself as an inspired bard, much less as a prophet doctrinal to his age. But he is not self-absorbed either; the movement inward to self and grotto is answered by a movement outward, as the poet stoops to truth and moralizes his song. To move outward is indeed to acknowledge the limitations of retirement, and it entails immersion in a

---

38. "On Looking into Pope's Milton," *Études Anglaises*, 27 (1974), 488.

society in which the Roman ideal is beginning to look incongruous if not impossible.

Meanwhile, the rhymes remain. By the end of his life Pope had become, if not exactly a culture hero, at least the unchallenged poetic master of his age.[39] To be sure, there was something intimidating about his authority. Shenstone remarked some years after his death that Pope was the most correct writer since Virgil but the greatest genius only since Dryden, and added wryly, "I durst not have censured Mr. Pope's writings in his lifetime, you say. True. A writer surrounded with all his fame, engaging with another that is hardly known, is a man in armour attacking another in his night-gown and slippers."[40] Indeed, it is a consequence of Pope's carefully tended self-image that his asperities and duplicities were so often denounced. People are harder on those who proclaim morality than on those—like Byron, for instance—who flout it. As Auden observes, "Only a minor talent can be a perfect gentleman; a major talent is always more than a bit of a cad."[41] But it is also true that Pope's self-image, projected in the poems, has always had much to do with the ways in which they have been admired. Gilbert Wakefield, at the very end of the eighteenth century, offers a list of qualities in which Pope stands "without a rival in ancient or modern times," which is most easily read if rearranged as a Sternean list:

delicacy of feeling,

accuracy of judgement,

poignancy of wit,

urbanity of humour,

vivacity of fancy,

discernment of human character,

solemnity of pathos,

---

39. See the testimonies quoted by Mack, *Alexander Pope*, pp. 760–61.

40. William Shenstone, "On Writing and Books," *The Works in Verse and Prose of William Shenstone* (Edinburgh, 1765), II, 133.

41. W. H. Auden, *The Dyer's Hand and Other Essays* (New York: Vintage, 1968), p. 21.

pregnancy of sentiment,
rectitude of taste,
comprehensive diction,
melodious numbers,
and dignified morality.[42]

Most of these attributes belong as much to the poet as to the poems.

Thus far, we have been considering Pope's ideal self-image as he chose to project it: a man who may not have been fully at home in the world, but who managed to shape a local world in which he could indeed be at home as poet, gentleman, friend, and son. Always, however, he claimed to speak for his society as a whole, giving advice and reproving misbehavior as if he were Mr. Spectator himself. We can explore the complications that this posture entailed by considering a subject Pope found both painful and fascinating, women in society and in relation to himself and his art.

One might conjecture that Pope's sense of isolation and vulnerability intensified his need to prescribe social behavior. Certainly, as Ellen Pollak has shown, his poems are filled with rhetorical attempts to reconcile or minimize contradictions in sexual codes.[43] In his highly conventionalized society, no conventions were stronger than those governing relations between the sexes, and given his physical handicaps, Pope had reason to be more keenly aware of them than most. Recent scholarship has abundantly demonstrated that he had a good deal of sympathy with women, but also that he had a strong wish to be thought manly and even rakish, so that much of his work perpetuates old stereotypes. As in every other aspect of his life, Pope needed to see individuals as members of a hierarchy in which he himself was well placed.

Pope's early letters quite often address his physical nature

42. *Observations on Pope* (1796), p. v.
43. *The Poetics of Sexual Myth: Gender and Ideology in the Verse of Swift and Pope* (Chicago: University of Chicago Press, 1985).

with rueful irony, as when he calls himself "that little Alexander the women laugh at" (*Corr.* I, 114). "Age came upon him rapidly," Leslie Stephen remarks, "and he had sown his wild oats, such as they were, while still a young man."[44] Apart from one wounding and unconfirmed anecdote which Cibber told years later about Pope at a brothel, we know nothing whatever about Pope's sexual experience, but his references to sex increasingly suggest limitation and disappointment. Certainly his contemporaries assumed that frustration was his lot, as in Wilkes's sly ironies in his *Essay on Woman:* "Mr. Pope might indeed, and in all probability he actually, and frequently did handle this subject in a cursory way, but I dare say he never *went deep* into it."[45] In his lively translation of Horace's *Ode* IV.i, with its famous *Non sum qualis eram* ("I am not now, alas! the man") Pope implores Venus,

> Ah sound no more thy soft alarms,
> Nor circle sober fifty with thy charms.
> Mother too fierce of dear desires!
> Turn, turn to willing hearts your wanton fires.
> (*TE* IV, 151)

Pope was just a year short of "sober fifty," and one senses personal feelings in his protest against the *dulcium / mater saeva cupidinum.* Ben Jonson, incidentally, translates the phrase more darkly, "Sour mother of sweet loves."[46]

References to sex in Pope's poems seldom suggest the simple gratification of desire. Disgust is as likely as celebration, as in an image which Pope adds to Horace:

> While bashful Jenny, ev'n at morning prayer,
> Spreads her fore-buttocks to the navel bare.
> (*Satire* I.ii.33–34)

44. *Alexander Pope*, p. 84.
45. John Wilkes, *An Essay on Woman, by Pego Borewell . . . And a Commentary of the Rev. Dr. Warburton* (1762), quoted by Calhoun Winton, "John Wilkes and 'An Essay on Woman,'" in *A Provision of Human Nature: Essays on Fielding and Others in Honor of Marian Austin Locke*, ed. Donald Kay (University: University of Alabama Press, 1977), p. 127.
46. *Under-wood* No. 88, *Ode the First: The Fourth Book, To Venus.*

Later in the same poem, desire is described through oblique
hints:

> Suppose that honest part that rules us all
> Should rise, and say—"Sir Robert! or Sir Paul!
> Did I demand, in my most vig'rous hour,
> A thing descended from the conqueror?"
>
> (87–90)

"Thing" is a euphemism for *cunnum,* as Pope emphasizes in
a Scriblerian footnote attributed to Bentley (*TE IV,* 82).

Perhaps some insight into Pope's feelings is offered by an
epigram on the manuscript title page of *Sappho to Phaon:*

> Poor Gellius keeps, or rather starves two maids,
> Seldom he feeds, but often f——s the jades.
> He stops one mouth that t'other may not mutter,
> So what they want in bread, they have in butter.

Whether or not the lines are by Pope, he certainly transcribed
them; Mack conjectures that they refer to his mistress-
keeping friend Henry Cromwell.[47] In this private jotting, euphemism is exploded, in an opposite procedure to *Sappho to
Phaon:*

> Then fiercer joys—I blush to mention these,
> Yet while I blush, confess how much they please!
>
> (153–54)

These lines evidently pleased Pope, for Mack notes (p. 82)
that in the margin of the manuscript he wrote "Pulcherrimé."
It is hard not to suspect that Pope envies Gellius. His name
may, as Mack suggests, imply tiresome pedantry about the
classics, but that doesn't stop him from having—and pleasing—as many women as he wants.

In *The Rape of the Lock,* which in formalist terms is undoubt-

---

47. Maynard Mack, *The Last and Greatest Art: Some Unpublished Poetical
Manuscripts of Alexander Pope* (Newark: University of Delaware Press, 1984),
p. 72. The epigram (not in *TE:* first published 1976) is on p. 74.

edly Pope's most perfect poem, he strives throughout to identify himself with the male "we," who are attracted by women
but know how to keep them in their place:

> Fair tresses man's imperial race insnare,
> And beauty draws us with a single hair.
> (I.27–28)

This note of amused detachment is fundamental to the poem.
Pope's "we," to be sure, never moralizes as brusquely as a
cruder satirist like Edward Young:

> Women were made to give our eyes delight;
> A female sloven is an odious sight.[48]

But Pope does gaze down upon women from an Olympian
height, reducing their hearts to toyshops (I.100) and their
interests to flirtation and cards, and his language embeds
condescension in its alliterative mockery: "practiced to lisp"
(IV.33), "And little hearts to flutter at a beau" (I.90).

In Young's heavily moralistic poem, stylized dress is directly emblematic of stylized behavior, and therefore point-
less if sexual truth is openly admitted:

> Vain is the task to petticoats assigned,
> If wanton language shows a naked mind.
> (p. 96)

In Pope, very differently, the whole point of stylization is to
whet the appetite, and the barrier is for show only.

> To fifty chosen sylphs, of special note,
> We trust th' important charge, the petticoat:
> Oft have we known that sev'nfold fence to fail,
> Though stiff with hoops, and armed with ribs of whale.
> (II.117–20)

As in Fragonard's painting of the swing, sophisticated gar-
ments are a systematic enticement veiling the beauties that

---

48. *Satire VI*, in Young, *Love of Fame, the Universal Passion: In Seven Characteristical Satires*, 5th ed. (1752), p. 115.

well-bred women conceal. Gilbert West wrote in a poem addressed to Pope, with a reference to "upper air" that may well recall the sylphs of the *Rape,*

> Tossed to and fro, up flew the giddy fair,
> And screamed, and laughed, and played in upper air.
> The flutt'ring coats the rapid motion find,
> And one by one admit the swelling wind:
> At length the last, white, subtle veil withdrew,
> And those mysterious charms exposed to view.[49]

In the *Rape* the sexual truth is finally admitted when Belinda wishes the Baron had been "content to seize / Hairs less in sight, or any hairs but these" (IV.175–76). This sort of innuendo was remarkably popular, reflecting no doubt a powerful taboo.[50] Pope certainly wants to suggest that beauty enhances or even sublimates the coarser passions. In the poem, this is a beauty which the artist creates; in life, it is a beauty which artistic vision can help us to see. Studying painting at this time, Pope wrote to Gay, "I become by Mr. Jervas's help, *Elegans Formarum Spectator.* I begin to discover beauties that were till now imperceptible to me. Every corner of an eye, or turn of a nose or ear, the smallest degree of light or shade on a cheek, or in a dimple, have charms to distract me" (*Corr.* I, 187).

It needs to be emphasized that the attraction *is* attraction, in the almost magical sense which that word once had. The

---

49. *Stowe: The Gardens of the Right Honourable Richard Lord Viscount Cobham, Addressed to Mr. Pope* (1732), p. 15. West, who published the poem anonymously, was Cobham's nephew.

50. In a burlesque poem by Pope's very conventional friend Fenton, the devil loses a bargained-for soul because he is unable to straighten a hair:

> The dame produced a single hair,
> But whence it came I cannot swear;
> Yet this I will affirm is true,
> It curled like any bottle-screw. . . .
> If I, quoth he, conceive its nature,
> This hair has flourished nigh the water.

Elijah Fenton, *The Fair Nun: A Tale*, in *Poems on Several Occasions* (1717), pp. 64–65.

sylphs, objectifications of Belinda's mind or self, may be flimsy, but they are breathtakingly lovely too:

> Some to the sun their insect-wings unfold,
> Waft on the breeze, or sink in clouds of gold.
> Transparent forms, too fine for mortal sight,
> Their fluid bodies half dissolved in light.
> (II.59–62)

In *The Rape of the Lock* the world of desire is seen from outside by a poet who recognizes its duplicities even as he longs for its rewards.

> What guards the purity of melting maids,
> In courtly balls, and midnight masquerades,
> Safe from the treach'rous friend, the daring spark,
> The glance by day, the whisper in the dark;
> When kind occasion prompts their warm desires,
> When music softens, and when dancing fires?
> 'Tis but their sylph, the wise celestials know,
> Though Honour is the word with men below.
> (I.71–78)

What makes it all so complicated is the doubleness of Pope's attitude toward Belinda's power. On the one hand she is the victim and the Baron the aggressor. On the other hand she is a huntress who has caught him in her "hairy sprindges" (II.25), and she capitalizes on the convention that beauty frees its possessor from ordinary limitations.

> If to her share some female errors fall,
> Look on her face, and you'll forget 'em all.
> (II.17–18)

In a dedicatory poem, *To Belinda on the Rape of the Lock*, Pope identifies "mankind" as the common foe of women, and commiserates interestingly with what he sees as female weakness:

> Nature to your undoing arms mankind
> With strength of body, artifice of mind;
> But gives your feeble sex, made up of fears,
> No guard but virtue, no redress but tears.
> (15–18)

The second line is echoed in Pope's *Iliad*, where Hector addresses Ajax during a heroic combat:

> Whom heav'n adorns, superior to thy kind,
> With strength of body, and with worth of mind.
> (VII.350–51)

In another passage "strength of body" is joined with "force of mind" (IX.73–74). In the lines to Belinda, "artifice," which *The Rape of the Lock* might have led one to associate with women, is frankly ascribed to male seducers, but this is hardly encouraging since it leaves women "feeble," weeping helplessly if their virtue should fail. (And this poem, like the final lines of the *Rape* itself, turns out to be an unabashed tribute to Pope's own achievement:) just as Lucrece "lives unblemished" in art (21), so Arabella Fermor should feel flattered that art will gain her immortality.

> But would your charms to distant times extend,
> Let Jervas paint them, and let Pope commend.
> Who censure most, more precious hairs would lose,
> To have the Rape recorded by his muse.
> (27–30)

These lines plainly say that Pope's art is ample compensation for the humiliating "rape." Surely the *Rape* has embodied Pope's own voyeuristic enjoyment. And if a sensible woman would lose "more precious hairs," then Pope almost seems to be saying that his muse accomplishes a rape of its own. The lock belongs neither to Belinda nor to the Baron now, but to the poet. Pope was clearly delighted with a poem by Lady Winchilsea that reassured him that he would not be torn apart by enraged women as Orpheus was:

> But you our follies gently treat,
>   And spin so fine the thread,
> You need not fear his awkward fate;
>   The *Lock* won't cost the *Head*.[51]

51. *To Mr. Pope*, included by Pope in *Poems on Several Occasions* (1717); reprinted in *Pope's Own Miscellany*, ed. Ault, p. 80.

In the world of *The Rape of the Lock*, the sophistication of sexual relations in early-eighteenth-century culture is sophisticated still further by poetic artifice. In *Eloisa to Abelard*, Pope imagines a pre-artificial state in which, as in Donne's lyrics, mutual understanding might be perfect and love might impose its own irresistible law:

> Oh happy state! when souls each other draw,
> When love is liberty, and nature, law:
> All then is full, possessing, and possessed,
> No craving void left aching in the breast.
>
> (91–94)

But if this was "once the lot of Abelard and me" (98), it is now lost forever, both because Abelard is far away and because his brutal castration has made sexual union impossible. Eloisa's lines here echo the beginning of Dryden's *Absalom and Achitophel*, which represents primitive Israel as a kind of happy state of nature:

> When nature prompted, and no law denied
> Promiscuous use of concubine and bride.
>
> (4–5)

Dryden's motive was to excuse the tireless philandering of Charles II; Pope's is to ratify the moral law that contradicts nature's promptings, and to relegate gratification to an irrecoverable past. In the *Essay on Man* the line from *Eloisa* is repeated in a description of the lost state of nature:

> Converse and love mankind might strongly draw,
> When love was liberty, and nature law.
>
> (III.207–8)

The sylphs fail to protect Belinda because she has "an earthly lover lurking at her heart" (III.144), which seems to mean that she really wants the Baron and ought to accept him. In *Eloisa* desire is criminal, in a fallen world in which criminality only intensifies desire: "How glowing guilt exalts the keen delight" (230). "Nature" is forced to surrender since consummation is impossible, but desire still refuses to abate:

> Nature stands checked; religion disapproves;
> Ev'n thou art cold—yet Eloisa loves.
>
> (259–60)

But it has to be said that Pope quickly withdraws from the darkest implications of *Eloisa*. Self-reproach never reaches the depths of loathed obsession that has haunted other poets:

> Past reason hunted, and, no sooner had,
> Past reason hated, as a swallowed bait.[52]

Neither Eloisa nor Pope is ever past reason. When the poem begins she has been struggling with turbulent emotions for a long time; we come in late, as it were, at the moment when she is putting it down on paper. The act of writing imposes clarity, and of course it gives permanent existence to what would otherwise be evanescent. The final lines of the poem, calling across the centuries to the poet who will share and sing her grief, constitute a tribute to the superiority of art to life. Pope may be frustrated in the world of experience, but he can still raise frustration to the level of art. Just as Eloisa survives in European memory, so Pope will be remembered and recreated by his readers. Language is used first to protect reality and then to replace it. As Gillian Beer argues in a subtle essay, an Ovidian heroic epistle like *Eloisa to Abelard* works to exorcise sexual guilt and to assert an identification between the female letter writer and the male poet. "Come!" is the reiterated plea, but the desired lover is forever absent. All that remains is language, as in Aphra Behn's wonderful phrase "With outstretched voice I cry."[53]

In the years that followed *The Rape of the Lock* and *Eloisa to Abelard*, Pope's actual relations with women—apart from a

---

52. William Shakespeare, Sonnet 129, "Th' expense of spirit in a waste of shame."

53. "'Our Unnatural No-voice': The Heroic Epistle, Pope, and Women's Gothic," *Yearbook of English Studies*, 12 (1982), 125–51. Behn is quoted (p. 141) from her version of Ovid's *Oenone to Paris*.

temporary passion for Lady Mary Wortley Montagu[54]—revolved principally about Martha and Theresa Blount, unmarried sisters in a Catholic family with whom Pope was on close terms for most of his life. At first he was attracted most to the beautiful and fickle Theresa, but later he gave his strongest affection to Martha (nicknamed Patty), whom he praised in a late letter to Swift: "Mrs. Patty Bl[ount] is one of the most considerate and mindful women in the world, toward others, the least so with regard to herself. . . . I scarce know two more women worth naming to you; the rest are ladies, run after music, and play at cards" (*Corr.* IV, 177–78). The distinction between women and ladies is telling, implying a critique of socially deformed behavior.

The precise nature of Pope's relationship with Martha Blount is unclear. Fifty years ago Sherburn said tartly, "Whether she was Pope's mistress is now nobody's business."[55] These days it is likelier to seem everybody's business, but the evidence remains inconclusive. Certainly Pope provided munificently for her in his will.[56] But from the much earlier period of *Eloisa*, the surviving letters suggest deep unhappiness at being esteemed rather than loved. Pope writes to both sisters in 1717, with a bitter reference to his deformity,

> Let me open my whole heart to you: I have sometimes found myself inclined to be in love with you: and as I have reason to know from your temper and conduct how miserably I should be used in that circumstance, it is worth my while to avoid it: it is enough to be disagreeable, without adding fool to it, by constant slavery. I have heard indeed of women that have had a kindness for men of my make; but it has been after enjoyment, never before; and I know to my cost you have had no taste of that talent in me, which most ladies would not only like better, but understand better, than any other I have.
>
> (*Corr.* I, 456)

54. As Patricia Meyer Spacks shows, Lady Mary must have found Pope's flirtatious letters presumptuous and hectoring; the cool generalities and emotional reserve of her replies indicate a refusal to let him fictionalize and fantasize her. "Imaginations Warm and Tender: Pope and Lady Mary," *South Atlantic Quarterly*, 83 (1984), 207–15.

55. *Early Career*, p. 291.

56. Reprinted by Mack, *The Garden and the City*, p. 265.

Since they refuse to try his physical talent, he must make do with his poetic talent. In another letter Pope returns to his favorite theme of poetic immortality, but very strikingly modulates into the sexual interest that underlies the poetic:

> A poor translator . . . comforts himself to reflect that he shall be remembered when people have forgot what colours you wore, and when those at whom you dress shall be dust! This is the pride of a poet, let me see if you dare own what is the pride of a woman, perhaps one article of it may be, to despise those who think themselves of some value, and to show your friends you can live without thinking of 'em at all. Do, keep your own secrets, that such fellows as I may laugh at ye in the valley of Jehosaphat, where cunning will be the foolishest thing in nature, and those white bums which I die to see will be shown to all the world.
>
> (*Corr.* I, 515)

Female pride encourages the Blount sisters to pretend indifference to Pope; or is it that they really *are* indifferent? The secret will remain locked up until the Last Judgment, which is a long time to wait either for secrets or for a view of white bums.

The *Epistle to a Lady,* many years later, ends by telling Martha that Apollo "to you gave sense, good humor, and a poet" (292). But as Pope dryly wrote to Caryll,

> Your . . . question about intending marriage made me laugh; for if that line meant any such thing, it must be over. 'Tis in the preterperfect tense, *Gave a Poet.* 'Tis a new sort of father for marriage: he [Apollo] gave me long ago to Belinda, as he did Homer to Achilles, and 'tis a mercy he has not given me to more ladies, but that I am almost as little inclined to celebrate that way, as the other.
>
> (*Corr.* III, 451)

For Pope to address *To a Lady* to Martha Blount is thus to place the work in a complicated personal context. Mack rather complacently declares that *To a Lady* is "the finest tribute that any eighteenth-century woman ever received."[57] Recent readings,

---

57. *Alexander Pope,* p. 340.

however, have brought out the extent to which Pope was committed to the idea that women are good only when passive, and are defined by relationships to men.[58]

Still, it is possible to make too much of the conventional pieties with which Pope ends the poem, and to overlook the fascination with which he paints the portraits that he condemns. The notorious line "But ev'ry woman is at heart a rake" (216) reflects a shocking, but also exciting, freedom from the male retirement ideal of Twickenham—decorous, controlled, carefully harmonious, living out a life of classical models. Women may be subject to the tyranny of social critics, but so long as they avoid public disgrace they are less bound by emotional rules than men, either because society encourages them to express emotion more freely, or else because their natures are swayed unpredictably. Not just the ferocious Atossa, but Flavia too has an excess of "spirit" and must therefore suffer all her life:

> Wise wretch! with pleasures too refined to please,
> With too much spirit to be e'er at ease,
> With too much quickness ever to be taught,
> With too much thinking to have common thought:
> Who purchase pain with all that joy can give,
> And die of nothing but a rage to live.
>
> (95–100)

The violated ideal here is one which Pope always sought to obey, and the violation reflects impulses which he certainly felt in himself.

Forms mask the reality of feeling, and feeling itself—the subject of the eighteenth-century preoccupation with "sensibility"—is a mask for something else. In the language of Eliot's Popean imitation,

> For varying forms, one definition's right:
> Unreal emotions, and real appetites.[59]

58. See esp. Pollak, *The Poetics of Sexual Myth*, ch. 4.
59. T. S. Eliot, *The Waste Land: A Facsimile and Transcript of the Original Drafts*, ed. Valerie Eliot (New York: Harcourt Brace Jovanovich, 1971), p. 41.

Annotating the line "Bred to disguise, in public 'tis you hide" (203), Warburton comments, "Female education is an art of teaching not to *be*, but to *appear*."[60] But is not this the basis of Pope's own lifelong behavior? Young's satire on women contains the couplet

> For her own breakfast she'll project a scheme,
> Nor take her tea without a stratagem.

Johnson very strikingly applied this to Pope himself: "In all his intercourse with mankind he had great delight in artifice, and endeavoured to attain all his purposes by indirect and unsuspected methods. 'He hardly drank tea without a stratagem.'"[61] One might say that Pope badly wants social forms to shape emotional experience, and is indignant with women—but also stimulated by them—for betraying the inadequacy of this wish.

Pope's customary mode, when it is not abusive, is all too close to Blake's parodic *Imitation of Pope: A Compliment to the Ladies*, with its carefully graded hierarchy:

> Wondrous the gods, more wondrous are the men,
> More wondrous wondrous still the cock and hen,
> More wondrous still the table, stool and chair;
> But ah! more wondrous still the charming fair.

Instead of permitting his own experience of subordination and marginality to inform his idea of women, Pope chose to displace upon them those traits which he distrusted in himself, and to present himself as the spokesman for a masculine culture. On this view, woman in his poems "displays his troublesome emotions while he dictates her behavior."[62] If he was condemned to sexual disappointment, Pope could still immortalize whichever "fair charmers" he chose; and if he was the little Alexander whom the ladies laughed at, he could still be the great poet who laughed at the ladies.

60. Pope's *Works* (1751), III, 207–8.
61. Young, *Satire* VI, p. 114; Johnson, *Lives*, III, 200.
62. Carol Virginia Pohli, "'The Point Where Sense and Dulness Meet': What Pope Knows about Knowing and about Women," *Eighteenth-Century Studies*, 19 (1985–86), 218.

2

Society, Money, Class

The line "Let us be fixed, and our own masters still" concludes a poem that ruefully acknowledges Pope's disappointment at inheriting no estate from his father, and makes
pointed reference to his temporary occupancy at Twickenham. The descriptions he applies to himself are spoken in the
original not by Horace but by a dispossessed tenant farmer:

> My lands are sold, my father's house is gone;
> I'll hire another's, is not that my own? . . .
> Pray heav'n it last! (cries Swift) as you go on:
> I wish to God this house had been your own. . . .
> Let lands and houses have what lords they will,
> Let us be fixed, and our own masters still.
> *(Satire* II.ii.155–80)

The humbleness of his life and estate are constant themes in
Pope's writing. In a letter to Ralph Allen he quotes Horace's
Parvum parva decent, "Small things befit small folk,"[1] and in
another to Fortescue he expatiates more largely:

> Mine are *poor* vanities, a few of the *worse sort* of laurels. I began
> my life without any views, and hope to end it without any
> regrets. I have raised no estate, nor aimed at it, though I in-
> herited none. I have lived decently, and not servilely, that's
> enough for me: I shall die poor, but not dishonoured; and if
> nobody weeps for me, nobody will curse my memory. Let
> greater men say this, if they can, and let them be *good*, if they
> dare.
> *(Corr.* IV, 156)

---

1. Horace's *Epistle* I.vii.44, quoted by Pope in *Corr.* IV, 191. (H. Rushton
Fairclough's translation, Horace, *Satires, Epistles and Ars Poetica*, Loeb Classical Library [London: Heinemann, 1929], p. 299.)

The note of high-minded poverty is explicit in lines addressed to Bolingbroke from Pope's grotto:

> Let such, such only, tread this sacred floor,
> Who dare to love their country, and be poor.[2]

Pope scholars have responded sympathetically to this image of modest competence at the lower margin of the propertied world. Mack describes Pope as "a species of country 'squire,' occupant and improver of a small 'estate,' living off annuities, investments, a small inheritance, and other revenues not gained by shopkeeping."[3]

In such a perspective, Pope's relation to the social and political world is heavily idealized. Living in quasi-Roman retirement with a small income on a small estate, he contrives to entertain a few valued friends and watches from afar the political battles of the great world. But politics need not be considered, as it usually is, as the day-to-day maneuvers of Walpole and his enemies. In a larger view, politics embraces the whole structure of wealth, property, and privilege in which a man like Pope was immersed, and we need to take that larger view before returning to the controversies of court and parliament. In Durkheim's terms, society confronts us as a *thing*, an intractable structure into which the individual must learn to fit. Some of the most powerful eighteenth-century novels, from *Robinson Crusoe* to *Caleb Williams*, are concerned with the difficulty of doing so, but the novels are also filled with narrative versions of the role playing to which Pope was deeply and consciously committed. As Peter Berger puts it, "We *want* to obey the rules. We *want* the parts that society has assigned to us."[4] But Pope was well aware that the rules themselves cried out for examination, and that his

---

2. *Verses on a Grotto by the River Thames at Twickenham* (TE VI, 382–83), included by Pope in a letter to Bolingbroke in 1740, *Corr.* IV, 262.

3. Maynard Mack, *The Garden and the City: Retirement and Politics in the Later Poetry of Pope, 1731–1743* (Toronto: University of Toronto Press, 1969), p. 233.

4. *Invitation to Sociology: A Humanistic Perspective* (New York: Doubleday, Anchor, 1963), p. 93.

own social status had to be created rather than taken for granted.

First, let us consider Pope's money, the necessary basis for his life as poet and gentleman, and a subject of more interest than is usually recognized. Unfortunately, reliable information is lacking. Late in the century Johnson and Warton, who had presumably consulted persons who knew Pope, estimated that he had an income of about £800 per year.[5] This would have been no small sum. In 1688, the year of Pope's birth, Gregory King thought that half the families in the country had incomes under £40 per year; Johnson wrote in the *Life of Savage,* published after Pope's death, that £50 per year would keep a family from want.[6] This would normally mean that more than one member of the family would have to work, for modern historians tell us that a laborer's annual income was less than £20 per year.[7] Conversion of these figures into modern buying power is notoriously difficult, but one authority suggests multiplying by 60,[8] which would give Pope an income of approximately £50,000 in 1980 pounds.

Some of this money came from Pope's father. Warburton thought that he retired from business with £15,000 or £20,000. Without explanation Sherburn objects, "That seems a large estimate," and puts the figure at £10,000 with the coy observation, "Such a fortune was the modest desideratum of heroes of fiction in the days of *David Simple.*"[9] Heroes of fiction aside, it would have amounted to more than half a million pounds in modern money, and Sherburn also mentions that Pope's father bought a fourteen-acre estate at Binfield for only

5. Samuel Johnson, *Life of Pope,* in *Lives of the English Poets,* ed. G. B. Hill (Oxford: Clarendon, 1905), III, 203; Joseph Warton's edition of Pope's *Works* (1797), I, lxxi.

6. King is cited by Roy Porter, *English Society in the Eighteenth Century* (Harmondsworth: Penguin, 1982), p. 28; Johnson, *Lives,* II, 398.

7. See John Burnett, *History of the Cost of Living* (Harmondsworth: Penguin, 1969), pp. 164–66.

8. Porter, *English Society in the Eighteenth Century,* p. 13 ("Conversion Tables").

9. George Sherburn, *The Early Career of Alexander Pope* (Oxford: Clarendon, 1934), p. 34.

£445 (p. 36). Fearful of anti-Catholic confiscations, the elder
Pope lived off the principal rather than investing it, so the
poet inherited only a few thousand pounds.[10]

Whatever his inheritance, it is important to note that during Pope's childhood money was simply *there*, a fact that con-
tributes to the almost preternatural tranquillity he ascribes to
his father:

> Stranger to civil and religious rage,
> The good man walked innoxious through his age. . . .
> By nature honest, by experience wise,
> Healthy by temp'rance and by exercise . . .
> Oh grant me thus to live, and thus to die!
> Who sprung from kings shall know less joy than I.
> (*To Arbuthnot* 394–405)

Pope's early experience of automatic income no doubt contributed to his later irritation at having to earn it. Johnson
resented, on behalf of all wage-laboring writers, Pope's easy
contempt: "The great topic of his ridicule is poverty: the
crimes with which he reproaches his antagonists are their
debts, their habitation in the Mint, and their want of a dinner."[11] And Pope's words do seem unfeeling, if not smug:

> Yet then did Gildon draw his venal quill;
> I wished the man a dinner, and sat still:
> Yet then did Dennis rave in furious fret;
> I never answered, I was not in debt.
> If want provoked, or madness made them print,
> I waged no war with Bedlam or the Mint.
> (*To Arbuthnot*, 151–56)

Needing more income than his investments could provide,
Pope brought off a remarkable coup by offering his translation
of Homer in an expensive subscription. Leslie Stephen, in his

---

10. According to Spence, Pope told Martha Blount that he inherited between £3,000 and £4,000. Joseph Spence, *Observations, Anecdotes, and Characters of Books and Men*, ed. James M. Osborn (Oxford: Clarendon, 1966), I, 7.
11. *Lives*, III, 204. The Mint was a refuge in which a debtor might evade
arrest.

survey of literature and society in the eighteenth century, explains what this implies in social as well as financial terms:

> He had no [monetary] interest in the general sale, which was large enough to make his publisher's fortune. The publisher meanwhile supplied him gratuitously with the copies for which the subscribers paid him six guineas apiece. That means that he received a kind of commission from the upper class to execute the translation.[12]

Stephen estimates that Pope made £9,000 from both the *Iliad* and the *Odyssey*; Sherburn is unclear about the *Iliad* but puts the *Odyssey* profits at over £5,000.[13] One may not be altogether sympathetic, therefore, when Pope laments,

> Hibernian politics, O Swift! thy fate;
> And Pope's, ten years to comment and translate.
> (*Dunciad* III.331–32)

Still less edifying is the original version in the three-book *Dunciad*,

> Hibernian politics, O Swift, thy doom,
> And Pope's, translating three whole years with Broome.[14]

William Broome and Elijah Fenton, who between them translated half of the *Odyssey* (Broome wrote all the notes) got £800, or a sixth of Pope's share. Broome wrote to Fenton when Pope was pretending to have done nearly all of the translation, but ascribing some weaker parts of it to his collaborators, "The mines of gold and silver belong to the monarch, as privileges of his supremacy, but coarser metals are left for the use of the owner of the soil" (*Corr.* II, 390). A few months earlier Broome had bitterly remarked, "I fear we have hunted with the lion, who, like his predecessor in Phaedrus, will take

---

12. *English Literature and Society in the Eighteenth Century* (London: Duckworth, 1904), p. 51.
13. Leslie Stephen, *Alexander Pope* (New York: Harper, 1902), p. 63; Sherburn, *Early Career*, p. 259.
14. *Dunciad Variorum* III.327–28, in *TE* V, 190–91. When Broome objected to this passage Pope made the revision, but managed to insert yet another insult to Broome in the final *Dunciad* (I.146, *TE* V, 280).

the first share merely because he is a lion, the second because he is more brave; the third because he is of most importance; and if either of us shall presume to touch the fourth, woe be to us" (*Corr.* II, 344).

There was nothing unworldly about Pope—his letters are full of shrewd investment planning—but clearly he did not care to think of himself as a wage earner, however exalted; and as Sherburn observes, "Nothing annoyed the poet more than to have his father called a farmer or a hatter."[15] The ideal expressed in the *Ode on Solitude*, which Pope claimed to have written at the age of twelve, is based upon inherited property:

> Happy the man, whose wish and care
> A few paternal acres bound,
> Content to breathe his native air,
>   In his own ground.

But in fact Pope's father moved twice, and the Binfield estate was only a temporary home. The poet's sense of being an outsider was certainly heightened when the family was forced to sell; he wrote to his Catholic friend Caryll, "I write this from Windsor Forest, which I am come to take my last look and leave of. We here bid our papist-neighbours adieu, much as those who go to be hanged do their fellow-prisoners, who are condemned to follow 'em a few weeks after" (*Corr.* I, 336–37). Pope often remarks that the estate at Twickenham was rented rather than owned, and this too may have been for prudential reasons, since Catholics were legally prohibited from buying land. In any case many Twickenham properties were being rented at the time.[16] Late in life Pope had the chance to purchase the estate for £1,000, but chose not to do so (*Corr.* IV, 446).

Pope was fond of describing his estate as diminutive:

> I am as busy in three inches of gardening, as any man can be in threescore acres. I fancy myself like the fellow that spent

---

15. *Early Career*, p. 30.
16. See Peter Dixon, *The World of Pope's Satires* (London: Methuen, 1968), pp. 142–43.

his life in cutting the twelve apostles in one cherry-stone. I have a theatre, an arcade, a bowling green, a grove, and what not, in a bit of ground that would have been but a plate of sallet to Nebuchadnezzar, the first day he was turned to graze.

(*Corr.* II, 328)

But this was written to an earl. Nebuchadnezzar would have had to be a voracious feeder, since Pope's theater, arcade, bowling green, and gardens occupied five acres. These contained, among other things, four leaden urns, sixteen stone ones, three statues and four "bustos" of classical figures, and an elaborate assemblage of shells and minerals in the grotto, on which Martha Blount (almost certainly underestimating) said he spent a thousand pounds.[17] Mack speaks of Pope's "small house" but mentions elsewhere that it had "ten or twelve rooms";[18] among its furnishings were over fifty portraits of Pope's friends.

It is worth remembering, then, that all of this Horatian ease was founded on plenty of money by almost anyone's standards. In this context it is interesting to ponder the difficulty Pope has in dealing with the question of wealth, faced as he was—like everyone else in his time—by enormous changes in the structure of life that could be only dimly understood.[19] His conception is essentially ethical, based on the proper use of wealth and haunted by the avarice that drives men to accumulate endlessly:

If wealth alone then make and keep us blest,
Still, still be getting, never, never rest.
(*Epistle* I.vi.95–96)

But unlike the simple greed that a medieval satirist might expose, the modern kind works by manipulation of mysteri-

17. Spence, *Observations*, I, 157. On the urns and statues see Mack, *The Garden and the City*, p. 28n.
18. *The Garden and the City*, pp. 32, 16n.
19. Much valuable work has been done in recent years on the implications of the "financial revolution" for Pope's culture. For a good summary see David B. Morris, *Alexander Pope: The Genius of Sense* (Cambridge, Mass.: Harvard University Press, 1984), ch. 7.

ous abstractions, "blest paper-credit" (*To Bathurst*, 69). "Every valuable, every pleasant thing," Pope wrote after the collapse of the South Sea Bubble, in which he had heavily invested, "is sunk in an ocean of avarice and corruption. The son of a first minister is a proper match for a daughter of a late South Sea director,—so money upon money increases, copulates, and multiplies, and guineas beget guineas in *saecula saeculorum*" (*Corr.* II, 182). Horace says mildly, "With many their money grows with interest unobserved," *multis occulto crescit res faenore.*[20] Pope turns this into a masterful outburst of controlled revulsion:

> While with the silent growth of ten percent,
> In dirt and darkness hundreds stink content.
> (*Epistle* I.i.132–33)

Beyond the indecency with which money reproduces itself, Pope despises its conspicuous consumption by parasites like the woman-about-town Con Philips, as he indicates with a disgusted "fusion of the metaphors of land and sex":[21]

> "Treat on, treat on," is her eternal note,
> And lands and tenements go down her throat.
> (*Satire* I.ii.13–14)

Very likely Pope thought that an honest merchant like his father could not have survived in the world of speculative finance; he uses *honest* in its traditional sense of "virtuous" rather than its modern sense of "dealing fairly":[22]

> Asleep and naked as an Indian lay,
> An honest factor stole a gem away.
> (*To Bathurst*, 361–62)

Honesty in its prudential sense, as in Defoe's fiction, can easily be a mask for theft. And from such thefts the greatest of family dynasties may be created, as the ensuing lines hint:

20. *Epistle* I.i.80, in Fairclough's Loeb edition, pp. 256–57.
21. Frank Stack, *Pope and Horace: Studies in Imitation* (Cambridge: Cambridge University Press, 1985), p. 84.
22. See Dixon, *World of Pope's Satires*, pp. 131–32.

He pledged it to the knight; the knight had wit,
So kept the diamond, and the rogue was bit.

Johnson quotes these lines to illustrate *bite:* "To cheat; to trick;
to defraud: a low phrase."[23] And they carry a further meaning, since *bit* closely echoes *Pitt.* Thomas Pitt—whose grand-
son and great-grandson became prime ministers—was notorious for unscrupulously acquiring and selling the famous
Pitt Diamond.

It was normal for Pope and his contemporaries to think in
ethical terms: Pitt was slippery, Con Philips sleazy. But it was
also apparent that money was being newly professionalized,
controlled by behind-the-scenes manipulators whose waxen
seals, in Swift's metaphor, resemble the effigies of witchcraft:

Conceive the works of midnight hags,
Tormenting fools behind their backs;
Thus bankers o'er their bills and bags
Sit squeezing images of wax.[24]

Commercial sex, gambling losses, and the unwise purchase
of mortgages merge into a single Satanic pattern, as in the
lines Pope added to his imitation of Donne:

And when rank widows purchase luscious nights,
Or when a duke to Jansen punts at White's,
Or city heir in mortgage melts away,
Satan himself feels far less joy than they.[25]

Pope's conservatism runs much deeper than partisan dislike of Whigs. Its foundation is an idea of simplicity which
the modern world is felt to violate, an attitude as old as Plato.
The *Republic* is, in its positive aspect, an idealized vision of a
harmonious community. But in its negative aspect it expresses indignation at a wave of complexities, or specializa-
tions, which are felt to be overwhelming traditional simplic-

23. Samuel Johnson, *A Dictionary of the English Language* (1755).
24. Jonathan Swift, *The Run upon the Bankers*, 29–32.
25. *The Second Satire of Dr. John Donne*, 87–90. At White's gaming house
the duke of Bedford lost £3,800 to Janssen in a single twenty-five-hour period
(*TE* IV, 141n).

ity. Philosophy has fallen to sophists who cultivate rhetoric rather than truth. Law is in the hands of similar types, and the proliferation of statutes is a symptom of their ability to pervert justice. Medicine has become an elaborate specialty although Plato claims, just as many eighteenth-century writers would, that a well-balanced person can stay healthy with no need for doctors, who cater to the ills that luxurious living creates. And the arts likewise are degenerating, poetry turning sensational, music complicated and emotional.

Pope's animus comes from just this kind of classical attitude, spiced by Juvenal's diatribes against corruption in imperial Rome. He was deeply sympathetic with—and deeply influenced by—Bolingbroke's criticism of paper credit, stockjobbing, and commercial monopolies, and by his commitment to the landed gentry, who felt themselves robbed by the new financial manipulators. "They have bodies," Bolingbroke's periodical *The Craftsman* said of the giant companies, "but no souls, nor consequently consciences."[26] Anyone could see that money was no simple medium of exchange, but rather an incarnation of power. Bolingbroke explicitly says, "The power of money, as the world is now constituted, is real power."[27]

What remained less obvious was the extent to which money simply objectified power that had previously disguised itself in ethical and patriarchal terms. The immense popularity, in the generation after Pope, of Goldsmith's *Deserted Village* and *Vicar of Wakefield* is partly explained by their heartfelt nostalgia for a lost social ideal. Goldsmith wrote in *The Traveller,*

> As Nature's ties decay,
> As duty, love, and honour fail to sway,

26. No. 246 (31 Aug. 1734), quoted by Isaac Kramnick, *Bolingbroke and His Circle: The Politics of Nostalgia in the Age of Walpole* (Cambridge, Mass.: Harvard University Press, 1968), p. 72. Kramnick's third chapter, "Bolingbroke and the New England," is a concise and valuable survey of the subject.

27. Henry St. John, Viscount Bolingbroke, *The Works of Lord Bolingbroke* (Philadelphia, 1841), II, 166; quoted by Kramnick, *Bolingbroke and His Circle,* p. 78.

Fictitious bonds, the bonds of wealth and law,
Still gather strength and force unwilling awe.
(349–52)

Pope's nostalgia is similar but his vision is darker, and one of his last satires rises to an emblematic vision of the triumph of Vice:

Our youth, all liv'ried o'er with foreign gold,
Before her dance; behind her crawl the old!
(*Epilogue* I.155–56)

Pope's social theory is fascinating because its inner conflict is so naked: on the one hand, a passionate affirmation of society as a self-regulating order; on the other, a passionate revulsion against actual behavior and the perversions of order that ensue. The ideal is a universal harmony, ethical and aesthetic as well as political, that is symbolized in the *concordia discors* of *Windsor-Forest* and can be paralleled in such contemporaries as Shaftesbury:

Harmony is harmony by nature, let men judge ever so ridiculously of music. So is symmetry and proportion founded still in nature, let men's fancy prove ever so barbarous, or their fashions ever so Gothic in their architecture, sculpture, or whatever other designing art. 'Tis the same case, where life and manners are concerned. Virtue has the same fixed standard. The same numbers, harmony, and proportion will have place in morals; and are discoverable in the characters and affections of mankind.[28]

Speaking of wealthy landowners who neither revel nor stint, Donne says tersely, "None starve, none surfeit so." Pope characteristically develops the thought into a couplet that rhetorically embodies the "just mean" it extols:

28. Anthony Ashley Cooper, third earl of Shaftesbury, *Characteristicks* (4th ed., 1732), I, 353; quoted by Mack, *The Garden and the City*, pp. 34–35. The classic account of *concordia discors* in *Windsor-Forest* is E. R. Wasserman's in *The Subtler Language: Critical Readings of Neoclassic and Romantic Poems* (Baltimore: Johns Hopkins University Press, 1959), ch. 4.

> And all mankind might that just mean observe,
> In which none e'er could surfeit, none could starve.[29]

In Pope's political theory, as in the eighteenth century generally right down to the framing of the American Constitution, competing "interests" harmonize almost miraculously,

> Till jarring int'rests of themselves create
> Th' according music of a well-mixed state.
> (*Essay on Man* III.293–94)

This harmony is inseparable from social and political hierarchy, as Pope emphasizes a few lines later:

> Draw to one point, and to one centre bring
> Beast, man, or angel, servant, lord, or king.
> (301–2)

A major function of eighteenth-century conservative writing is to justify the status quo, making power palatable by affirming that it knows its obligations and limits. To preserve such a system from the suspicion of exploitation, it is necessary to defend it with the rhetoric of fairness and mutual advantage. Thus the legal system, as E. P. Thompson describes it, was massively manipulated by the governing elite, but they still paid allegiance to the idea of law both in theory and in practice, and permitted their power to be curtailed by it. If they had not done so, rulers as well as ruled would have had to perceive the system as a mere sham.[30] For this very reason eighteenth-century conservatives—Swift, Pope, Goldsmith, Johnson, Burke—were fiercely critical of abuses and "corruption": they had a crucial stake in believing that the (uncorrupted) system was sound. There may be a sense in which, as Thompson puts it, "the ascendant Hanoverian Whigs appeared as no more than a sort of state banditry."[31] But that does not mean that the state itself was perceived as

29. *The Second Satire of Dr. John Donne*, 119–20. Donne's original is quoted in *TE* IV, 142.
30. *Whigs and Hunters: The Origin of the Black Act* (New York: Pantheon, 1975), esp. pp. 258–69.
31. Ibid., p. 294.

criminal. Thompson has not succeeded in proving that Pope experienced a drastic political conversion when his brother-in-law and nephew were arrested for deer stealing, and Pat Rogers, who ably makes the case against Thompson, comments that the method of the Waltham Black poachers "was recognisably that of gangsters at large."[32]

What is ultimately at issue is what sociologists call legitimation: abuses are shown to be *only* abuses, exceptions that prove the social rule. Hierarchy is presented not as a convenient way of structuring society, but as the inevitable norm. In *Gulliver's Travels*, even the utopian school system in Lilliput returns children to their original social class, and the Houyhnhnms not only control the Yahoos but are stratified by class with bays on top and sorrels below. Laputa allegorizes a corrupt courtier system, but even there a good nobleman, Lord Munodi, shows how a superior ought to relate to his dependents. Pope's poems are filled with praise of similar figures, from great magnates like Bathurst and Burlington down to modest figures like the Man of Ross, who serves as a focus for local charity. Making inquiries about the original, Pope says "I was determined the ground work at least should be *Truth*," but adds, "If any man shall ever happen to endeavour to emulate the Man of Ross, 'twill be no manner of harm if I make him think he was something more charitable and more beneficent than really he was, for so much more good it would put the imitator upon doing."[33]

Without question this is a double theodicy, in Max Weber's sense, that justifies the social order as well as the cosmic, and indeed conflates the two. From a modern perspective it is impossible not to flinch at lines like these, in which Pope lauds his friend Bathurst:

> To want or worth well-weighed, be bounty giv'n,
> And ease, or emulate, the care of Heav'n.

---

32. "Blacks and Poetry and Pope," in Pat Rogers, *Eighteenth Century Encounters: Studies in Literature and Society in the Age of Walpole* (Brighton: Harvester, 1985), p. 78.

33. Letter to Tonson, *Corr.* III, 290. The portrait of the Man of Ross appears in the *Epistle to Bathurst*, 249 ff.

> Whose measure full o'erflows on human race
> Mend Fortune's fault, and justify her grace.
>
> > (*To Bathurst* 229–32)

Dixon comments sardonically, "Christianity no longer requires men to sell all they have and give to the poor," and quotes Bishop Butler: "As Solomon expresses it in brief, and with much force, 'the rich ruleth over the poor.' And this their general intercourse, with the superiority on one hand, and dependence on the other, are in no sort accidental, but arise necessarily from a settled providential disposition of things, for their common good."[34] It is certainly true that the rich, in this conception, have the right to pick and choose in enacting the will of heaven: "To want or worth well-weighed, be bounty giv'n." But it is also true that they are morally obligated to do it. Few modern people give an eighth of their income to charity as Pope did.[35] Still, Warburton's paraphrase of the lines in *To Bathurst* brings out their complacency: "Such of the rich whose full measure overflows on human race, repair the wrongs of Fortune done to the indigent; and, at the same time, justify the favours she had bestowed upon themselves."[36] As in *Tom Jones*, Providence gives moral goodness while Fortune gives (or withholds) money.

Behind all of Pope's ruminations on this topic lies a dilemma. On the one hand, human desire and greed supply the motor that drives the divinely appointed system:

> Thus God and Nature linked the gen'ral frame,
> And bade self-love and social be the same.
>
> > (*Essay on Man*, III.317–18)

On the other hand, self-love is in practice directly contrary to the precepts of Christianity, which commands us to love our neighbors as ourselves.

---

34. *World of Pope's Satires*, pp. 149–50.
35. See Johnson, *Lives*, III, referring to a 1729 letter from Pope to Swift (*Corr.* III, 57).
36. Pope's *Works* (1751), III, 243.

> Yet, to be just to these poor men of pelf,
> Each does but hate his neighbour as himself.
>
> *(To Bathurst,* 109–10)

The contradiction is far from peculiar to Pope; it lies at the heart of a culture which still imagines itself in traditional ethical terms, but which is committed to a radical individualism in which the sanctity of property is the chief preoccupation of law and government alike. According to Locke, "Government has no other end but the preservation of property," and William Blackstone saw property as the basis of law, founded not just in reason but in the "imagination" and "affections" too: "There is nothing which so generally strikes the imagination, and engages the affections of mankind, as the right of property; or that sole and despotic dominion which one man claims and exercises over the external things of the world, in total exclusion of the right of any other individual in the universe." [37] Defoe, who was twice bankrupt, struggled in vain in *Moll Flanders* to reconcile ethical probity with economic survival, and in *Robinson Crusoe* he reconciled them only through a fantasy of total mastery in total isolation.

Once society is introduced, self-love turns to selfishness and disorder overwhelms order. But the notion of acquisitiveness as the motor of a self-governing machine was deeply attractive in the eighteenth century, and forms the basis of Adam Smith's economic thought—which betrays the same unhappiness about human consequences that Pope's poems do. [38] The notion of checks and balances as an ideal *concordia* continued to capture the imaginations of many hardheaded people. The same Blackstone, soaring into rhyme, hymned "Britannia's Law" as a perfectly calibrated engine:

> Observe how parts with parts unite
> In one harmonious rule of right;

37. John Locke, *The Second Treatise of Government;* Blackstone, *Commentaries on the Laws of England;* both quoted by Douglas Hay, "Property, Authority and the Criminal Law," in Hay et al., *Albion's Fatal Tree: Crime and Society in Eighteenth-Century England* (New York: Pantheon, 1975), pp. 18–19.

38. See Laura Brown, *Alexander Pope* (Oxford: Blackwell, 1985), pp. 79–93.

> See countless wheels distinctly tend
> By various laws to one great end.[39]

In the *Essay on Man* Pope sketches the way in which primitive man learned his politics from "the ant's republic, and the realm of bees," but the analogy works subversively to show how inferior man is even to the insects in disposing of wealth and property:

> How those in common all their wealth bestow,
> And anarchy without confusion know;
> And these for ever, though a monarch reign,
> Their sep'rate cells and properties maintain.
> (III.185–88)

The *Epistles to Several Persons*, which Warburton reentitled the *Moral Essays*, are filled with uneasy references to charity performed uncharitably:

> Not always actions show the man: we find
> Who does a kindness, is not therefore kind.
> (*To Cobham*, 61–62)

> Yet hence the poor are clothed, the hungry fed;
> Health to himself, and to his infants bread
> The lab'rer bears: What his hard heart denies,
> His charitable vanity supplies.
> (*To Burlington*, 169–72)

Traditional ethics defines charity by the intention, not the result. But Pope is keenly aware that some people, quite deliberately, perform actions that look "kind" but are done without kindness. So he is obliged to look instead to the effects: the rich builder's vanity produces the effects of charity without any trace of charity itself. This generalizes "charity" into an inevitable condition of things, which works itself out whether people intend it or not.

> Ask we what makes one keep, and one bestow?
> That POW'R who bids the ocean ebb and flow,

39. [William Blackstone], *The Lawyer's Farewell to His Muse, Written in the Year 1744*, in Dodsley's *Collection of Poems by Several Hands* (1770), IV, 226.

Bids seed-time, harvest, equal course maintain,
Through reconciled extremes of drought and rain.
(*To Bathurst*, 165–68)

Pope does not ask why certain people happen to be rich, but only why one rich person spends while another saves. And as Laura Brown comments, the cycles of finance merge into those of nature.[40]

Providentialism is thus translated, quite baldly, into a socioeconomic system, and is surprisingly similar at bottom to nineteenth-century laissez-faire, however different Pope's rhetoric may make it seem. And indeed his realism often tends to contradict the high-minded pieties of other passages that work from picturesque analogy rather than from social experience: self-love expanding to social like ripples in a lake (*Essay on Man* IV.361–72), or the loving support of vine by elm:

Man, like the gen'rous vine, supported lives;
The strength he gains is from th' embrace he gives.
(III.311–12)

It is easy enough to expose Pope's difficulties here, but they were deeply embedded in his culture, and we ought to admire the disillusioned insight in his poems that often subverts official orthodoxy. Defoe is far more incoherent than Pope, the commercial boosterism of his tracts belied at every point by the grim realism of his novels. And there is nothing in Pope like Addison's unctuous tribute to the Royal Exchange:

As I am a great lover of mankind, my heart naturally overflows with pleasure at the sight of a happy and prosperous multitude, insomuch that at many public solemnities I cannot forbear expressing my joy with tears that have stolen down my cheeks. For this reason I am wonderfully delighted to see such a body of men thriving in their own private fortunes, and at the same time promoting the public stock.
(*Spectator* 69)

It would be too easy to say that Pope did not understand what he took from Hobbes and Mandeville. He understood

40. *Alexander Pope*, pp. 109–11.

it, but he did not know how to reconcile it with the social optimism in which he also wanted to believe.

> Force first made conquest, and that conquest, law;
> Till superstition taught the tyrant awe,
> Then shared the tyranny, then lent it aid,
> And gods of conqu'rors, slaves of subjects made.
>
> *(Essay on Man* III.245–48)

From this it is but a step, though not a step Pope would dream of taking, to Hume's natural history of religion and Blake's satire on superstition and tyranny.

The full ambiguity of the economic system, which Pope of course sees as the behavior of individuals rather than as a system, is apparent in the twistings of the *Epistle to Bathurst*. The operations of natural appetite, normally hailed as the mechanism that keeps society running, are held up to disquieting suspicion:

> What Nature wants (a phrase I much distrust)
> Extends to luxury, extends to lust:
> And if we count among the needs of life
> Another's toil, why not another's wife?
>
> (25–28)

Warburton, not surprisingly, suppressed that last couplet because of its "bad reasoning," and Bateson is careful to smooth the matter over: "The 'bad reasoning' is his rather than Pope's. The lines merely expand the preceding couplet, 'Another's toil' defining 'luxury', and 'another's wife' illustrating 'lust'. Their omission makes the transition unpleasantly abrupt" (*TE* III-ii, 88n). Much more is involved, however, than an abrupt transition. Pope does indeed believe that "we" count another's toil among the needs of life, and he comes close to recognizing the ethical abyss that this threatens to open up.

The whole paradox of selfish means producing selfless ends is unforgettably imaged later on in *To Bathurst*, immediately after the lines about seedtime and harvest.

> Who sees pale Mammon pine amidst his store,
> Sees but a backward steward for the poor;

> This year a reservoir, to keep and spare,
> The next a fountain, spouting through his heir,
> In lavish streams to quench a country's thirst,
> And men and dogs shall drink him till they burst.
> (171–76)

Good stewardship is a central ideal for Pope,[41] but here it seems that backward stewardship gets results just as much as frontward does. Miserliness becomes a reservoir and gross extravagance a fountain, both of which are positive images (though "spouting" suggests sarcasm). But one is then staggered by the bursting dogs and men, an appalling vision whose moral disgust resembles Spenser's description of Error's whelps that devour their dam:

> Having all satisfied their bloody thirst,
> Their bellies swolne he saw with fulness burst.[42]

When the Man of Ross finally appears in *To Bathurst*, his selfless generosity is like light shining through the moral murk, but it also seems rather incredible, attested as it is by lisping babes:

> Who taught that heav'n-directed spire to rise?
> The Man of Ross, each lisping babe replies.
> Behold the market-place with poor o'erspread!
> The Man of Ross divides the weekly bread:
> Behold yon alms-house, neat, but void of state,
> Where Age and Want sit smiling at the gate. . . .
> (261–66)

There is no reason why the poor should not be imagined as a body rather than separately, or why Age and Want should not smile like figures in an emblem, but all the same one senses that Pope prefers not to think of them as individuals. There is no place in his imaginative world for the underside of economic life, poverty as a condition that is experienced rather than as an object on which to bestow charity. Such

---

41. As Howard Erskine-Hill demonstrates in rich detail in *The Social Milieu of Alexander Pope* (New Haven: Yale University Press, 1975).

42. Edmund Spenser, *The Faerie Queene*, I.i.26.

matters, for the most part, were segregated into the novel in the eighteenth century, though Lonsdale's magnificent anthology offers some memorable expressions in "subliterary" poems:

> I rose betimes to go I knew not where,
> By eventide I found that I was there;
> And as I went I fell upon a strand,
> Where all men do obey, but none command.
> I asked the name of this unpleasant shore;
> They said, "It is the Province of the Poor,
> And lies upon the coast of Want and Wrong,
> Which you will find as you do pass along."[43]

If we focus for a moment on the recipients of charity rather than on the donors, we may be startled to learn that something like half of the eighteenth-century population was unable to earn even a subsistence income, and was therefore dependent to some extent on public or private charity.[44] It is also worth remarking that in literature as in landscape painting, people actually working are hard to find except as picturesque types.[45] When farm laborers appear they are joyous partners with bountiful Ceres, and are "tempted" to pluck nature's bounty as Pope does his host's grapes and peaches:

> Here Ceres' gifts in waving prospect stand,
> And nodding tempt the joyful reaper's hand.
> (*Windsor-Forest* 39–40)

Ceres, to be sure, gives her fruits to those who work for them, as in Gay's lines that command the privileged hunter to stay out of the fields while the goddess rewards the reapers:

---

43. John Wright, *The Poor Man's Province* (1727), in *The New Oxford Book of Eighteenth Century Verse*, ed. Roger Lonsdale (Oxford: Oxford University Press, 1984), p. 196. This poem is clearly influenced by Bunyan, both in manner and in poetic style (see the poems prefixed to the two parts of *The Pilgrim's Progress*).

44. See W. A. Speck, *Stability and Strife: England, 1714–1760* (Cambridge, Mass.: Harvard University Press, 1977), pp. 34–35.

45. See Raymond Williams, *The Country and the City* (London: Chatto and Windus, 1973), and John Barrell, *The Dark Side of the Landscape: The Rural Poor in English Painting, 1730–1840* (Cambridge: Cambridge University Press, 1980).

Let the keen hunter from the chase refrain,
Nor render all the plowman's labour vain,
When Ceres pours out plenty from her horn,
And clothes the fields with golden ears of corn.
Now, now, ye reapers, to your task repair,
Haste, save the product of the bounteous year.[46]

But Ceres and the reapers are both seen from outside.

Only rarely do we hear, as from the "thresher poet" Stephen Duck, that it is not the laborers but the farmer who stands to profit—and that he too has a landlord to fear:

Soon as the harvest hath laid bare the plains,
And barns well filled reward the farmer's pains,
What corn each sheaf will yield intent to hear,
And guess from thence the profits of the year,
Or else impending ruin to prevent
By paying, timely, threat'ning landlord's rent,
He calls his threshers forth: around we stand,
With deep attention waiting his command.[47]

Six years later, after being taken up by the court, Duck revised the opening lines:

Soon as the golden harvest quits the plains,
And CERES' gifts reward the farmer's pains. . . .[48]

Raymond Williams has commented bitterly on Duck's transformation into a singer of groves, nymphs, and swains: "He wrote *Gratitude: A Pastoral:* those two words, together, are the essential history."[49] But there is a still deeper pathos in Duck's awareness of the cultural gulf that must always exist between himself and his benefactors. Pope's friend Spence, Oxford professor of poetry and one of Duck's patrons, reported, "It seems plain to me that he has got English just as we get Latin.

46. John Gay, *Rural Sports*, II. 281–86.
47. *The Thresher's Labour* (1730), in *The New Oxford Book of Eighteenth Century Verse*, p. 224.
48. *The Thresher's Labour* (1736), reprinted in facsimile with Mary Collier's *The Woman's Labour* by Moira Ferguson, Augustan Reprint Society No. 230 (Los Angeles: William Andrews Clark Memorial Library, 1985), p. 11.
49. *The Country and the City*, p. 89.

Most of his language in conversation, as well as in his poems, is acquired by reading." According to Spence, Duck said of his own poems, "Gentlemen, indeed, might like 'em, because they were made by a poor fellow in a barn; but that he knew as well as anybody that they were not really good in themselves."[50]

I do not mean to suggest that Pope should have written about the pains of labor, let alone adopted the laborer's point of view; I only want to emphasize how uncongenial the fact of labor is to his imaginative world. Just as in Fielding's fiction, circumlocution is needed to talk about such people, as when Mallet tells Pope that a farm woman is unusually good looking: "Here, indeed, to atone for the rest of her country-women, I met with the greatest beauty I ever saw, and yet this plebeian angel, this goddess of low degree, was doing the humble office of a jack, or in plain English, turning a spit" (*Corr.* III, 422). And just as in Fielding, the workers one sees tend to be servants of one kind or another, normally regarded as venal and vulgar. Thus the sewer goddess Cloacina responds to the link-boys who light one's way through city streets, and to the watermen who row one across the Thames:

> List'ning delighted to the jest unclean
> Of link-boys vile, and watermen obscene.
> (*Dunciad* II.99–100)

In Gay the nighttime cruelty of London is still more vivid, and is identified with abusers of charity:

> The lurking thief, who while the daylight shone,
> Made the walls echo with his begging tone:
> That crutch which late compassion moved, shall wound
> Thy bleeding head, and fell thee to the ground.
> Though thou art tempted by the link-man's call,
> Yet trust him not along the lonely wall;
> In the mid-way he'll quench the flaming brand,
> And share the booty with the pilf'ring band.[51]

---

50. Joseph Spence, *A Full and Authentick Account of Stephen Duck, the Wiltshire Poet* (1731), pp. 10, 26.
51. John Gay, *Trivia*, I, 135–42.

One might recall Wimsatt's sarcasm about Gay's *Trivia* as an accurate representation of London.[52]

The city, indeed, is usually inimical to Pope, "an external force, a thing with energy and destiny of its own, inhuman, beyond his power to order."[53] Retirement means suburban living, in which the poet lurks in hiding, just barely within earshot of the busy world:

> Know, all the distant din that world can keep
> Rolls o'er my grotto, and but soothes my sleep.
>   (*Satire* II.i, 123–24)

The enthusiast in Joseph Warton's poem, very similarly, gets pleasure from being *just far enough* from the city:

> Oft near some crowded city would I walk,
> Listening the far-off noises, rattling cars,
> Loud shouts of joy, sad shrieks of sorrow, knells
> Full slowly tolling, instruments of trade,
> Striking mine ears with one deep-swelling hum.[54]

This is a world where people are supposed to know their place, whether rural or urban, and where they look silly or wicked when they fail to do so. In a note to the *Dunciad* Pope quite casually suggests that social "high" is to moral "true" as social "low" is to moral "false": "*Order* here is to be understood extensively, both as civil and moral, the distinctions between high and low in society, and true and false in individuals" (*TE* V, 340–41n). And in a striking addition to Horace he makes it clear that to act like a servant is to be literally degraded:

> See good Sir George of ragged livery stript,
> By worthier footmen pissed upon and whipped!
>   (*Satire* I.ii.55–56)

Thomas Edwards comments that the adulterer in disguise "pretends to change his status when he stoops to actions un-

---

52. See p. 6 above.
53. Max Byrd, *London Transformed: Images of the City in the Eighteenth Century* (New Haven: Yale University Press, 1978), p. 79.
54. *The Enthusiast: Or, the Lover of Nature, A Poem* (1744), p. 13.

worthy of it, but his pretense becomes his real condition; and he is punished by his inferiors, who could not have touched him had he kept to his proper role."[55]

Mallet's term *plebeian* is really as good as any, since it is anachronistic to invoke the notion of competing classes that derives from the industrial revolution and reflects a world of far greater social mobility than that of Pope's England. E. P. Thompson prefers to call eighteenth-century workers "plebs" because they lacked class consciousness, and he stresses such patterns of reciprocity as "gentry-crowd" and "paternalism-deference."[56] The common eighteenth-century term was *mob*, a contraction of the Latin *mobile vulgus*, which Johnson defines as "the crowd; a tumultuous rout," and illustrates from Addison's *Freeholder*: "A cluster of *mob* were making themselves merry with their betters." Pope's contemptuous line about the wits of the Restoration, "The mob of gentlemen who wrote with ease" (*Epistle* II.i.108), gets an added sting from this context. And while Thompson sees plebeian culture as "an ever-present threat to official descriptions of reality" (p. 164), one may say that Pope was virtually oblivious to it, even while he himself strove to reject certain aspects of the official description. His collaborator Fenton saw clearly that the retirement ideal meant superiority to ordinary work:

> Like the great Trojan, mantled in a cloud,
> Himself unseen he sees the lab'ring crowd.[57]

It is only fair to add that Pope's letters are full of complaints about Fenton's preternatural indolence, and that according to Johnson, "a woman that once waited on him in a lodging told him, as she said, that he would 'lie a-bed, and be fed with a

---

55. *This Dark Estate: A Reading of Pope* (Berkeley: University of California Press, 1963), p. 79.
56. "Eighteenth-Century English Society: Class Struggle without Class?" *Social History*, 3 (1978), 145, 150.
57. Elijah Fenton, *An Epistle to Thomas Lambard, Esq.*, in *Poems on Several Occasions* (1717), p. 202.

spoon.'"[58] Pope was never idle, and his labor brought him money, but he was always uncomfortable about the implications, which were easier to sense than to get into focus.

Meanwhile, he certainly did get into focus his revulsion at a society based on acquisition. It may perhaps be true, as Laura Brown claims, that his rhetoric sometimes reflects the values of commodification and imperialism, though "the grotesque superimposition of mercantile spoils upon the English landscape" seems as much hers as Pope's.[59] At any rate, after his early poems Pope fought against both tendencies with all the eloquence he could summon.

> Admire we then what earth's low entrails hold,
> Arabian shores, or Indian seas infold?
> All the mad trade of fools and slaves for gold?
> *(Epistle* I.vi.11–13)

Moreover, Pope diagnosed the disease as psychological, a crazed greed motivated not by rational calculation but by "wild desire":

> Fly then, on all the wings of wild desire!
> Admire whate'er the maddest can admire.
> Is wealth thy passion? Hence! from Pole to Pole,
> Where winds can carry, or where waves can roll,
> For Indian spices, for Peruvian gold,
> Prevent the greedy, and out-bid the bold;
> Advance thy golden mountain to the skies;
> On the broad base of fifty thousand rise.
> (67–74)

Money is a fact of life, but Pope keeps trying to see it as a fact of *ethical* life; it is no wonder that he wrote two major epistles "Of the Use of Riches." Lord Burlington, addressee of one of these, was a theorist and practitioner of classical

---

58. Samuel Johnson, *Life of Fenton*, in *Lives of the English Poets*, II, 262. Broome wrote to Pope of Fenton, "I will tell you a true story: when he was with me at Sturston he often fished; this gave him an opportunity of sitting still and being silent; but he left it off because the fish bit. He could not bear the fatigue of pulling up the rod and baiting the hook" (*Corr.* II, 358).

59. *Alexander Pope*, pp. 43–44.

architecture, and represents for Pope moral and aesthetic harmony united with practical usefulness.[60] The emphasis in Pope's writings is never on wealth for its own sake, but on wealth as conducive to human happiness:

> You show us, Rome was glorious, not profuse,
> And pompous buildings once were things of use.
>
> (*To Burlington*, 23–24)

Tenant of an elegant villa and believer in the moral role of the aristocracy, Pope placed his faith in great magnates like Burlington, an allegiance which has caused distaste in many readers. "Next to the pleasure of contemplating his possessions," Johnson remarks acidly, "seems to be that of enumerating the men of high rank with whom he was acquainted."[61] That Pope cared a great deal about these relationships is obvious; his letters record visits to over fifty country seats of gentlemen and lords.[62] But if he loved to cultivate "the great," it is also true that he often felt awkward in his relations with them. His letters have many hints at this, as when he writes to Bathurst, "Other people of my rank may respect you, and so do I, but I love you so much more, that I forget many degrees of that respect" (*Corr.* III, 137). Similarly he all but apologizes for offering condolences when Oxford has lost a son: "My Lord, forgive me: a more general and common style would better suit the distance between us: but humanity renders men as equal, as death does" (*Corr.* II, 337). Even as an insider Pope remains outside.

It is worth emphasizing that Pope never flatters great men in the way earlier writers routinely did (and many of his contemporaries too). Dryden, praising a translation by the earl of Mulgrave, declares abjectly,

---

60. See William A. Gibson, "Three Principles of Renaissance Architectural Theory in Pope's *Epistle to Burlington*," *Studies in English Literature*, 11 (1971), 487–505.

61. *Lives*, III, 204.

62. As Morris Brownell notes, *Alexander Pope and the Arts of Georgian England* (Oxford: Clarendon, 1978), p. 186.

How will sweet Ovid's ghost be pleased to hear
His fame augmented by an English peer.[63]

An Ode to the Earl of Cadogan by the workmanlike Welsted,
soon to find himself in the *Dunciad*, opens with humble def-
erence:

While careful crowds your levees wait,
The pomp and anguish of the great;
Accept this verse, illustrious chief,
From business no undue relief.[64]

Even Locke, in the "Epistle Dedicatory" to his great *Essay,*
pretends to believe that Lord Pembroke is a far deeper thinker
than himself: "This, my lord, shows what a present I here
make to your lordship; just such as the poor man does to his
rich and great neighbour, by whom the basket of flowers or
fruit is not ill taken, though he has more plenty of his own
growth, and in much greater perfection."[65] Pope's flattery of
the great never goes so far as this; he never pretends that
they excel him in anything except wealth and position. But
they do excel him in those. A historian speaks of "the three
key variables: wealth, power, and status."[66] These three are
by no means always in harmony: the eighteenth century was
a time when status based on money increasingly threatened
status based on birth.[67] Pope managed to accumulate a fair
amount of wealth, but his status was always uncertain, and
only as a literary figure did he have any power at all.

63. John Dryden, *To the Earl of Roscommon, on His Excellent Essay on Translated Verse,* 59–60.
64. Leonard Welsted, *Epistles, Odes, &c. Written on Several Subjects* (1724),
p. 50.
65. John Locke, *An Essay concerning Human Understanding,* ed. Alexander
Campbell Fraser (New York: Dover, 1959), I, 5.
66. Lawrence Stone, *The Past and the Present* (Boston: Routledge & Kegan
Paul, 1981), p. 22.
67. See Michael McKeon, "Generic Transformation and Social Change:
Rethinking the Rise of the Novel," *Cultural Critique,* 1 (1985), 171.

3

Politics and History

The landed interest to which Pope's friends belonged was being rudely pushed aside by two centers of power, the financial City and the job-bestowing Westminster court. We have already touched on the former, and noticed that money-making was perceived as the behavior of individuals rather than as the operation of a system. As for the court, Pope like others tended to exaggerate the obsolescent structure of personal relationships centering on the monarch, which had been weakened by the playboy Charles II, further damaged by Dutch William, and fatally wounded by the German Georges. Robert Walpole emerged as the new symbolic center and the target of two decades of satirists: Swift in *Gulliver's Travels*, Gay in *The Beggar's Opera*, Johnson in *London*, Fielding in *Jonathan Wild*, Pope in a long series of poems. The power of the newly "prime" minister was troubling and hard to make sense of; kings had always had their Sejanuses, but now Sejanus had his king. As Pope came to see it, Walpole the "wizard" had abandoned all principles but hypocritical loyalty to the monarch, and this was somehow the secret of his ascendancy:

> Lost is his God, his country, ev'ry thing;
> And nothing left but homage to a king!
> (*Dunciad* IV.523–24)

But a good deal of bewilderment centered on the relative impotence of the monarch, who remained invested with the symbolism of supreme power but clearly did not wield it. In a fine anecdote, Queen Caroline is supposed to have asked Walpole how much it would cost to enclose St. James's Park as private property. "Only a *crown*, Madam," Walpole answered.[1]

Writing four decades after Pope's death, Joseph Warton called attention to the obsessive frequency with which Pope made "king" a term of abuse:

> Our author is so perpetually expressing an affected contempt for kings, that it becomes almost a nauseous cant;
> —the pride of kings—
> —some monster of a king—
> —pity kings—the gift of kings—
> —Gods of kings—much above a king—
> —Settle wrote of kings—&c.—
> Hawkins Brown laughed at him for this affectation, in the pleasant Imitations of English poets, on Tobacco.
> Come, let me taste thee, *unexcis'd by kings!*[2]

Conservative though they were, Pope and his allies were determined to demystify kingship, purging it of the quasi-religious associations that it still had for Dryden. "No imaginable things," Swift wrote in verse, "can differ more than God and kings."[3]

In his first *Epistle* Horace distances himself from the Roman people, *populus Romanus* (I.i.70), and says that he avoids what they love because, as in Aesop's fable, all the footprints lead into their den and none come out. Pope drastically alters this passage by applying it instead to the court, the distributor of lucrative "places," which makes it a creator of beasts and murderer of virtue (*Epistle* I.i.103–19). The rhetorical climax of the *Epistle to Arbuthnot* is the portrait of Lord John Hervey as Sporus, painted eunuch and shallow poet, and the climax of the portrait of Sporus is the revelation that he has the ear of Queen Caroline as Satan did Eve's:

---

1. Robert Walpole, as reported by his son Horace Walpole, *Memoirs of the Reign of King George the Second* (1847), II, 220–21; quoted by E. P. Thompson, "Eighteenth-Century English Society: Class Struggle without Class?" *Social History*, 3 (1978), 151.
2. *An Essay on the Writings and Genius of Pope* (1782), II, 324.
3. Jonathan Swift, *A Libel on the Reverend Dr. Delany*, 195–96.

> Or at the ear of Eve, familiar toad,
> Half froth, half venom, spits himself abroad,
> In puns, or politics, or tales, or lies,
> Or spite, or smut, or rhymes, or blasphemies. . . .
>
> (319–22)

Politics, in this context, is merely another ingredient in the court gossip mill, just as in *The Rape of the Lock* it is interchangeable with routine seductions and other social recreations:

> Here Britain's statesmen oft the fall foredoom
> Of foreign tyrants, and of nymphs at home;
> Here thou, great Anna! whom three realms obey,
> Dost sometimes counsel take—and sometimes tea.
>
> (III.5–8)

Pope consistently stayed clear of all that. He wrote accurately enough to Swift, "Courts I see not, courtiers I know not, kings I adore not, queens I compliment not; so am never like to be in fashion, or in dependance" (*Corr.* II, 469).

Whatever resentment Pope may have felt at the years of Homer translation, they freed him from ignoble dependence on titled patrons, "fed with soft dedication all day long" (*To Arbuthnot*, 233), and from the role of domestic intellectual who pays for sustenance with wit,

> A constant critic at the great man's board,
> To fetch and carry nonsense for my Lord.
>
> (*Essay on Criticism*, 416–17)

A sympathetic Swift more than once extolled Pope's independence:

> Hail! happy Pope, whose generous mind,
> Detesting all the statesman kind!
> Contemning courts, at courts unseen,
> Refused the visits of a queen . . .
> His heart too great, though fortune little,
> To lick a rascal statesman's spittle.[4]

4. Ibid., 71–74, 81–82.

Colley Cibber, preposterous laureate and hero of the revised *Dunciad*, was despicable above all for pleasing the court
so abjectly, while Gay sought a "place" in vain and Young
paid ignominiously for his pension of £200 a year:

> Harmonious Cibber entertains
> The court with annual birthday strains;
> Whence Gay was banished in disgrace,
> Where Pope will never show his face;
> Where Young must torture his invention
> To flatter knaves, or lose his pension.[5]

Walpole was the direct source of the pension, and Young said
so explicitly in a poem addressed to him:

> At this the muse shall kindle, and aspire:
> My breast, O Walpole, glows with grateful fire.
> The streams of royal bounty, turned by thee,
> Refresh the dry domains of poesy.[6]

Pope ironically compared George Augustus to the Roman
emperor, to the disadvantage of the British king; Young did
the same thing without the irony.

> Such is the prince's worth, of whom I speak,
> The Roman would not blush at the mistake.[7]

But Young's groveling is most pathetic when performed for
lesser figures, Sir Spencer Compton for example:

> Thee, Compton, born o'er senates to preside,
> Their dignity to raise, their councils guide;
> Deep to discern, and widely to survey,
> And kingdoms' fates, without ambition, weigh. . . .[8]

The *Dictionary of National Biography* says of Compton, "By the
public as well as by his subordinates he was regarded as a
mere cipher. Wanting in decision, and possessing but very

---

5. Jonathan Swift, *On Poetry: A Rhapsody*, 321–26.
6. Edward Young, *The Installment: To the Right Hon. Sir Robert Walpole,
Knight of the Most Noble Order of the Garter.*
7. Edward Young, *Satire IV*, final lines, in Young, *Love of Fame, the Universal Passion: In Seven Characteristical Satires.*
8. Ibid., opening lines.

ordinary abilities, he was neither suited to become a leader
of men nor a framer of measures. . . . He was the butt of the
satirists and caricaturists of the day."[9]
Pope's enemy Welsted explicitly invoked the Augustan
analogy in a fawning hymn to the duke of Chandos:

> Th' approaching times my raptured thought engage;
> I see arise a new Augustan Age.
> Here, stretched at ease, beneath the beechen boughs,
> The sylvan poet sings his faithful vows;
> Others, retiring from the vulgar throng,
> At leisure meditate an epic song;
> Or choose the worthies of a former age,
> With all their pomp of grief to fill the stage;
> While, here, historians BRUNSWICK's praise sustain,
> Record his deeds, and lengthen out his reign.[10]

Poetry is invited to escape into pastoral love songs, epics remote from the vulgar throng, and tragedies set in the distant
past. Meanwhile, the principal work "here" is to celebrate
George Augustus. Against this form of servile Augustanism,
which Howard Weinbrot has exhaustively documented,[11]
Pope proudly contrasted himself, for instance in his *Epitaph,
For One Who Would Not Be Buried in Westminster Abbey:*

> Heroes, and KINGS! your distance keep:
> In peace let one poor poet sleep,
> Who never flattered folks like you:
> Let Horace blush, and Virgil too.
>   (*TE* VI, 376)

Most of the noblemen Pope admired stood apart from the
ruling order, at a time when fully one-quarter of the peerage

9. *Dictionary of National Biography* (Oxford: Oxford University Press, 1917),
IV, 906–7.
10. Leonard Welsted, *An Epistle to His Grace the Duke of Chandos*, in *Epistles,
Odes, &c. Written on Several Subjects* (1724), p. 45.
11. *Augustus Caesar in "Augustan" England* (Princeton: Princeton University Press, 1978). Weinbrot's severe findings, however, are qualified somewhat by Howard Erskine-Hill, who shows that Augustan culture was still
admired even if Augustan politics was not: *The Augustan Idea in English Literature* (London: Arnold, 1983).

held government office.[12] Like Marvell's General Fairfax, Pope's heroes are confined to domestic pleasures because they have renounced public glory or have been excluded from it.

> There, my retreat the best companions grace,
> Chiefs, out of war, and statesmen, out of place.
> There St. John mingles with my friendly bowl
> The feast of reason and the flow of soul:
> And he, whose lightning pierced th' Iberian lines
> Now forms my quincunx, and now ranks my vines,
> Or tames the genius of the stubborn plain
> Almost as quickly as he conquered Spain.
> *(Satire* II.i.125–32)

Both Bolingbroke (St. John) and Peterborough represent disaffection from Walpole and the government's policies.[13] But more than that, they represent Pope's conviction that statesmen out of power are nobler than statesmen in it. His enemies, of course, preferred not to accept Pope's valuations. Cibber complained in 1742, "Whenever the government censures a man of consequence for any extraordinary disaffection to it, then is Mr. Pope's time generously to brighten and lift him up with virtues, which never had been so conspicuous in him before."[14]

This interest in exclusion was not simply a consequence of political disappointment after the death of Queen Anne. Pope's very first mention of power, at the start of his youthful pastoral *Spring*, refers to its abdication by Sir William Trumbull:

> You, that too wise for pride, too good for pow'r,
> Enjoy the glory to be great no more,
> And carrying with you all the world can boast,
> To all the world illustriously are lost!
> (7–10)

---

12. See Roy Porter, *English Society in the Eighteenth Century* (Harmondsworth: Penguin, 1982), p. 73.

13. See Vincent Carretta, *The Snarling Muse: Verbal and Visual Political Satire from Pope to Churchill* (Philadelphia: University of Pennsylvania Press, 1983), pp. 108–9.

14. Colley Cibber, *A Letter from Mr. Cibber, to Mr. Pope* (1742), pp. 23–24.

Similarly, Pope's 1713 prologue to Addison's *Cato* treats politics as renunciation. In the martyred Cato, dying by his own hand,

> Her last good man dejected Rome adored,
> And honoured Caesar's less than Cato's sword.
>
> (35–36)

Caesar, by contrast, is "ignobly vain and impotently great" (29), a specialized notion of impotence that exalts the moral superiority of the loser. An outsider himself, Pope likes his admired great men to be outsiders too.

Swift might have seen Ireland as a degrading exile, but he wielded real political power there, and he well remembered the days when foppish courtiers in London had been compelled to pay attention to him:

> Now, Delaware again familiar grows,
> And in Swift's ear thrusts half his powdered nose.[15]

This intimacy with power was never possible for Pope; all avenues were closed to him by his Catholicism as well as by his physical condition. As he said to Gay, "Nature, temper, and habit, from my youth made me have but one strong desire; all other ambitions, my person, education, constitution, religion, &c. conspired to remove far from me. That desire was to fix and preserve a few lasting, dependable friendships" (*Corr.* III, 138).

To some extent this was a prudential posture, like that of Edward Blount writing to Pope in 1715:

> 'Tis a great many years since I fell in love with the character of Pomponius Atticus: I longed to imitate him a little, and have contrived hitherto, to be like him engaged in no party, but to be a faithful friend to some in both: I find myself very well in this way hitherto, and live in a certain peace of mind by it, which I am persuaded brings a man more content than all the perquisites of wild ambition.
>
> (*Corr.* I, 321)

15. Jonathan Swift, *The Author upon Himself*, 67–68.

This sounds bland enough, but it was written by an anxious Catholic at the time of the Jacobite rebellion: "What ruin have those unfortunate rash gentlemen drawn upon themselves and their miserable followers, and perchance upon many others too, who upon no account would be their followers?" (p. 320).

Making a virtue of necessity, Pope constantly asserted that he was above all parties, "while Tories call me Whig, and Whigs a Tory" (*Satire* II.i.68). Politics becomes something other people do, while Pope strives for a moderation that flows directly from his forthright honesty:

> I love to pour out all myself, as plain
> As downright Shippen, or as old Montaigne.
> (51–52)

Erskine-Hill suggests that since Shippen was a well-known parliamentary Jacobite, Pope implies "an honest mean" (line 66) that can embrace Shippen's political commitment as well as the "secluded self-examination" of Montaigne.[16] But it is somewhat misleading to say that the reference to Montaigne is "quite unpolitical," for Montaigne was explicitly antipolitical, reacting to life during the religious wars when soldiers invaded his house and might easily have killed him. Pope's "While Tories call me Whig," incidentally, comes directly from Montaigne's "Au Gibelin j'estois Guelphe, au Guelphe Gibelin."[17] Whatever Pope's private sympathy with Jacobitism may have been, and however much he identified with the opposition "patriots" in the late 1730s,[18] he continued to think of parties as destructive factions rather than as normal instruments of power. In a long political letter to the Patriot

---

16. *The Augustan Idea*, p. 298.
17. *Essais* III.xii, as noted by Claude Rawson, *Order from Confusion Sprung: Studies in Eighteenth-Century Literature from Swift to Cowper* (London: Allen & Unwin, 1985), p. 250.
18. See Bertrand A. Goldgar, *Walpole and the Wits: The Relation of Politics to Literature, 1722–1742* (Lincoln: University of Nebraska Press, 1976), pp. 177–78, and Brean S. Hammond, *Pope and Bolingbroke: A Study of Friendship and Influence* (Columbia: University of Missouri Press, 1984), pp. 160–65.

leader Lyttelton in 1738, he urged that the opposition collect all "honest men" together and resist the spirit of party, "for parties are but higher and more interested mobs" (*Corr.* IV, 144). If honesty is antithetical to party, and if party is synonymous with mob, then the possibilities for political action are slim. The only good statesman is a statesman out of place, which might seem a contradiction in terms, even to Pope, if the Roman ideal were not so deeply assimilated.

Since Pope and Swift are usually identified closely by scholars, the contrast between them here is worth driving home. Swift fought for decades to change things, and he knew that that was impossible without "interest" and party, though of course he deplored narrow interests and corrupt parties. Pope wrote loftily to Swift in 1726, two years after the triumph of the *Drapier's Letters,*

> Surely, without flattery, you are now above all parties of men, and it is high time to be so, after twenty or thirty years observation of the great world. . . . I question not, many men would be of your intimacy, that you might be of their interest: but God forbid an honest or witty man should be of any, but that of his country. They have scoundrels enough to write for their passions and their designs; let us write for truth, for honour, and for posterity. If you must needs write about politics at all, (but perhaps 'tis full as wise to play the fool any other way) surely it ought to be so as to preserve the dignity and integrity of your character with those times to come, which will most impartially judge of them.
>
> (*Corr.* II, 412–13)

The familiar terms are lined up once again: honesty, wit, truth, honor, and integrity on one side of the balance; party, interest, and politics on the other. Most tellingly of all, Pope is content to appeal to posterity: he wants Swift to write to be approved by unknown judges in "times to come," rather than to influence current affairs.

We have no immediate reply from Swift, but a letter to Pope a couple of years later is deeply thought-provoking:

> I look upon my Lord Bolingbroke and us two, as a peculiar triumvirate, who have nothing to expect, or to fear; and so far

fittest to converse with one another: only he and I are a little
subject to schemes, and often upon very weak appearances,
and this you have nothing to do with. I do profess without
affectation, that your kind opinion of me as a Patriot (since
you call it so) is what I do not deserve; because what I do is
owing to perfect rage and resentment, and the mortifying
sight of slavery, folly, and baseness about me, among which I
am forced to live. And I will take my oath that you have more
virtue in an hour, than I in seven years; for you despise the
follies, and hate the vices of mankind, without the least ill
effect on your temper; and with regard to particular men, you
are inclined always rather to think the better, whereas with me
it is always directly contrary. I hope however, this is not in you
from a superior principle of virtue, but from your situation,
which hath made all parties and interests indifferent to you,
who can be under no concern about high and low church,
Whig and Tory, or who is first Minister.

(Corr. II, 497)

If rage and resentment are weaknesses, than Pope is more
virtuous than Swift. But if folly and baseness ought to impel
one to change things, then Pope's posture begins to look passive and escapist. And the final point is clearly the crucial
one: someone whose "situation" excludes him can easily find
reasons to praise the excluded life.

Swift mentions Bolingbroke as still "subject to schemes,"
but as impotent to carry them out. Pope's veneration for—
not to mention "quasi-feminine passivity" toward[19]—Henry
St. John, Viscount Bolingbroke, lies at the very center of his
paradoxical antipolitics. Secretary of state under Queen
Anne, Bolingbroke was forced into exile in France upon the
accession of George I, unwisely associated himself there with
the Pretender, and returned to lead the opposition in England
in the 1720s (though he was forbidden to reenter Parliament).
At that time any opposition was regarded as suspiciously
disloyal, and therefore had to be defended by strong assertions of "patriotism." It is impossible to determine, two and
a half centuries later, whether Bolingbroke sincerely espoused his political ideals, motivated by nostalgia for a van-

---

19. Hammond, *Pope and Bolingbroke*, p. 1.

ishing social order,[20] or whether he cynically manipulated them in order to regain power. At all events, as Quentin Skinner argues in a penetrating essay, Bolingbroke was obliged to act *as if* ideals were crucial, and consequently they influenced his political practice if not his actual beliefs.[21]

Superiority to mere party was a favorite principle of Bolingbroke's, and his *Idea of a Patriot King* was a fantasy of national unity that might cohere around the prince of Wales if ever he came to the throne. In the meantime Bolingbroke pondered political motives with bitter cynicism:

> A man who has not seen the inside of parties, nor had opportunities to examine nearly their secret motives, can hardly conceive how little a share principle of any sort, though principle of some sort or other be always pretended, has in the determination of their conduct. Reason has small effect on numbers. A turn of imagination, often as violent and as sudden as a gust of wind, determines their conduct: and passion is taken, by others, and by themselves too, when it grows into habit especially, for principle.[22]

Like Pope's, Bolingbroke's emphasis is resolutely ethical, and therefore bleakly disillusioned. Power has to be exercised by individuals, individuals succumb to "passion," and all values collapse into hypocrisy and greed.

> If a people is growing corrupt, there is no need of capacity to contrive, nor of insinuation to gain, nor of plausibility to seduce, nor of eloquence to persuade, nor of authority to impose, nor of courage to attempt. The most incapable, awkward, ungracious, shocking, profligate, and timorous wretches, invested with power, and masters of the purse, will be sufficient for the work, when the people are complices in

---

20. This is the thesis of Isaac Kramnick, *Bolingbroke and His Circle: The Politics of Nostalgia in the Age of Walpole* (Cambridge, Mass.: Harvard University Press, 1968).

21. "The Principles and Practice of Opposition: The Case of Bolingbroke versus Walpole," in *Historical Perspectives: Studies in English Thought and Society,* ed. Neil McKendrick (London: Europa, 1974), pp. 93–128.

22. Henry St. John, Viscount Bolingbroke, *The Idea of a Patriot King* (1749), ed. Sydney W. Jackman (Indianapolis: Bobbs-Merrill, 1965), p. 59.

it. Luxury is rapacious; let them feed it: the more it is fed, the more profuse it will grow.

(p. 36)

Whatever its actual political purpose may have been, this kind of rhetoric was deeply nostalgic, and Pope eagerly joins in, telling Swift that he has made friends with "young men, who look rather to the past age than the present, and therefore the future may have some hopes of them" (*Corr.* IV, 51). Once more, posterity is to be the arbiter. To live in the past and future would be dangerous if it were not impossible, and one sees the point of the prominstry epigram that described Walpole rather than Bolingbroke as beneficiary of history:

> On history he grounds his hope;
> Let St. John trust for fame to Pope.[23]

After Pope's death Warburton, quarreling publicly with Bolingbroke, said of Pope that "the folly which ran through his whole life was, in trying to *extract friendship from politics.*"[24] Warburton no doubt meant that a political friend was undependable, but one might well adapt the thought differently and suggest that Pope wanted a friendship purged of the grossness of politics, even while Bolingbroke raged inwardly at his political impotence. Warton remarks that Addison "always called him, in the language of Shakespeare, 'that cankered Bolingbroke.'"[25] Bolingbroke's own answer to Warburton is revealing: *A Familiar Epistle to the Most Impudent Man Living* identifies Warburton as "the bully of Mr. P's memory, into whose acquaintance, at the latter end of the poor man's life, you was introduced by your nauseous flattery," and concludes with an assertion of injured rank: "In a word, be less insolent to those, that are far above you in every form of life,

23. Epigram in the *Daily Gazetteer* for 9 Apr. 1740, quoted by Goldgar, *Walpole and the Wits*, p. 18.

24. [William Warburton], *A Letter to the Editor of the Letters on the Spirit of Patriotism* (1749), p. 23.

25. *Essay on . . . Pope*, I, 260.

to ladies of the first quality, and to men of the greatest eminency."[26]

If Bolingbroke saw politics as a congeries of schemes by corruptible individuals, with the only hope an enlightened aristocracy and a Patriot King, it is no wonder that Pope entertained similar views. The corollary is a belief that personal behavior is all that really counts in the end:

> For forms of government, let fools contest;
> Whate'er is best administered is best.
> *(Essay on Man* III.303–4)

Warburton had to step in here to save Pope from his apparent meaning:

> The reader will not be displeased to see the poet's own apology, as I find it written in the year 1740, in his own hand, in the margin of a book where he found these two celebrated lines misapplied. "The author of these lines was far from meaning that no one form of government is, in itself, better than another (as, that mixed or limited monarchy, for example, is not preferable to absolute) but that no form of government, however excellent or preferable in itself, can be sufficient to make a people happy, unless it be administered with integrity. On the contrary, the best sort of government, when the *form* of it is preserved, and the *administration* corrupt, is most dangerous."[27]

Perhaps Pope does not mean, after all, that a bad system is good if administered by good men, and intends only the tautology (as Nuttall puts it) that "things will not be far wrong as long as they are done right."[28] At any rate, the focus certainly remains on corruption, very much in the traditional Renaissance-classical way.

26. Henry St. John, Viscount Bolingbroke, *A Familiar Epistle*, pp. 12, 23–24. Both pamphlets are reprinted in facsimile by the Augustan Reprint Society (Los Angeles: William Andrews Clark Memorial Library and UCLA, 1978), with an introduction by Donald T. Siebert, Jr.

27. Pope's *Works* (1751), III, 106n. Warburton's transcription is accurate, as comparison with the original shows (*TE* III-i, 124n; a longer version of the note is given on p. 170).

28. A. D. Nuttall, *Pope's "Essay on Man"* (London: Allen & Unwin, 1984), p. 127.

With the hindsight of two centuries, it is possible to see how far-reaching were the political developments in Pope's lifetime, and how little he was in a position to recognize their ultimate significance. Without doubt Walpole established himself at the center of a Whig oligarchy, gaining complete control of both Parliament and court, and without doubt his shrewd quid-pro-quo transactions often deserve the name of bribery. But to think of this simply as "corruption," with a band of honest men holding out virtuously against the self-ishness of "faction," is to place a narrowly ethical interpreta-tion upon a profound movement toward centralization and political stability. The selling of places in the rapidly modern-izing bureaucracy was the means by which a new and reliable order was established. As J. H. Plumb has argued, instability rather than stability is the norm in most societies, and the Whig hegemony of the 1720s was anything but inevitable, ending as it did a state of unstable competition that had been endemic since the revolution of 1688 (the year of Pope's birth).[29] Political stability was won not by clever political ma-neuvers, or even by wholesale "corruption" of officeholders, but by forging a consensus that offered something to every important center of power. Significant opposition was essen-tially co-opted, and many erstwhile Tories found it expedient to become Whigs.

Above all, consensus rested on an idealization of "law," metaphors of which pervade Pope's poems at many points.[30] Most Whig justifications of the Revolution settlement of 1688 did not appeal to the sovereignty of the people, as Locke's contract theory might suggest, since Whigs tended to be men of property anxious to defend their privileges. Instead, they relied on the rule of law, understood as a traditional structure of rights and obligations that bound both king and people. The ideal, accordingly, was a golden mean between royal tyr-

29. *The Growth of Political Stability in England, 1675–1725* (Harmondsworth: Penguin, 1969).
30. See Laura Brown, *Alexander Pope* (Oxford: Blackwell, 1985), pp. 56–67.

anny and mob anarchy.[31] One ought not to exaggerate, as some modern interpreters do, the ideological hypocrisy of defenses of law. H. T. Dickinson's conclusion deserves to be considered: "The rule of law does of course have both a conservative and a liberal dimension. The law can be an instrument by which men of property seek to define and defend their privileged position, but it can also be a weapon which even the most humble subjects might use to protect their rights."[32] But as Charles Davenant—in his own time a very influential political writer—had pointed out early in the century, "a tyranny that governs by the sword has few friends but men of the sword; but a legal tyranny (where the people are only called upon to confirm iniquity with their own voices) has of its side the rich, the fearful, the lazy, those that know the law and get by it, ambitious churchmen, and all those whose livelihood depends upon the quiet posture of affairs."[33] From this perspective, the eighteenth century sustained its "quiet posture" at the cost of loathsome corruption: "Every one is upon the scrape for himself, without any regard to his country; each cheating, raking, and plundering what he can, and in a more profligate degree than ever yet was known."[34] For Davenant as for Pope, the answer was not greater democracy but less. Davenant proposed restricting seats in Parliament to the landed gentry, in terms that nakedly express his stake in the status quo: "He who has a large estate will not consent to have the laws subverted, which are his firmest security. . . . They who are well born will desire to preserve that constitution of which they and their ancestors have always been a part."[35]

31. See H. T. Dickinson, *Liberty and Property: Political Ideology in Eighteenth-Century Britain* (New York: Holmes & Meier, 1977), pp. 70–90.

32. Ibid., p. 90.

33. "Of Private Men's Duty in the Administration of Public Affairs," *Political and Commercial Works* (1771), II, 301. Davenant died in 1714.

34. Davenant, *Works*, III, 302.

35. Ibid., V, 52. Dickinson, who quotes this passage, remarks that a law of 1711 provided that candidates for county elections should possess real estate worth £600 a year, and borough candidates £300 per year (*Liberty and Property*, p. 115).

Pope and Swift, of course, continued to think in personal terms: Queen Anne's Tory ministry fell because Oxford and Bolingbroke inexplicably quarreled, and Bolingbroke's enemies then vindictively drove him into exile instead of hailing him as the nation's savior. Their interpretation of political affairs reflects a cynicism that was born—like Swift's misanthropy—of disappointed idealism. If the majority of politicians seemed to be grabbing whatever they could and shamelessly exchanging favors with each other, then a principled opposition had to believe that the ascendant politicians lacked all principle. The Scriblerian and Patriot view that an in-group manipulates affairs is strangely prophetic of the "prosopography" of historians in the 1930s, whose experience of their own era led them to see self-serving elites as the mainspring of historical action. A weakness of prosopographers, Lawrence Stone comments, "has been their relative unwillingness to build into their perspective of history a role for ideas, prejudices, passions, ideologies, ideals, or principles."[36] Pope, very similarly, tended to ignore the possibility that Walpole and his allies might have been motivated by ideals, or even ideas. Not until Burke did a powerful theorist argue that ideals are compatible with parties, and indeed are impotent apart from them.

It needs to be added that opposition condemned Pope—like most of the other "wits"—to marginality, even if his marginal position lent eloquence to denunciations of power which he could not share and did not wholly understand. For Dryden as for Swift, politics means action in times of crisis. For Pope it means inaction, and "Dulness" becomes a black "vortex" that swallows up all possibility of healthy change:

> The gath'ring number, as it moves along,
> Involves a vast involuntary throng,
> Who gently drawn, and struggling less and less,
> Roll in her vortex, and her pow'r confess.
> (*Dunciad* IV.81–84)

36. *The Past and the Present* (Boston: Routledge & Kegan Paul, 1981), p. 63.

At the same time, one need not exaggerate the despair implied by Pope's late satires. To some extent it represents simply a rhetorical ploy against the Walpole administration in its waning years, when it was starting to look vulnerable. It is significant that Pope now reproaches Horace for a smooth irony that can compromise with power:

> His sly, polite, insinuating style
> Could please at court, and make Augustus smile:
> An artful manager, that crept between
> His friend and shame, and was a kind of screen.
> (*Epilogue* I.19–22)

Horace is conflated with Walpole, the notoriously artful manager who was often satirized as a "screen" protecting the king. The lines that follow, however, are remarkable for their hints that the gulf between Walpole and Pope is not so deep after all:

> See Sir ROBERT!—hum—
> And never laugh—for all my life to come?
> Seen him I have, but in his happier hour
> Of social pleasure, ill-exchanged for pow'r;
> Seen him, uncumbered with the venal tribe,
> Smile without art, and win without a bribe.
> Would he oblige me? let me only find
> He does not think me what he thinks mankind.
> Come, come, at all I laugh he laughs, no doubt,
> The only diff'rence is, I dare laugh out.
> (27–36)

One of Walpole's maxims was that every man has his price; Pope compliments himself by proposing that Walpole think him different from all the others. But he also pays a compliment to Walpole as social companion—the man as distinct from the politician—and a complicity is implied in the suggestion that Walpole and Pope both laugh at the same things, though only the satirist-outsider can afford to do it openly.

Swift's treatment of the same theme is much more sardonic:

> Now, Chartres at Sir Robert's levee,
> Tells, with a sneer, the tidings heavy:

"Why, is he dead without his shoes?"
(Cries Bob) "I'm sorry for the news;
Oh, were the wretch but living still,
And in his place my good friend Will;
Or, had a mitre on his head
Provided Bolingbroke were dead."[37]

Walpole wouldn't mind if Swift continued to live, or even if he had his longed-for bishopric, so long as Bolingbroke or William Pulteney (Walpole's erstwhile "good friend Will") could be dead in his place. Walpole countenances Swift's existence only if Swift can do him no harm by living and no good by dying. Swift characteristically directs irony against himself in a way that Pope seldom does. Pope compliments himself on refusing to be bought; Swift recognizes that he and Pope are much more interested in Walpole than Walpole is in them.

Pope's ambiguous feelings about political power help to explain why many of his contemporaries found it hard to accept him as the noblest Roman of them all. There is something quixotic in the pose of dropout from one's age. In a pamphlet attack on Pope, Lord John Hervey, the despised Sporus, shrewdly observes that censorious authors cannot easily escape the errors they condemn,

> But lash the times as swimmers do the tide,
> And kick and cuff the stream on which they ride.[38]

Abusing Hervey's behavior at court, Pope had written in *To Arbuthnot*,

> So well-bred spaniels civilly delight
> In mumbling of the game they dare not bite.
> (313–14)

Hervey's retort is less witty, but hardly foolish:

> For all the taste he ever has of joy,
> Is like some yelping mungril to annoy
> And tease that passenger he can't destroy.
> (p. 6)

37. Jonathan Swift, *Verses on the Death of Dr. Swift,* 189–96.
38. *The Difference between Verbal and Practical Virtue* (1742), p. 1.

No doubt the highborn Hervey intends a social sneer in calling Pope a mongrel, but the analogy still holds: if we are all dogs, then a court fawner and an out-of-court yelper are not so different as the outsider wants to believe.

> I am his Highness' dog at Kew;
> Pray tell me sir, whose dog are you?
>
> (*TE* VI, 372)

One easily imagines the mortification of a courtier bending over to read the inscription, and perceiving that he himself is as much a domestic animal as the dog is. But as Empson says,

> The joke carries a certain praise for the underdog; the point is not that men are slaves but that they find it suits them and remain good-humoured. The dog is proud of being the prince's dog and expects no one to take offence at the question. There is also a hearty independence in its lack of respect for the inquirer.[39]

And when David Morris asks us to deduce from this scene "a poet who is self-possessed and independent,"[40] we might also recall the poem's full title: *Epigram: Engraved on the Collar of a Dog Which I Gave to His Royal Highness*. His Royal Highness was Frederick, the feckless prince of Wales from whom Pope's political friends expected great things, and Pope was embarrassed by Swift's lines praising his contempt of courts:

> I've had another vexation, from the sight of a paper of verses said to be Dr. Swift's, which has done more by praising me than all the libels could by abusing me, [and] seriously troubled me; as indeed one indiscreet friend can at any time hurt a man more than a hundred silly enemies. I can hardly bring myself to think it his, or that it is possible his head should be so giddy.
>
> (*Corr.* III, 91)

---

39. William Empson, *Some Versions of Pastoral* (New York: New Directions, 1960), p. 247.
40. *Alexander Pope: The Genius of Sense* (Cambridge, Mass.: Harvard University Press, 1984), p. 213.

Colley Cibber makes a point similar to Hervey's, quoting the epigram (presumably by Pope himself) inserted in the notes to the *Dunciad:*

> In merry old England it once was a rule,
> The king had his poet, and also his fool:
> But now we're so frugal, I'd have you to know it,
> That C[ibbe]r can serve both for fool and for poet.
>
> (*TE* V, 187)

"A king's fool," Cibber comments, "was nobody's fool but his master's," and he offers this counter-epigram:

> The fools of old, if fame says true,
> Were chiefly chosen for their wit;
> Why then, called fools? because, like you,
> Dear Pope, too bold in showing it.

Cibber concludes triumphantly, "And so, if I am the king's fool; now, sir, pray whose fool are you?" Quoting the line in *To Arbuthnot,* "And has not Colley still his lord, and whore?" (97), Cibber retorts tellingly, "As to the first part of the charge, the *Lord;* Why—we have both had him, and sometimes the *same* Lord."[41]

Immersed in the politics of personality, Pope had little sense of the great mutations of history that generate significant change. He was well aware that behavior can be historically conditioned, praising Shakespeare for distinguishing the "manners" of Coriolanus's time from those of Caesar's, and remarking to Spence, "Facts in ancient history are not very instructive now; the principles of acting vary so often and so greatly. The actions of a great man were quite different even in Scipio's and Julius Caesar's times."[42] But this does not mean that universal principles are chimerical; rather, they should be sought at a deeper level than the vagaries of par-

---

41. *A Letter from Mr. Cibber, to Mr. Pope* (1742), pp. 39–40, 45.

42. Preface to *The Works of Shakespeare,* in *Literary Criticism of Alexander Pope,* ed. Bertrand A. Goldgar (Lincoln: University of Nebraska Press, 1965), p. 166; Joseph Spence, *Observations, Anecdotes, and Characters of Books and Men,* ed. James M. Osborn (Oxford: Clarendon, 1966), I, 241.

ticular actions. Until the latter part of the eighteenth century it was universally believed that historic events should be studied as moral *exempla;* history was seen as "the empirical part of moral philosophy."[43] In Bolingbroke's words,

> There are certain general principles, and rules of life and conduct, which always must be true, because they are conformable to the invariable nature of things. He who studies history as he would study philosophy will soon distinguish and collect them, and by doing so will soon form to himself a general system of ethics and politics on the surest foundations, on the trial of these principles and rules in all ages, and on the confirmation of them by universal experience.[44]

Later on in the century, the Enlightenment search for universal principles would break down into historicism, a recognition that human experience is evolutionary rather than fixed. But for Pope the variations in behavior were accidental rather than essential, and he aspired to survey the experience of "man" in a single view: "His time a moment, and a point his space" (*Essay on Man*, I.72).

Society is not a vast organism growing by slow evolution, but the sum total of actions that flow from human irrationality, as in the Virgilian *furor* that pervades *Windsor-Forest*.[45] Society is filled with energy of an endlessly repetitive kind: "Heir urges heir, like wave impelling wave" (*Epistle* II.ii.253). The couplets in *Windsor-Forest* balance fields against woods, hills against valleys, as elements in a harmonious picture; in this later poem, in a passage much expanded from Horace, all human achievements are doomed to collapse:

> Let rising granaries and temples here,
> There mingled farms and pyramids appear,
> Link towns to towns with avenues of oak,
> Enclose whole downs in walls, 'tis all a joke!

43. George H. Nadel, "Philosophy of History before Historicism," *History and Theory*, 3 (1963), 312.

44. Henry St. John, Viscount Bolingbroke, *Of the Study of History*, in Bolingbroke's *Works* (1777), II, 290.

45. See Morris, *Alexander Pope*, pp. 110–15.

Inexorable death shall level all,
And trees, and stones, and farms, and farmer fall.
                                        (258–63)

This is not so much a vision of historical change as of ceaseless mutability, compatible perhaps with the providentialism
that keeps the social machine running, but very dark in tone.

Even in his last years Pope apparently dreamed of national
renewal. His projected epic on Brutus, legendary founder of
Britain, would have been a sort of Patriot manifesto, with a
prince who punishes evil ministers, suppresses religious and
political tyranny, and exhibits benevolence as his ruling passion.[46] In the few lines that survive from the invocation, Pope
offers himself (in more or less Miltonic blank verse) as "my
country's poet" (*TE* VI, 404). But the ultimate tendency of
epic, as Pope understands it, was to submerge politics and
even history in the immense cycles of existence. When Zeus
tells Poseidon in the *Iliad* that he can obliterate the Greek
fortifications, Pope makes him speak with melancholy grandeur:

> But yon proud work no future age shall view,
> No trace remain where once the glory grew.
> The sapped foundations by thy force shall fall,
> And whelmed beneath thy waves, drop the huge wall:
> Vast drifts of sand shall change the former shore,
> The ruin vanished, and the name no more.
>   (VII.550–55)

Such a vision easily transposes into apocalypse. The *Dunciad* ends with the suicide of civilization, in which "universal
darkness buries all" (IV.656), and the image echoes Agamemnon's prophecy of the destruction of Troy,

> When Priam's pow'rs and Priam's self shall fall,
> And one prodigious ruin swallow all.
>   (*Iliad* IV.198–99)

46. See Donald T. Torchiana, "Brutus: Pope's Last Hero," *Journal of English
and Germanic Philology,* 61 (1962), 853–67, and Miriam Leranbaum, *Alexander
Pope's "Opus Magnum," 1729–1744* (Oxford: Clarendon, 1977), ch. 7.

Less melodramatic passages also hint, with a different but equally moving eloquence, that only the end of things can put an end to political degradation:

> But past the sense of human miseries,
> All tears are wiped for ever from all eyes,
> No cheek is known to blush, no heart to throb,
> Save when they lose a question, or a job.
>
> (*Epilogue* I.101–4)

The Twickenham footnote for this passage misleadingly points to Isaiah; the reference is in fact to Revelation, "And God shall wipe away all tears from their eyes; and there shall be no more death, neither sorrow, nor crying, neither shall there be any more pain: for the former things are passed away."[47] In a world of endless recurrence, political favor is the power that banishes misery and wipes tears from eyes, and political disfavor is the power that restores them. And this will always be so until that final apocalypse when former things pass away.

47. Revelation 21:4; the same phrase occurs at 7:17. At Isaiah 25:8 the wording is different ("the Lord God will wipe away tears from off all faces"). See also Milton's *Lycidas*, line 181.

4

The Vocation of Satire

Although Swift was a lifelong satirist, Pope was not. Of the three great poems of his twenties—*An Essay on Criticism, Windsor-Forest,* and *The Rape of the Lock*—only the last is satiric, and it is as much a comedy as a satire. Pope devoted the next decade to Homer, whom he translated with the utmost seriousness—Dryden's *Aeneid* is much jauntier and more ironic—and only in his forties did he turn to satire, with the first version of the *Dunciad* and the Horatian imitations.

Yet it is certainly as a satirist that posterity best remembers Pope. Why satire, then? Mack, after expounding the retirement ideal, explains the transition by invoking the coarse and unscrupulous Walpole:

> So the stage was set. Here was a man in high place who was widely believed to represent all that was vicious in government. He was backed by a court which seemed to uphold all that was hostile to true cultivation. No writer having classical views of the function of his art, certainly no satirist, could avoid coming to terms sooner or later with such a man. It was simply a matter of time.[1]

So Pope was goaded to it; he became a satirist because the age demanded it.

Another way of thinking about satire, more disquieting perhaps to literary criticism, is with reference to temperament rather than genre. In this view, people become satirists because they have hostilities to release, either overtly or co-

1. Maynard Mack, *The Garden and the City: Retirement and Politics in the Later Poetry of Pope, 1731–1743* (Toronto: University of Toronto Press, 1969), p. 128.

vertly, and satire affords a plausibly constructive way of doing it.[2] In 1730 Lyttelton made the ghost of Virgil plead with Pope to forswear satire:

> Why would'st thou force thy genius from its end?
> Formed to delight, why striv'st thou to offend?
> When every soft, engaging muse is thine,
> Why court the least attractive of the nine?[3]

Pope's public image certainly grew bitter enough, creating the paradox to which Spence alludes: "All the people well acquainted with Mr. Pope looked on him as a most friendly, open, charitable, and generous-hearted man;—all the world almost, that did not know him, were got into a mode of having very different ideas of him: how proper this makes it to publish these Anecdotes after my death."[4] In each of the foregoing chapters we have considered elements of Pope's experience that were disturbing and at times unassimilable, even while we recognized the strength of his desire to comprehend and assimilate. Satire, I suggest, is a kind of writing that responds to both aspects of Pope's experience, allowing rebellious and even anarchic impulses to define themselves as custodians of moral order. He wanted to be (and to seem) generous and wise *and also* bitterly satiric. Throughout the

2. A classic expression of this view is Robert C. Elliott, *The Power of Satire: Magic, Ritual, Art* (Princeton: Princeton University Press, 1960). This approach is fruitfully applied to Pope by David B. Morris, *Alexander Pope: The Genius of Sense* (Cambridge, Mass.: Harvard University Press, 1984), ch. 8, "The Muse of Pain." In his recent biography Mack emphasizes Pope's status as unfortunate victim: "Theobald's lacerating attack on his Shakespeare, Curll's highly embarrassing publication at this same moment of his youthful unbuttoned letters to Henry Cromwell, and the accumulating irritation of many unprovoked attacks all helped dictate the excursion into satire from which the *Art of Sinking* and the *Dunciad* resulted" (*Alexander Pope: A Life* [New York: Norton, 1985], p. 511).

3. George Lyttelton, *An Epistle from Rome to Mr. Pope*, p. 7, in *A Collection of Pieces in Verse and Prose, Which Have Been Publish'd on Occasion of the Dunciad* (1732). In the 1776 posthumous edition of Lyttelton's *Works* (III, 100), the first of these couplets is omitted.

4. On the first leaf of the manuscript of Joseph Spence's *Anecdotes*, quoted by George Sherburn, *The Early Career of Alexander Pope* (Oxford: Clarendon, 1934), p. 7.

/

rest of his career he was constantly readjusting his image, and as Spence's remark confirms, he was never able to get it the way he wanted it.

Pope's painful position as a satirist is inseparable from the growth of the mass reading public for whom his kind of art—classical, elitist, and demanding—was increasingly uninviting. The sort of "poetry" that general readers consume has been described as "easily understood on first reading or hearing, stale and conventional in its phrasing and imagery, heavily sentimental, and filled with uncomplicated messages about life."[5] This is the art of Grub Street, which has maintained its appeal from Welsted down to Rod McKuen. Pope breezily mocks an earlier era when humane letters were neglected in favor of "the classics of an age that heard of none" (*Dunciad* I.148). But he faces with increasing bitterness an antihierarchical world in which the classics are again neglected, and in which the great traditional themes are preempted by unworthy scribblers. "Almost all non-satiric poetry written before 1800," Christopher Clausen remarks, "dealt with one or more of five broad areas in human experience: love, death, religion, war, and external nature."[6] Before he stooped to truth, Pope addressed all of these themes: nature and war in *Windsor-Forest,* love in *The Rape of the Lock* and *Eloisa to Abelard,* death in the *Elegy to the Memory of an Unfortunate Lady,* religion in *Messiah.* In his later career satire displaced all of them, with *An Essay on Man* the exception that proves the rule, an attempt to recover religious themes for an irreligious age.

One of Pope's favorite roles as satirist, in addition to those of naïf and *vir bonus,* was that of a Biblical prophet denouncing a wicked world.[7] But unlike Milton or Blake, Pope was reluctant to accept the alienation that the prophetic role entailed. From his earliest years he was anxious not to seem

5. Christopher Clausen, *The Place of Poetry: Two Centuries of an Art in Crisis* (Lexington: University Press of Kentucky, 1981), p. 121.

6. Ibid., p. 124.

7. See Maynard Mack, "The Muse of Satire," *Yale Review,* 41 (1951), 80–92.

unsympathetic in his wit. The much reiterated term *good humor* probably still carried some traces of the old humor psychology, implying a favorable disposition of elements in the self. (Johnson defines *disposition* as "temper of mind,"[8] and *temperament* too goes back to the "tempering" of the bodily "humors.") Pope's early mentor Walsh wrote that "the two best qualities in conversation are good humour and good breeding," and added, "There are some men so surly and ill-natured, and so ill-bred, that though we can hardly deny them to have wit, yet we can say, at least, that we are sorry they have it."[9] Pope was always careful to exhibit good humor and good breeding, and of course he could not be indifferent to the changing idea of humor in his time, which was moving from psychological deformation (as in Jonson's plays) to lovable eccentricity and a hearty openness to one's fellows.[10]

Swift was famous for never laughing openly, and according to Johnson, Pope resembled him: "He sometimes condescended to be jocular with servants or inferiors; but by no merriment, either of others or his own, was he ever seen excited to laughter."[11] Johnson's own definition of the noun *laugh* suggests why Pope might constrain himself: "The convulsion caused by merriment; an inarticulate expression of sudden merriment." Sudden, convulsive, and inarticulate behavior was not likely to appeal to Pope, and we might usefully apply Mary Douglas's anthropological insight, "The more value people set on social constraints, the more the value they set on symbols of bodily control."[12] For Pope, laughter was both a necessary expression of honest feeling and a temptation whose symptoms required explanation if not apology. In an early letter to Henry Cromwell he ex-

8. Samuel Johnson, *A Dictionary of the English Language* (1755).

9. William Walsh, Preface (written 1692) to *The Works of William Walsh, Esq.; In Prose and Verse* (1736), p. iv.

10. See Stuart M. Tave, *The Amiable Humorist* (Chicago: University of Chicago Press, 1960).

11. Samuel Johnson, *Life of Pope*, in *Lives of the English Poets*, ed. G. B. Hill (Oxford: Clarendon, 1905), III, 202.

12. *Natural Symbols: Explorations in Cosmology* (New York: Vintage, 1973), p. 16.

pressly rejects the Hobbesian theory that laughter is "a rec-
ommending our selves to our own favour, by comparison
with the weakness of another," and goes on to admit that
among close friends his demeanor is not always so inflexible
as good breeding might demand:

> I must confess the iniquity of my countenance before you; sev-
> eral muscles of my face sometimes take an impertinent liberty
> with my judgment, but then my judgment soon rises, and sets
> all right again about my mouth: and I find I value no man so
> much, as he in whose sight I have been playing the fool. I
> cannot be *Sub-Persona* before a man I love; and not to laugh
> with honesty, when nature prompts, or folly (which is more a
> second nature than any thing I know) is but a knavish hypo-
> critical way of making a mask of one's own face. —To con-
> clude, those that are my friends I *laugh with,* and those that
> are not I *laugh at.*
>
> (*Corr.* I, 111–12)

"Sub-Persona" would be "under a mask," and among friends
one's face ought not to be a mask. But in public or among
those one despises, the mask is resumed. "He has given his
imagination full scope," Orrery remarked, "and yet has preserved a perpetual guard upon his conduct. The constitution
of his body and mind might early incline him to habits of
caution and reserve. The treatment which he met afterwards
from an innumerable tribe of adversaries confirmed these
habits."[13]

In *The Rape of the Lock,* comic laughter is conceived of as a
means of reconciliation. Pope told Spence long afterward that
when Robert Lord Petre cut off Arabella Fermor's lock, the
two families became estranged and a friend "desired me to
write a poem to make a jest of it, and laugh them together
again."[14] There is certainly satire in the poem, but as Warton
says it is "delicate" and "oblique"; elsewhere he calls it "that

13. John Boyle, fifth earl of Orrery, writing on Pope in *Remarks on the Life
and Writings of Dr. Swift* (1752), 224–25, quoted by Mack, *Alexander Pope,* p.
840n; see also Mack's discussion of this point, pp. 103–4.

14. Joseph Spence, *Observations, Anecdotes, and Characters of Books and Men,*
ed. James M. Osborn (Oxford: Clarendon, 1966), I, 44.

most delicious poem, in which satire wears the cestus of Venus."[15] In Garth's *Dispensary,* Pope's immediate model, the world of "frail nymphs" and pleasure-seeking swains is far grimmer:

> How sanguine swains their amorous hours repent,
> When pleasure's past, and pains are permanent;
> And how frail nymphs, oft by abortion, aim
> To lose a substance, to preserve a name.[16]

In *The Rape of the Lock* sexuality is refined into courtship, and if sexual intercourse does take place it is imagined as leading to marriage, not to the clap. The preservation of Belinda's good name is a central theme of the poem, but one cannot imagine an abortion as the price of it.

Pope's transition to satire involves a renunciation of the comic. If Fielding's art moves from *Jonathan Wild* to *Tom Jones,* Pope's goes the opposite way. In addition, he increasingly names names. "Satire is a sort of glass," Swift observes, "wherein beholders do generally discover everybody's face but their own";[17] Pope makes the faces unmistakable. The early *Rape of the Lock,* to be sure, was based on identifiable people, and Pope professed surprise that some of them took offense: "Sir Plume blusters, I hear; nay, the celebrated lady herself is offended, and, which is stranger, not at herself, but me" (*Corr.* I, 151). But the general tone was affectionate rather than punitive, and in any case the reader is not asked to make a judgment upon these individual persons, as in most of Pope's later satires. "This whimsical piece of work," Pope wrote after completing the revised version, ". . . is at once the most a satire, and the most inoffensive, of anything of mine. People who would rather it were let alone laugh at it, and seem heartily merry, at the same time that they are un-

---

15. Joseph Warton, *An Essay on the Writings and Genius of Pope* (1756), I, 205, and edition of *The Works of Alexander Pope* (1797), I, xx.

16. Samuel Garth, *The Dispensary,* 3rd ed. (1699), Canto III, p. 34.

17. Jonathan Swift, "The Preface of the Author" to *The Battle of the Books,* in *Gulliver's Travels and Other Writings,* ed. Louis A. Landa (Boston: Houghton Mifflin, 1960), p. 358.

easy. 'Tis a sort of writing very like tickling" (*Corr.* I, 211). The comic resolution, incidentally, was confined to art: while Arabella's lock was enshrined in the poetic heavens, she herself married a Mr. Perkins shortly after the poem was published. Lord Petre also married in 1712, and was dead of the smallpox a year later, before the enlarged edition appeared.[18]

In this fundamental change of direction in Pope's career, the hinge is the memorable portrait of Addison as Atticus, drafted in 1715, printed after Addison's death (perhaps without Pope's consent) in 1722, enlarged into a *Fragment of a Satire* in the 1727 *Works*, and finally incorporated in *To Arbuthnot* in 1735:

> Peace to all such! but were there one whose fires
> True genius kindles, and fair fame inspires. . . .
> Should such a man, too fond to rule alone,
> Bear, like the Turk, no brother near the throne. . . .
> Damn with faint praise, assent with civil leer,
> And without sneering, teach the rest to sneer;
> Willing to wound, and yet afraid to strike,
> Just hint a fault, and hesitate dislike. . . .
> Like Cato, give his little senate laws,
> And sit attentive to his own applause. . . .
>   (*Arbuthnot* 193–210)

The portrait of course describes a type, but it is filled with specific allusions: Addison had compared Pope in the *Spectator* to the jealous Turk,[19] and Pope's prologue to Addison's *Cato* included the line "While Cato gives his little senate laws" (23).

Not long before the 1722 publication, Atterbury wrote to say that manuscript versions were much admired: "No small piece of your writing has been ever sought after so much; it has pleased every man without exception, to whom it has been read. Since you now therefore know where your real strength lies, I hope you will not suffer that talent to lie unemployed" (*Corr.* II, 104–5). So long as Addison and his works

18. See *TE* II, 92–94, 372–74.
19. See *TE* IV, 110n, citing *Spectator* 253 and the lines by Denham from which Addison borrowed the analogy.

were familiar, the Atticus portrait got its best effects from the reader's shock at perceiving the covert faults of this great and good man. Pope's Victorian editor Elwin commented indignantly, "Addison has never been convicted of an untruthful word or a dishonourable act; Pope's career was a labyrinth of deceit, and he abounded in audacious malignant inventions."[20] To Pope, of course, Addison was not a cultural institution but a living contemporary, a man whom Ambrose Phillips was accustomed to address as "Joe."[21] We now know that Pope had strong provocation from Addison's covert hostility, patronizing a rival translation of Homer by Thomas Tickell, which many people suspected he had written himself.[22] But today, when Addison is only a dim name to most educated readers, the rights and wrongs of the quarrel seem less important. What is notable is the brilliance with which Pope turns personal animus into an unforgettable image of controlled duplicity, which Addison masked from most observers and perhaps from himself as well.

The best criticism of the Atticus portrait is not a generic or formal one, but the blunt judgment of Chesterton:

> Pope was not such a fool as to try to make out that Addison was a fool. He knew that Addison was not a fool, and he knew that Addison knew it. But hatred in Pope's case had become so great and, I was almost going to say, so pure that it illuminated all things as love illuminates all things. He said what was really wrong with Addison; and in calm and clear and everlasting colours he painted the picture of the evil of the literary temperament.[23]

20. *The Works of Alexander Pope*, ed. Whitwell Elwin and W. J. Courthope, 10 vols. (London: Murray, 1871–1889), I, 327.

21. See the anecdote of Garrick quoted by G. B. Hill in his edition of Johnson's *Lives*, III, 314, n. 5. ("'That,' said Quin, 'was to let you know how familiar he was with Addison.'")

22. See Norman Ault, *New Light on Pope* (London: Methuen, 1949), pp. 101–27. The original Atticus portrait contains a couplet, dropped in *To Arbuthnot*, that alludes to the competition between Pope's translation and Tickell's: "Who when two wits on rival themes contest, / Approves them both, but likes the worst the best" (*TE* VI, 143).

23. G. K. Chesterton, "Pope and the Art of Satire," in *Essays and Poems*, ed. Wilfrid Sheed (Harmondsworth: Penguin, 1958), p. 123.

Art operates here to intensify lived experience. Even Pope's favorite antitheses, which had once seemed artificial feats of skill, are now intrinsic to the subject: "Willing to wound, and yet afraid to strike." Pope did not revise the language much in this piece, but he did take pains over the *mot juste* at the start of that line: "pleased to wound" in 1722, "wishing to wound" in 1727.[24] "Willing to wound" is subtler: does Addison "will" the wound deliberately, or is he just "willing" in the passive sense of letting it happen?

Addison, both in life and in the *Spectator,* is the ultimate exemplar of the eighteenth-century ideal of breeding, control, and good humor. He thus embodies the very virtues that Pope constantly praises, which makes the revelation of hypocrisy all the more telling, but also all the more necessary to relieve Pope's feelings. Addison's identification with the victorious Whigs did not help: he was the quintessential insider to Pope's outsider. C. S. Lewis shrewdly comments, "I do not believe for one moment that he was the fiendlike Atticus; but one sees how inevitably he must have appeared so to the losers. He is so cool, so infuriatingly sensible, and yet he effects more than they."[25] A frontal attack would have been self-destructive, for as Paulson observes, Addison filled the *Spectator* with Horatian poses and piously abjured satiric harshness: "I had once gone through half a satyr, but found so many motions of humanity rising in me towards the persons whom I had severely treated, that I threw it into the fire without even finishing it."[26] Pope had to debunk the genial Addison by a superior subtlety of wit.

The social rituals of the age made it necessary for Pope and Addison to reach an outward truce, whatever they may have felt within. In 1715 Pope showed the Atticus manuscript to Addison, with a clear threat to publish it if further provoked,

24. *TE* VI, 143, 285.
25. "Addison," in *Eighteenth-Century English Literature: Modern Essays in Criticism,* ed. James L. Clifford (New York: Oxford University Press, 1959), p. 146.
26. *Spectator* 355; see Ronald Paulson, *The Fictions of Satire* (Baltimore: Johns Hopkins University Press, 1967), pp. 211, 216.

and repeated the Turk metaphor in a letter to his friend
Craggs:

> If our principles be well considered, I must appear a brave
> Whig, and Mr. Tickell a rank Tory; I translated Homer for the
> public in general, he to gratify the inordinate desires of one
> man only. We have, it seems, a great Turk in poetry, who can
> never bear a brother on the throne; and has his mutes too, a
> set of nodders, winkers, and whisperers, whose business is to
> strangle all other offsprings of wit in their birth. . . . But after
> all I have said of this great man, there is no rupture between
> us: we are each of us so civil and obliging, that neither thinks
> he is obliged. And I for my part treat with him, as we do with
> the Grand Monarch [Louis XIV], who has too many great qual-
> ities not to be respected, though we know he watches any
> occasion to oppress us.
>
> *(Corr.* I, 306–7)

Clearly Addison was a dangerous enemy, with his winking
and whispering informers. One of these was Thomas Burnet,
later defamed in the *Dunciad,* who wrote to his friend Duck-
ett, "It has very often made me smile at the pitiful soul of the
man, when I have seen Addison caressing Pope, whom at the
same time he hates worse than Beelzebub and by whom he
has been more than once lampooned."[27]

In the first of his own inoffensive satires (1725), Edward
Young publicly implored Pope to come forward as the Horace
of his age:

> Why slumbers Pope, who leads the tuneful train,
> Nor hears that virtue, which he loves, complain? . . .
> Doubly distrest, what author shall we find
> Discreetly daring, and severely kind,
> The courtly Roman's shining path to tread,
> And sharply smile prevailing folly dead?[28]

Young's ponderous oxymorons express the ideal which readers expected of Pope: daring but discreet, severe but kind

27. Letter of 1 June 1716, quoted by Sherburn, *Early Career,* p. 116.
28. *Love of Fame, The Universal Passion: In Seven Characteristical Satires,* 5th
ed. (1752), p. 15.

(though gentle, yet not dull). Of his own satires Young declared, "I am not conscious of the least malevolence to any particular person through all the characters." Pope soon came to see that he needed to name individuals.[29]

To forestall sympathy with the host of satiric victims, Pope was careful to invite rather than abuse the reader, particularly in the openings of his poems:

> There are (I scarce can think it, but am told)
> There are to whom my satire seems too bold. . . .
>
> (*Satire* II.i.1–2)

The fine parenthesis—not in Horace—suspends the point until one reaches the second line, and conveys a nice touch of playful irony, such as would be achieved in conversation by facial expression and tone of voice. Immediately afterward, Pope names names:

> Scarce to wise Peter complaisant enough,
> And something said to Chartres much too rough.
>
> (3–4)

We don't want to be identified with these slimy characters, and we are presumably glad of the invitation to share a pose of superiority to them. The famous opening to *Arbuthnot* works very similarly:

> Shut, shut the door, good John! fatigued I said,
> Tie up the knocker, say I'm sick, I'm dead. . . .
>
> (1–2)

No reader wants to be excluded, and the poem cunningly invites us *inside* the closing door.

In his sixth satire Young trumpets exalted claims for his art:

29. Irvin Ehrenpreis quotes this remark (from Young's *Preface*) and interestingly contrasts Young's generalities with Pope's naming of names: "The Cistern and the Fountain: Art and Reality in Pope and Gray," in Ehrenpreis, *Literary Meaning and Augustan Values* (Charlottesville: University Press of Virginia, 1974), pp. 76–93.

> Rise then, my muse, in honest fury rise;
> They dread a satire, who defy the skies.
>
> (p. 125)

When Pope echoes this thought he puts it very differently:

> Yes, I am proud; I must be proud to see
> Men not afraid of God, afraid of me.
>
> (*Epilogue* II.208–9)

It is not his "muse" but *himself* that bad men dread, and Pope openly takes pride in this achievement. Horace says that Lucilius was a friend to virtue and its friends, and Pope unabashedly applies the description (in capital letters) to himself, "TO VIRTUE ONLY and HER FRIENDS, A FRIEND" (*Satire* II.i.121). Pope's "friends" can easily be understood to mean "Patriot" politicians, as a progovernment writer retorted in an apostrophe to Prejudice:

> See Pope to thy almighty influence bend,
> To virtue and to Bolingbroke a friend.[30]

Pope might not reject the implication. His satire is personal in both senses, attacks *on* specific persons *by* a specific person whose friendships help to define and justify him.

To support his role as censor, Pope repeatedly asserts the sanative function of his art:

> Hence satire rose, that just the medium hit,
> And heals with morals what it hurts with wit.
>
> (*Epistle* II.i.261–62)

Pope follows the Horatian original in contrasting malice with flattery, but he adds the idea that satire hits the "medium." Its role, then, is to find or make order in disorder, wounding only in order to cure. But hitting the medium is still hitting, and Pope often presses the metaphor of slashing or stabbing:

> Satire's my weapon, but I'm too discreet
> To run amuck, and tilt at all I meet.
>
> (*Satire* II.i.69–70)

30. The *Daily Courant* for 16 June 1733, quoted by Bertrand A. Goldgar, *Walpole and the Wits: The Relation of Politics to Literature, 1722–1742* (Lincoln: University of Nebraska Press, 1976), p. 129.

Horace, very differently, says that his sheathed dagger and pen will protect him but "never of my free will assail any man alive."[31] There is no parallel in Horace for Pope's line later in the same imitation: "What? armed for virtue when I point the pen" (105). And Pope's final satire reiterates the image: "Yes, the last pen for freedom let me draw" (*Epilogue* II.248).

An engraving in Warburton's edition of Pope's *Works* (see fig. 3) illustrates the metaphor "O sacred weapon, left for truth's defence" (*Epilogue* II.212) with the point of (Athena's?) spear touching the quill and a blindfolded Justice holding an unsheathed sword. A lovely youth (or maiden?) is revealed behind the satiric mask, smoke rises heavenward from the desk-altar, and an aging Pope in wig and robe looks up abstractedly while yielding his pen to the spirit of satire or else accepting it from her. The impression is of satire's justice and authority in an atmosphere of calmness—even weariness—and total absence of malice. The allegorical image is a kind of repastoralizing; Pope stoops to truth only to rise again.

But it *is* truth, as Pope understands it, to which he stoops. At the very end of the *Epilogue to the Satires* he writes,

> Truth guards the poet, sanctifies the line,
> And makes immortal, verse as mean as mine.
>
> (246–47)

Its intrinsic subjects would make satire mean (that is, "low") if they were merely the inventions of art; its power and moral value derive from its commitment to real people and real events. Young's pieties aside, many of Pope's admirers agreed that the weapon was used rightly only if specific victims were named. In Walter Harte's words,

> The random shaft, impetuous in the dark,
> Sings on unseen, and quivers in the mark.
> 'Tis justice, and not anger, makes us write,
> Such sons of darkness must be dragged to light.[32]

31. H. Rushton Fairclough's Loeb Classical Library edition of Horace's *Satires, Epistles and Ars Poetica* (London: Heinemann, 1929), p. 131.

32. *An Essay on Satire*, p. 24, in Richard Savage's volume *A Collection of Pieces in Verse and Prose, Which Have Been Publish'd on Occasion of the Dunciad* (1732).

Plate XVIII.

Vol. IV. facing p. 299.

T. Hayman inv. et del.

C. Grignion Sculp.

O Sacred Weapon, left for Truth's Defence,
Sole Dread of Folly, Vice and Insolence!
To all but Heaven-directed Hands denied,
The Muse may give thee, but the Gods must guide.

Ep. 2 to y.Satires.

3. Engraving after Francis Hayman, facing the *Epilogue to the Satires*
in vol. 4 of Warburton's edition of Pope's *Works* (1751). By permission
of the Folger Shakespeare Library.

Once names were attached to the figures in the *Dunciad,* Johnson recalled, readers "delighted in the visible effect of those shafts of malice, which they had hitherto contemplated as shot into the air."[33] Pope himself wrote persuasively to Arbuthnot, "To attack vices in the abstract, without touching persons, may be safe fighting indeed, but it is fighting with shadows. General propositions are obscure, misty, and uncertain, compared with plain, full, and home examples" (*Corr.* III, 419). Satire would be an indiscriminate weapon if names were not named, as Pope indicated in an ironic mock attack on himself: "The extent of this man's malice is beyond being confined to any One. Every thrust of his satyr, like the sword of a giant, tranfixes [*sic*] four or five, and serves up spitted lords and gentlemen with less ceremony than skewered larks at their own tables."[34] With what amusement or pain did Pope imagine himself as a mighty giant?

A satirist who claims to embody "the strong antipathy of good to bad" (*Epilogue* II.198) must depend upon consensus, a shared notion of the good. As Hume concludes his survey of morals,

> When a man denominates another his *enemy,* his *rival,* his *antagonist,* his *adversary,* he is understood to speak the language of self-love and to express sentiments peculiar to himself and arising from his particular circumstances and situation. But when he bestows on any man the epithets of *vicious* or *odious* or *depraved,* he then speaks another language and expresses sentiments in which he expects all his audience are to concur with him. He must here, therefore, depart from his private and particular situation and must choose a point of view common to him with others; he must move some universal principle of the human frame and touch a string to which all mankind have an accord and symphony.[35]

33. *Lives,* III, 150.

34. *A Master Key to Popery, or, A True and Perfect Key to Pope's Epistle to the Earl of Burlington,* transcribed by Lady Burlington and reprinted by John Butt, *Pope and His Contemporaries: Essays Presented to George Sherburn,* ed. James L. Clifford and Louis A. Landa (Oxford: Clarendon, 1949), p. 55.

35. David Hume, *An Inquiry concerning the Principles of Morals* (1751), ed. Charles W. Hendel (Indianapolis: Bobbs-Merrill, Library of Liberal Arts, 1957), IX.i ("Conclusion"), p. 93.

In seeking to achieve this kind of "symphony" with his fellows, Pope was not just defending himself against attacks. In the deepest sense, he was trying to participate in his culture even while he criticized its faults. Unlike a Romantic artist, who might glory in apartness, Pope saw the function of literature very much in social terms, in the spirit of Lucien Goldmann's remark that a work of art achieves significant structure when it approximates "a conclusion towards which all the members of a certain social group are tending."[36] Goldmann does not mean, of course, that the artist merely reproduces what everyone already knows. "The work constitutes a collective achievement through the individual consciousness of its creator, an achievement which will afterwards reveal to the group what it was moving towards 'without knowing it,' in its ideas, its feelings and its behavior" (p. 115). When Pope's satires turn most bleak and desperate, it is because he doubts the possibility of playing this cultural role.

Pope's most elaborate, indeed obsessive, work of satire was the *Dunciad*, which appeared in four major revisions from 1728 to 1743, with minor variants in more than a dozen other editions. In its sprawling fertility of defamation, it struck the public as a peculiar and offending object that was not easily assimilated.[37] As Johnson notes, it was not so much a poem as a place into which one could be "put," often for good cause:

> Osborne was a man entirely destitute of shame, without sense of any disgrace but that of poverty. He told me, when he was doing that which raised Pope's resentment, that he should be put into *The Dunciad;* but he had the fate of Cassandra. I gave no credit to his prediction till in time I saw it accomplished.[38]

For almost two decades the *Dunciad* was a continuing presence, outlasting many of its original inhabitants.

---

36. "'Genetic Structuralism' in the Sociology of Literature," tr. Petra Morrison, in *Sociology of Literature and Drama*, ed. Elizabeth Burns and Tom Burns (Harmondsworth: Penguin, 1973), p. 113.

37. See Emrys Jones, "Pope and Dulness," in *Pope: A Collection of Critical Essays*, ed. J. V. Guerinot (Englewood Cliffs, N.J.: Prentice-Hall, 1972), pp. 124–57.

38. *Lives*, III, 187.

> Know, Eusden thirsts no more for sack or praise;
> He sleeps among the dull of ancient days.
>
> (I.293–94)

Those who were lucky were occasionally able to get out, as Broome did when he got Pope to delete an insulting allusion: "I thank you for the obliging alteration intended in your poem. If I were of your church, I should say it was a kind of releasement from purgatory and from the company of condemned reprobate poets and authors" (*Corr.* III, 512).

Many of the victims were, like Osborne, selected because of personal grudges. The great classical scholar Bentley said, "I talked against his Homer, and the portentous cub never forgives."[39] But whatever Pope's motives for inserting new victims, he always maintained that they belonged in the *Dunciad* for two quite divergent reasons: they were real people who had behaved disgracefully, and they were also replicable types who could be replaced at any time.

> There may arise some obscurity in chronology from the names in the poem, by the inevitable removal of some authors, and insertion of others, in their niches. For whoever will consider the unity of the whole design, will be sensible, that the *poem was not made for these authors, but these authors for the poem:* and I should judge they were clapped in as they rose, fresh and fresh, and changed from day to day, in like manner as when the old boughs wither, we thrust new ones into a chimney. . . .
>
> Yet we judged it better to preserve them as they are, than to change them for *fictitious names,* by which the satyr would only be multiplied, and applied to many instead of one. Had the hero, for instance, been called *Codrus,* how many would have affirmed him to be Mr. W—— Mr. D—— Sir R—— B——, etc., but now, all that unjust scandal is saved, by calling him *Theobald,* which by good luck happens to be the name of a real person.[40]

The splendid ironies of this passage warn us of the hopelessness of subjecting the *Dunciad* to conventional literary criti-

39. James Henry Monk, *The Life of Richard Bentley, D.D.* (London: Rivington, 1833), II, 372.
40. Appendix I to the three-book Variorum *Dunciad, TE* V, 205–6.

cism, seeking for instance to demonstrate what Pope calls "the unity of the whole design." The hero is named Theobald lest we wrongly identify him with someone else, and by good luck there happens to be "a real person" named Theobald; but the reality of Lewis Theobald is gravely compromised by his ghostly existence in the *Dunciad*.

The actual Theobald outlived his antiheroism (by a curious coincidence his lifetime exactly paralleled Pope's, 1688–1744) since the *Dunciad*s of the 1740s saw him superseded by Colley Cibber. Admirers of the poem as a work of art have not taken Johnson's criticism as seriously as they should:

> Unhappily the two heroes were of opposite characters, and Pope was unwilling to lose what he had already written; he has therefore depraved his poem by giving to Cibber the old books, the cold pedantry and sluggish pertinacity of Theobald. . . . He was able to hurt none but himself: by transferring the same ridicule from one to another he destroyed its efficacy; for, by showing that what he had said of one he was ready to say of another, he reduced himself to the insignificance of his own magpie, who from his cage calls cuckold at a venture.[41]

Johnson alludes to Pope's dismissal of "the man to books confined" whose opinions are not based on personal experience:

> The coxcomb bird, so talkative and grave,
> That from his cage cries Cuckold, Whore, and Knave,
> Though many a passenger he rightly call,
> You hold him no philosopher at all.
>
> (*To Cobham*, 5–8)

But Pope goes on, very interestingly, to suggest that experience is itself a form of "reading," and no more valid intrinsically than what is read in books:

> And yet the fate of all extremes is such,
> Men may be read, as well as books too much.
>
> (9–10)

Whatever the *Dunciad*'s sources in personal resentment, it

---

41. *Lives*, III, 186–87.

stands or falls as a "reading" of English civilization, with the premise—just as in Swift's *Tale of a Tub*—that an outpouring of ephemeral writing is symptomatic of fearful cultural decay. Pope's repeated claims of righteousness can get oppressive, and his targets can seem peculiar. Modern commentators are unnecessarily solemn when they represent butterfly collecting and French cooking (two prominent topics of the fourth book of the *Dunciad*) as symptoms of the death of civilization. It is refreshing to read the lines that Lady Mary puts into Pope's mouth:

> When I see smoking on a booby's board
> Fat ortolans, and pies of Perigord,
> My self am moved to high poetic rage
> (The Homer, and the Horace of the age).[42]

The world of the *Dunciad*, like every other element of Pope's imaginative world, is a complex union of personal feelings, public facts, and literary invention. Most of its victims were obscure and uninteresting in their own time, and are still more so in ours. That Pope could not leave them or the poem alone suggests how deeply the satiric vocation appealed to him, and how attractive he found the satiric mode of representing reality. By naming names while claiming to expose the defects of contemporary culture, he was enabled to raise his sense of confusion and frustration to the level of myth—a procedure in which modern criticism has been glad to cooperate.

Since critics commonly refer to Pope's victims as "the Dunces," it is worth emphasizing that few of them actually deserve that name, or at least they deserve it no more than most modern academics do. Consider James Ralph, friend of Franklin and Fielding, who wrote a poem called *Night* and also, injudiciously as it turned out, responded to the original *Dunciad* with a blank verse poem called *Sawney* (a vulgar nick-

---

42. *Pope to Bolingbroke*, in Mary Wortley Montagu, *Essays and Poems*, ed. Robert Halsband and Isobel Grundy (Oxford: Clarendon, 1977), p. 283.

name for "Alexander"). Alluding superbly to Shakespeare's moon "making night hideous," Pope retaliated promptly:

> Silence, ye wolves! while Ralph to Cynthia howls,
> And makes Night hideous—answer him ye owls![43]

The Twickenham editors describe Ralph as the author of political tracts and "a number of almost worthless plays and poems" (*TE* V, 452–53). *Sawney* is certainly a labored performance, but it is far from foolish. Ralph's shrewd skepticism about *Eloisa to Abelard*, for example, identifies the real ambiguity of that poem:

> But innocence
> And virtue were forgot, and 'tis the nun,
> The enamoured, raging, longing nun that gives
> The verse a name: extract her tender thought,
> Her hot desires, and all the rest will shrink
> From fame, like parchment shriv'ling in the blaze.[44]

Still more interesting is Ralph's much later *The Case of Authors by Profession or Trade* (1758), which clarifies the socio-economic issues that lurk in the footnotes of the *Dunciad*. Ralph earnestly pleads the right of authors to get paid for their work, and compares the garreteer to a slave in the mines:

> Both must drudge *and* starve; and neither can hope for deliverance. The compiler must compile; the composer must compose on; sick or well; in spirit or out; whether furnished with matter or not; till, by the joint pressure of labour, penury, and sorrow, he has worn out his parts, his constitution, and all the little stock of reputation he had acquired among the *Trade;* who were all, perhaps, that ever heard of his name.
>
> (p.22)

Ralph recalls Oldmixon, one of Pope's stock targets, as "submitting to labour at the press like a horse in a mill, till he became as blind and as wretched" (p. 3). And he ends with

---

43. Footnote to *Dunciad* III.159–60 in the three-book version (*TE* V, 165). In the four-book *Dunciad* the lines on Ralph are III.165–66.

44. *Sawney: An Heroic Poem, Occasion'd by the Dunciad* (1728), p. 12.

a semiserious call for unionization: "Combine! And perhaps you would need neither patrons nor establishments! Combine, and you might out-combine the very booksellers themselves!" (p. 67).

Ralph's indignation helps us to see how profoundly Pope thinks of literature as a preserve for those with the right qualifications. Our poet, Martinus Scriblerus says, "lived in those days, when (after providence had permitted the invention of printing as a scourge for the sins of the learned) paper also became so cheap, and printers so numerous, that a deluge of authors covered the land" (*TE* V, 49). There is a good deal of snobbery in Pope's dismissal of Ralph, as appears in a note to the lines about making night hideous: "He was wholly illiterate, and knew no language not even French. . . . He ended at last in the common sink of all such writers, a political newspaper" (*TE* V, 165). It is one thing to write clear English and quite another to be "literate" in other languages; it is one thing to write for a political newspaper and quite another to satirize politics in the accents of Horace or Juvenal.

In fact it is the very obscurity of Pope's enemies that maddens him even as he drags them into the light.

> The first objection I have heard made to the poem is, that the persons are too obscure for satyre. The persons themselves, rather than allow the objection, would forgive the satyre; and if one could be tempted to afford it a serious answer, were not all assassinates, popular insurrections, the insolence of the rabble without doors and of domestics within, most wrongfully chastised, if the meanness of offenders indemnified them from punishment?[45]

In Pope's imagination hack writers are very like insolent servants or an insolent mob, and their challenge to traditional literary hierarchy is a sort of popular insurrection. Worst of all, his victims often failed to grasp that they were victims, and went their own way with intolerable confidence. "Earless on high stood unabashed Defoe" (*Dunciad* II.147).

---

45. *A Letter to the Publisher*, ostensibly by William Cleland but almost certainly by Pope himself, at the beginning of the Variorum *Dunciad* (*TE* V, 14).

An embarrassing contradiction lies barely beneath the surface here. Pope's Twickenham *otium* was directly founded on commercial publication, as John Hughes noted in a 1714 poem urging him to secure his recompense before writing any "flowing numbers":

> If Britain his translated song would hear,
> First take the gold—then charm the list'ning ear;
> So shall thy father Homer smile to see
> His pension paid,—though late, and paid to thee.[46]

To translate Homer was to associate oneself with the greatest classical name, just as to edit Shakespeare was to associate with the greatest modern. But the Homer translation was shared out with collaborators, and the Shakespeare edition was largely produced by hired assistants; as Sherburn delicately puts it, "One can only infer that they eased Pope of a considerable amount of drudgery."[47] Theobald's chief offense against Pope was the exposure of scholarly defects in the Shakespeare edition, and Pope must have been especially pained by the recognition that he had entered an arena where he could be taken for Theobald's equal, or even inferior.

The public outcry over the division of labor on the *Odyssey* was still more damaging, for as Keener observes, "If a hack is one who writes for money and defrauds readers by supplying something less than what he offers, Pope, for the first time in his life, seemed to be a hack."[48] Pope's reaction, as expressed in a letter to Caryll, was to defend the product and meditate revenge:

> I'm glad you received the second set of the *Odyssey*. . . . I believe not only the future but the present age will soon allow it to be an exacter version than that of the *Iliad* where all the drudgery was my own. When I translate again I will be

---

46. *Advice to Mr. Pope, On His Intended Translation of Homer's Iliad, 1714,* in Hughes's *Poems on Several Occasions* (1735), II, 90. Pope occasionally corresponded with Hughes, and is listed as one of the subscribers to the volume.

47. *Early Career,* p. 234.

48. Frederick M. Keener, *An Essay on Pope* (New York: Columbia University Press, 1974), pp. 122–23; and see the whole of Keener's ch. 10.

hanged; nay I will do something to deserve to be hanged, which is worse, rather than drudge for such a world as is no judge of your labour. I'll sooner write something to anger it, than to please it.

(Corr. II, 341)

The *Dunciad* followed in due course.

Since in this light, satire not only allows Pope to release hostility, but permits him further to distinguish between acceptable and unacceptable aspects of himself. He writes for money and so do Ralph and Oldmixon, but he does not write *like* Ralph and Oldmixon. He calls names and so do his enemies, but they abuse indiscriminately and he does not. This is the clear subtext of the painful remark in the *Letter to the Publisher* that introduces the *Dunciad:* "Deformity becomes the object of ridicule when a man sets up for being handsome: and so must dulness when he sets up for a wit" (*TE* V, 17). In Swift's expansion of the idea, applied to his own satires,

> He spared a hump or crooked nose,
> Whose owners set not up for beaux.
> True genuine dullness moved his pity,
> Unless it offered to be witty.[49]

Pope had an elegant nose, but he also had a hump, and his enemies never tired of alluding to it. Pope's deformity ought not to be mocked, because he never "set up for being handsome"; as for his wit, nobody ever questioned that. But of course there were those who insisted that Pope's physical condition was far from irrelevant. The author of *The Curliad* in 1729, answering the first *Dunciad*, very shrewdly quoted Bacon's essay *On Deformity:*

> Whosoever hath any thing fixed in his person that doth induce contempt, hath also a perpetual spur in himself, to rescue and deliver himself from scorn. . . . It stirreth in them industry, and especially of this kind, to watch and observe the weakness of others, that they may have somewhat to repay.[50]

49. Jonathan Swift, *Verses on the Death of Dr. Swift,* 471–74.
50. *The Curliad: A Hypercritic upon the Dunciad Variorum* (1729), p. 33.

Dustin Griffin has splendidly shown that Hervey/Sporus is a horrible parody of Pope himself, an antitype who is in a deep sense an antiself, the thing Pope could be mistaken for by a careless or unsympathetic observer.[51] In a fine article Camille Paglia explores the ways in which Hervey was disturbing to Pope: his militant effeminacy, remorseless amorality, contempt for all politicians without exception (coupled with filial adoration of Queen Caroline), and tireless mockery directed at himself as well as at everybody else.[52] No wonder Warton said of Pope's Sporus portrait, "He has armed his muse with a scalping knife."[53] There is an obvious anguish in Pope's *Letter to a Noble Lord* addressed to Hervey and his ally Lady Mary:

> I am persuaded you can reproach me truly with no great faults, except my natural ones, which I am as ready to own, as to do all justice to the contrary beauties in you. It is true, my Lord, I am short, not well shaped, generally ill-dressed, if not sometimes dirty; . . . Your faces [are] so finished, that neither sickness nor passion can deprive them of colour.[54]

Pope's natural faults are manifest and cannot be concealed, he admits to "passion" that alters his (unpainted) features, and his ill shape is incorrigible.

In his later years Pope found himself outraged by a whole range of professions and pastimes, and the *Dunciad* became a vocation in itself. He was no longer the spokesman for his culture but its implacable censor, the outsider who admitted to standing outside.

> One of my amusements has been writing a poem, part of which is to abuse *Travelling* [Book IV of the *Dunciad*]. . . . I little thought three months ago to have drawn the whole polite world upon me, (as I formerly did the dunces of a lower spe-

51. *Alexander Pope: The Poet in the Poems* (Princeton: Princeton University Press, 1978), pp. 178–88.

52. "Lord Hervey and Pope," *Eighteenth-Century Studies*, 6 (1973), 348–71.

53. *Essay . . . on Pope*, II, 257.

54. *A Letter to a Noble Lord* (1733), in Warburton's edition of Pope's *Works* (1751), VIII, 261.

cies) as I certainly shall whenever I publish this poem. An army of virtuosi, medalists, Ciceroni, Royal Society-men, schools, universities, even florists, free thinkers, and Free Masons, will incompass me with fury: It will be once more, *Concurrere Bellum atque Virum.* But a good conscience, a bold spirit, and zeal for truth, at whatsoever expence, of whatever pretenders to science, or of all imposition either literary, moral, or political; these animated me, and these will support me.

(Corr. IV, 377)

It is true that the *Dunciad* is full of comedy, and that the apocalyptic ending suggests the curtain dropping on a bad play.[55] But it seems likely that when Pope placed an Ovidian couplet on the death of Orpheus as epigraph to the 1743 *Dunciad* (*TE* V, 247), he intended to suggest the Miltonic theme of a singer drowned out by dissonance and dismembered by a mob.[56] The epigraph (especially as Pope abridged it) can also suggest the power of the *Dunciad* to freeze its victims in their gropings, as Apollo did the serpents that attacked the severed Orphic head.[57] Poetry is power, but it is also inevitably an admission of weakness; its victims freeze on the page but not in life, and universal darkness does not really bury anything. One might almost suspect Pope of succumbing to the frenzy which he had helped the Scriblerians to diagnose, years before, in the furious John Dennis: "O destruction! Perdition! *Opera! Opera!* As poetry once raised a city, so when poetry fails, cities are overturned, and the world is no more." To this the doctor retorts, "He raves, he raves; Mr. Lintot, I pray you pinion down his arms, that he may do no mischief."[58]

Pope's satires made him an intensely controversial figure.

55. See Jones, "Pope and Dulness"; Griffin, *Alexander Pope,* pp. 251–61; and Donald Siebert, Jr., "Cibber and Satan: The *Dunciad* and Civilization," *Eighteenth-Century Studies,* 10 (1976–77), 203–21.

56. See John V. Regan, "Orpheus and the *Dunciad*'s Narrator," *Eighteenth-Century Studies,* 9 (1975), 87–101. Warburton deleted the epigraph in the 1751 edition.

57. See R. G. Peterson, "Renaissance Classicism in Pope's *Dunciad*," *Studies in English Literature,* 15 (1975), 431–45.

58. *The Narrative of Dr. Robert Norris, Concerning the Strange and Deplorable Frenzy of Mr. John Dennis* (1713), in *The Prose Works of Alexander Pope,* ed. Norman Ault (Oxford: Blackwell, 1936), p. 162.

Not counting attacks in newspapers, more than 150 pamphlets were published against him in his lifetime, starting with Dennis and ending with Cibber.[59] Broome, brooding on his inclusion in *Peri Bathous* (he was shortly to discover himself in the *Dunciad* too) wrote bitterly to Fenton,

> You ask me if I correspond with Mr. Pope. I do not. He has used me ill, he is ungrateful. He has now raised a spirit against him which he will not easily conjure down. He now keeps his muse as wizards are said to keep tame devils, only to send them abroad to plague their neighbours. I often resemble him to an hedgehog; he wraps himself up in his down, lies snug and warm, and sets his bristles out against all mankind. Sure he is fond of being hated.
>
> *(Corr.* II, 489)

But Pope in fact felt the attacks keenly, and a visitor remembered him looking up from one of Cibber's pamphlets and saying, with his features writhing in anguish, "These things are my diversion."[60] Clearly Pope was the kind of person who needs to be talked about, and also to know what is being said behind his back.

> All this may be; the people's voice is odd,
> It is, and it is not, the voice of God.
> *(Epistle* II.1.89–90)

Critics are the spokesmen of this public. It is not often remarked that the *Essay on Criticism* surveys an unusual topic for a very young poet; Pope was already trying to make himself master of the author-public relationship, identifying himself with the classics and demonstrating, proleptically as it were, that hostile criticism of him was bound to be wrong.

At times, then, it may be gratifying to be abused, since abuse at least implies celebrity, and "Pope" becomes a noun correlative with "poetry" and "wit":

> Poor Cornus sees his frantic wife elope,
> And curses wit, and poetry, and Pope.
> *(Arbuthnot* 25–26)

59. See J. V. Guerinot, *Pamphlet Attacks on Alexander Pope, 1711–1744: A Descriptive Bibliography* (London: Methuen, 1969).
60. Jonathan Richardson, quoted by Johnson, *Lives,* III, 188.

But a later passage in the same poem expresses weariness of the public role, caught in the toils of eternal invective:

> The tale revived, the lie so oft o'erthrown;
> Th' imputed trash, and dulness not his own;
> The morals blackened when the writings scape;
> The libelled person, and the pictured shape.
>
> (350–53)

The Romantic poets had at least the consolation of a prophetic vocation, in which isolation was a badge of honor. The urbane Pope was condemned to an *urbs* that he could not abide, or abide in. The inscription over his grotto entrance was a line from Horace, *Secretum iter et fallentis semita vitae,* "A secluded journey along the pathway of a life unnoticed."[61] This might seem a strange motto for an intransigent satirist, but together with the satire it embodies the paradox of Pope's career.

A recurring theme in the Horatian poems is the mysteriousness of poetic vocation.

> Why did I write? what sin to me unknown
> Dipped me in ink, my parents', or my own?
> As yet a child, nor yet a fool to fame,
> I lisped in numbers, for the numbers came.
>
> (*Arbuthnot* 125–28)

The lines half-acknowledge an element of compulsion even as they affirm a native gift that at first expressed itself artlessly. A deleted passage in the preface to the 1717 *Works* is more explicit about the psychological "sin" of poetry: "I was too young to resist temptations and I was very innocently in love with myself when I began to write and my first productions were the children of self love upon innocence." Pope interestingly compares his hopes of glory with the visionary powers of childhood: "[I] thought I had the greatest genius that ever was. I can't but regret those visions of my childhood

---

61. See Mack, *The Garden and the City,* p. 111.

which like the fine colours we then see when our eyes shut, are vanished for ever."[62]

The "fool to fame" mentioned in *Arbuthnot* was quickly taken up by older writers and was a popular success from the moment he began to publish. At the very outset of his career Pope chose to imitate Chaucer in the *Temple of Fame* and to ponder the emptiness of fame's rewards:

> How vain that second life in others' breath,
> Th' estate which wits inherit after death!
> Ease, health, and life, for this they must resign,
> (Unsure the tenure, but how vast the fine!)
>   (505–8)

Long afterward he ruefully acknowledged that even in one's lifetime, "others' breath" is empty:

> What's fame? a fancied life in others' breath,
> A thing beyond us, ev'n before our death.
> Just what you hear, you have, and what's unknown
> The same (my Lord) if Tully's or your own.
>   (*Essay on Man* IV.237–40)

"My Lord" is Bolingbroke, who was indeed tormented by longings for fame. From this perspective a poetic vocation is unappeasable, and the poet joins other self-deluding people—including "the cripple"—in compensating for satisfactions he can never attain:

> See the blind beggar dance, the cripple sing,
> The sot a hero, lunatic a king;
> The starving chemist in his golden views
> Supremely blest, the poet in his muse.
>   (*Essay on Man* II.267–70)

Poetry becomes a ruling passion in the narrow sense, an aid to delusion.

In our day it is common to detect a sexual impulse in ar-

---

62. Transcribed by Maynard Mack, "Pope's 1717 Preface with a Transcription of the Manuscript Text," in *Augustan Worlds*, ed. J. C. Hilson et al. (Leicester: Leicester University Press, 1978), p. 104,nn. 11 and 15. Pope first wrote "I then saw" before altering it to "we then see."

tistic creation. For Pope the analogy was likely to suggest incapacity and frustration, in the spirit of Cowley's startling remark that when he read Spenser as a boy he "was thus made a poet as irremediably as a child is made an eunuch."[63] Pope wrote to the poet Judith Cowper during the period of laborious translating,

> You (Madam) are in your honeymoon of poetry; you have seen only the smiles and enjoyed the caresses of Apollo. Nothing is so pleasant to a muse as the first children of the imagination; but when once she comes to find it mere conjugal duty, and the care of her numerous progeny daily grows upon her, 'tis all a sour tax for past pleasure.
>
> (*Corr.* I, 209)

As early as the *Essay on Criticism* Pope had expressed bitterness at public appropriation of one's talent, which was felt as alienated in still another version of the sexual metaphor:

> What is this wit which must our cares employ?
> The owner's wife, that other men enjoy.
> (500–1)

One's wit is not one's self, but rather an unfaithful spouse; its role is to seduce readers, but it is then the readers rather than the author who achieve gratification.

Pope's satire grows more strident and desperate until it exhausts itself and falls silent. "But why then publish?" (*To Arbuthnot*, 135). Not for patrons, whom Pope fervently despises; not for his friends, since they can read his poems in manuscript. And surely not for the reading public, whose customary tastes Pope scorns. Swift sardonically writes,

> Poor starveling bard, how small thy gains!
> How unproportioned to thy pains!
> And here a simile comes pat in:
> Though chickens take a month to fatten,
> The guests in less than half an hour
> Will more than half a score devour.

63. Abraham Cowley, "Of My Self," in *The Essays and Other Prose Writings*, ed. Alfred B. Gough (Oxford: Clarendon, 1915), p. 218.

> So, after toiling twenty days
> To earn a stock of pence and praise,
> Thy labours, grown the critic's prey,
> Are swallowed o'er a dish of tea;
> Gone, to be never heard of more,
> Gone, where the chickens went before.[64]

Poems are made to be consumed, and they are consumed all too casually and promptly. In his Homer, Pope succeeded in creating a consumer durable, but one that turned his career in a direction for which he felt distaste, or worse. Warton quotes a story of George II saying to Hervey, "You ought not to write verses, 'tis beneath your rank; leave such work to little Mr. Pope; it is his trade."[65] But even this sneer would have been more acceptable to Pope than another remark by the same king, "Who is this Pope that I hear so much about? I cannot discover what is his merit. Why will not my subjects write in prose?"[66]

At times, even toward the end, Pope allowed himself to hope that satire could change the world, or so he claimed at least.

> Ye tinsel insects! whom a court maintains,
> That counts your beauties only by your stains,
> Spin all your cobwebs o'er the eye of day!
> The muse's wing shall brush you all away!
>
> (*Epilogue* II.220–23)

At other times he probably brooded on the kinds of questions that one of Anthony Powell's characters asks: "Is art action, an alternative to action, the enemy of action, or nothing whatever to do with action? I have no objection to action. I merely find it impossible to locate."[67] Sometimes Pope resumed the pose of the amateur author who is above the fray, much to the disgust of Aaron Hill, who like Broome had been at pains to extricate himself from the *Dunciad:*

---

64. Jonathan Swift, *On Poetry: A Rhapsody,* 59–70.
65. Joseph Warton's edition of Pope's *Works* (1797), I, 229.
66. Prior's *Life of Malone* (1860), quoted in *TE* IV, 362.
67. *The Kindly Ones,* vol. 6 of *A Dance to the Music of Time* (Boston: Little, Brown, 1962), p. 76. The speaker is the musician Moreland.

I am sorry to hear you say, you never thought any great matters of your poetry. It is, in my opinion, the characteristic you
are to hope your distinction from; to be honest is the duty of
every plain man! Nor, since the soul of poetry is sentiment,
can a great poet want morality. But your honesty you possess
in common with a million, who will never be remembered;
whereas poetry is a peculiar, that will make it impossible you
should be forgotten.

(*Corr.* III, 168)

In Hill's opinion, satire was not really worthy of Pope's genius, and he challenged Pope to accept from others the truth-
telling he claimed for himself. "To imitate your love of truth,
with the frankness you have taught me, I wish the *great* qualities of your heart were as strong in you as the *good* ones; you
would then have been above that emotion and bitterness,
wherewith you remember things which want weight to deserve your anguish" (p. 167). Great satirist though he was,
Pope did indeed aspire to fame in other modes, as his cultivated image of genial politeness suggests. Swift wrote to Bolingbroke in 1730 that he expected to die in Ireland "in a rage,
like a poisoned rat in a hole" (*Corr.* III, 99). A few months
later Pope wrote to Swift, "I am just now writing (or rather
planning) a book, to make mankind look upon this life with
comfort and pleasure, and put morality in good humour"
(p. 117). That book was *An Essay on Man.*

PART TWO

IDEAS

5

Psychology

If the history of ideas is allowed to treat concepts as primary and lived experience as secondary, then it seriously distorts what it studies. A common scholarly procedure is to say, "Here are Pope's ideas; now we shall see how he used them in the poems." My procedure has been just the reverse: "Here is what experience felt like to Pope; now we shall look at the ideas he was attracted to and wanted to believe in." Even writers with an overt interest in metaphysics, Milton or Coleridge for instance, have deep temperamental reasons for choosing the ideas they do. And Pope, whose interest in metaphysics was limited and intermittent, was far less likely to have permitted philosophical ideas a privileged role.

A related temptation for scholars is to seize upon the work of some dominant thinker—Augustine or Aquinas for the Middle Ages, Kant or Hegel for the Romantics—and then to deduce the foundations of literary practice from him. Such a procedure yields results, since thinkers of genius inevitably share many preoccupations with others in their culture, but it yields deceptive ones, since their own special elaboration of them need not correspond to the practice of persons less theoretically inclined or working in different literary forms. For the early eighteenth century the inevitable philosopher is Locke, whom everybody read and whose ideas received the tribute of popularization in the *Spectator*. But even when an author like Sterne self-consciously dramatizes Lockean ideas, the literary result is profoundly different from the philosophical "source."[1] Historical hindsight permits us to see that the

1. See Duke Maskell, "Locke and Sterne, or Can Philosophy Influence Literature?" *Essays in Criticism*, 23 (1973), 22–40.

eighteenth century was a time of radical subjectivization, when epistemology replaced ontology as the focus of philosophical thought, and when Locke's brisk common sense rapidly collapsed into the paradoxes of Berkeley and Hume. Knowledge, according to Locke, is "nothing but the perception of the connection of, and agreement or disagreement and repugnancy of, any of our ideas."[2] This formulation participates in the seventeenth-century inquiry into language and knowledge as dynamic products of mental operations, not as discrete words and ideas.[3] As such it seems progressive and liberating. But it conceals a time bomb that was soon to detonate: the conclusion could easily be drawn that knowledge is merely mental, condemning us to a dreadful privacy.

We must be careful, however, not to project Romantic preoccupations backward into an age where they were only partly foreseen, and often were energetically resisted. This is especially important at a time when many literary critics are enthralled with the Romantic exploration of subjectivity, for as Denis Donoghue observes, "A theory of experience as consciousness soon becomes a theory of consciousness as virtue. In modern literature consciousness is the secular form of virtue."[4] Like most of his contemporaries, Pope longed to reaffirm the older forms of virtue and to free himself from the burden of consciousness. According to Warburton, Locke's *Essay* did not at first make a strong impression on Pope: "He had met with it early; but he used to say, it was quite insipid to him."[5]

Turning to psychology more narrowly considered, we may be likely, with our current interest in anarchic and unpredictable aspects of the self, to be struck by those passages in which Pope calls man a "chaos of thought and passion, all confused" (*Essay on Man* II.14) or asks,

---

2. John Locke, *An Essay concerning Human Understanding*, IV.i.2.
3. See Murray Cohen, *Sensible Words: Linguistic Practice in England, 1640–1785* (Baltimore: Johns Hopkins University Press, 1977).
4. *Ferocious Alphabets* (New York: Columbia University Press, 1984), p. 36.
5. William Warburton's edition of Pope's *Works* (1751), VII, 5n.

Our depths who fathoms, or our shallows finds,
Quick whirls, and shifting eddies, of our minds?
(*To Cobham* 29–30)

Pope is known to have admired Montaigne's essay *Of the In-consistency of Our Actions*, which memorably asserts, "We are all patchwork, and so shapeless and diverse in composition that each bit, each moment, plays its own game. And there is as much difference between us and ourselves as between us and others." But this means that human beings contain contradictory elements and play inconsistent roles, not that they are unintelligible. Immediately after this Montaigne quotes Seneca, "Consider it a great thing to play the part of one single man" [*unum hominem agere*]. And the essay concludes, "A sound intellect will refuse to judge men simply by their outward actions; we must probe the inside and discover what springs set men in motion" [*par quels ressorts se donne le branle*].[6] Montaigne's analysis, like Pope's adaptation of it, fits squarely in a classical tradition that despised inconstancy as a symptom of moral decay.[7]

Whether or not Pope flirts with the Lockean idea—much attacked by contemporary moralists—that the self is constantly recreated in the shifting currents of consciousness, he settles finally on something like the traditional view of the self as a permanent "substance," just as the *Memoirs of Scrib-lerus* makes extensive fun of Lockean paradoxes of identity.[8] "Crambe would tell his instructor that all men were not *singular*; that individuality could hardly be predicated of any man, for it was commonly said that a man *is* not the same he *was*, that madmen are *beside themselves*, and drunken men *come to themselves*; which shows that few men have that most

6. *The Complete Essays of Montaigne*, tr. Donald M. Frame (Stanford: Stanford University Press, 1965), II.i, p. 244.
7. See Thomas A. Stumpf, "Pope's *To Cobham, To a Lady*, and the Traditions of Inconstancy," *Studies in Philology*, 67 (1970), 339–58.
8. See Christopher Fox, "Locke and the Scriblerians: The Discussion of Identity in Early Eighteenth Century England," *Eighteenth-Century Studies*, 16 (1982), 1–25.

valuable logical endowment, individuality."[9] It appears indeed that Lockean psychology served more as a negative model than as a positive one: Locke's account of cognitive and linguistic error furnished a schema for satirizing solipsistic "pride." Rather than simply taking over his epistemological psychology, the satirists translated it into traditional moral terms, applied it to their satiric victims, and continued to imagine their own mental processes in more traditional ways.[10]

A few lines before the passage about the whirls and eddies Pope directly echoes Montaigne while lending his thought the structured confidence of the couplet:

> That each from other differs, first confess;
> Next, that he varies from himself no less.
> (*To Cobham*, 19–20)

To vary from oneself is not to lack an intelligible self, only to lapse into multiple roles. It is one thing to say—again, with Montaigne—that the "spring of action" is hard to locate, and quite another to doubt its existence.

> Oft in the passions' wild rotation tossed,
> Our spring of action to ourselves is lost:
> Tired, not determined, to the last we yield,
> And what comes then is master of the field.
> As the last image of that troubled heap,
> When sense subsides, and fancy sports in sleep,
> (Though past the recollection of the thought)
> Becomes the stuff of which our dream is wrought:
> Something as dim to our internal view,
> Is thus, perhaps, the cause of most we do.
> (41–50)

---

9. Pope et al., *Memoirs of . . . Martinus Scriblerus*, ed. Charles Kerby-Miller (New York: Russell and Russell, 1966), p. 119; see Locke's *Essay concerning Human Understanding*, II.xvii.20, and Samuel Clarke's rebuttal quoted by Kerby-Miller, p. 249.

10. See Peter M. Briggs, "Locke's *Essay* and the Strategies of Eighteenth-Century English Satire," in *Studies in Eighteenth-Century Culture*, vol. 10, ed. Harry C. Payne (Madison: University of Wisconsin Press, 1981), pp. 135–51.

If this passage implies the influence of the unconscious, it is a very different one from the all-powerful and purposive unconscious of Freud. This is rather a condition of randomness that prevails when reason and the senses are asleep.

The task, then, for Pope as for Seneca and Montaigne, is to understand our own springs of action and to play a role deliberately rather than by chance. When the sylphs desert Belinda because they find "an earthly lover lurking at her heart" (*Rape of the Lock* III.144), what is revealed is not unacceptable desire, as when Richardson's Clarissa realizes that she partly wants Lovelace, but desire of the most obvious kind, which Belinda needs to act upon. In a note on the famous passage in the *Iliad* where Athena restrains Achilles from attacking Agamemnon, Pope assumes that Homer is simply allegorizing a conscious debate within the hero's mind:

> Pallas the goddess of wisdom descends, and being seen only by him, pulls him back in the very instant of execution. . . . The allegory here may be allowed by every reader to be unforced: the prudence of Achilles checks him in the rashest moment of his anger, it works upon him unseen to others, but does not entirely prevail upon him to desist, till he remembers his own importance, and depends upon it that there will be a necessity of their courting him at any expence into the alliance again. Having persuaded himself by such reflections, he forbears to attack his general. . . .
>
> (*Iliad* I.261, *TE* VII, 99)

When Agamemnon much later says that *Ate* provoked him to steal Achilles' mistress, E. R. Dodds translates *Ate* as "divine temptation or infatuation" and shows that "like all insanity, it is ascribed, not to physiological or psychological causes, but to an external 'daemonic' agency."[11] Baffled perhaps, Pope leaves *Ate* in Greek: "Not by my self, but vengeful *Ate* driven" (XIX.92). But he cannot really imagine behavior that does not originate in the (conscious) self, and so in the notes he allegorizes again: "He cannot prevail with himself

11. *The Greeks and the Irrational* (Boston: Beacon, 1957), pp. 3, 5.

any way to lessen the dignity of the royal character, of which he everywhere appears jealous: something he is obliged to say in public, and not brooking directly to own himself in the wrong, he slurs it over with this tale" (*TE* VIII, 375).

In the *Essay on Criticism* Pope says,

> 'Tis with our judgments as our watches, none
> Go just alike, yet each believes his own.
>
> (9–10)

Watches are machines designed to tell time, which they do with only approximate success, but that does not mean that a true standard of time does not exist or that approximate success is failure. Human beings are machines made by God, and since it cannot be God's fault if the machines work imperfectly, any blame must attach to ourselves.

> Yet if we look more closely, we shall find
> Most have the seeds of judgment in their mind;
> Nature affords at least a glimm'ring light;
> The lines, though touched but faintly, are drawn right.
>
> (*Essay on Criticism* 19–22)

"Opinion" and "passions," Pope says in *To Cobham*, "discolor" and give a "tincture" to what we perceive (25–26). The distortion is easily explained by means of a scientific metaphor:

> The difference is as great between
> The optics seeing, as the objects seen.
>
> (23–24)

Or as Pope puts it in the *Essay on Man*,

> Meanwhile opinion gilds with varying rays
> Those painted clouds that beautify our days.
>
> (II.283–84)

We may prefer imaginary beauty to real disappointment, but the gilding cannot alter the clouds. Pope is remote here from Romantic thought; he believes that we psychologize reality, but not that reality itself is psychological.

For the most part, it needs to be emphasized, this is psychology seen from outside. "Know then thyself" (*Essay on*

Man II.1) is not an invitation to introspect, but a reference to the position of generic "man" in the universal order. Character is understood through signs, a process made difficult by the variousness of human beings, but not different in principle from other phenomena in nature.

> There's some peculiar in each leaf and grain,
> Some unmarked fibre, or some varying vein:
> Shall only Man be taken in the gross?
> Grant but as many sorts of mind as moss.
> *(To Cobham* 15–18)

Is this a hint that descriptive psychology might learn to codify the myriad types of personality, or an admission that the task is impossible? In any case, the attempt to see inside our minds can only produce dim sight—"something as dim to our internal view"—and rather than certainty we must be content with what Locke calls "the twilight, as I may so say, of probability."[12] Rather than peering within, therefore, we would do better to see ourselves as others see us. Nuttall comments, "To know oneself is to know (another) human being."[13]

Eighteenth-century writers and artists had constant recourse to a stylized code of the passions, which—as the novels and even Johnson's *Rambler* testify—were understood to express themselves in specific facial movements (we still speak of a person's "expression"). One scholar who has studied the subject finds, incidentally, that contempt may have been the passion most often displayed: "Its expression, unmistakable and withering, is one of the hallmarks of the structured and stable society of the eighteenth century."[14] Emotion is known because its outward signs are reliably displayed, in

12. John Locke, *Essay,* IV.xiv.2. On this topic see Douglas Lane Patey, *Probability and Literary Form: Philosophic Theory and Literary Practice in the Augustan Age* (Cambridge: Cambridge University Press, 1984), p. 103.

13. A. D. Nuttall, *Pope's "Essay on Man"* (London: Allen & Unwin, 1984), p. 79.

14. Alan T. McKenzie, "The Countenance You Show Me: Reading the Passions in the Eighteenth Century," *Georgia Review,* 32 (1978), 770.

the tableau manner of history painting.[15] It was in this sense that Dryden constantly hailed the power of the new psychology to identify "springs of action" and to reproduce them convincingly in the drama.[16] Aaron Hill, friend of Pope and Richardson, made still stronger claims: "The passions are (in a tragedy where well marked and expressed) what the keys are in a harpsichord. If they are aptly and skilfully touched, they will vibrate their different notes to the heart, and awaken in it the music of humanity."[17] This produces a behaviorist psychology in which to know the passions is to manipulate them, as an anonymous poet credited Walpole with doing:

> Strength of genius, by experience taught,
> Gives thee to sound the depths of human thought,
> To trace the various workings of the mind,
> And rule the secret springs, that rule mankind.[18]

If fancy can gild and discolor reality, it possesses a potential for harm, and at its extreme it can degenerate into madness. This is no frightening revelation of the deepest self, but rather a simple consequence of reason's unwise abdication. Usually, in fact, madness is seen as the irrational idée fixe of an otherwise rational person, like the kindly astronomer in Johnson's *Rasselas*, who believes that his thoughts influence the weather. As in Swift's *Mechanical Operation of the Spirit*, madness is an expression of physiology cut loose from mental control.

The Cave of Spleen in *The Rape of the Lock* is a sustained fantasy of aberrations:

---

15. See, for instance, Pope's note to *Iliad* XXI.41 ff., *TE* VIII, 423, and Morris R. Brownell's discussion in *Alexander Pope and the Arts of Georgian England* (Oxford: Clarendon, 1978), p. 48.

16. See, for example, *The Grounds of Criticism in Tragedy*, in John Dryden, *Of Dramatic Poesy and Other Critical Essays*, ed. George Watson (London: Everyman, 1962), I, 254.

17. *The Prompter*, no. 64 (20 June 1735).

18. *An Epistle to the Right Honourable Sir Robert Walpole*, in *The Flower-Piece: A Collection of Miscellany Poems* (1731), p. 50. The volume was edited by Matthew Concanen, familiar from the *Dunciad*.

> Men prove with child, as pow'rful fancy works,
> And maids turned bottles call aloud for corks.
>
> (IV.53–54)

Wakefield reports a tradition that Pope had in mind a specific case of neurosis ("hypochondria"):

> The fanciful person here alluded to was Dr. Edward Pelling, chaplain to several successive monarchs. Having studied himself into that disorder of mind vulgarly called the hyp, between the age of forty and fifty he imagined himself to be pregnant, and forebore all manner of exercise, lest motion should prove injurious to his ideal [i.e., imaginary] burden. Nor did the whim evaporate till his wife assured him, that she was really in his supposed condition. This lady was masculine and large-boned in the extreme; and our merry monarch Charles, being told of the strange conceit adopted by his chaplain, desired to see her. As she quitted his presence, he exclaimed with a good round oath, that if any woman could get her husband with child, it must be Mrs. Pelling.[19]

In the *Dunciad* madness is detected at the heart of a sick civilization, and just as in Swift it is seen as a form of solipsistic pride.[20] If pride is resisted, accordingly, reason can reassume its authority, as Pope says very clearly in the *Essay on Criticism*:

> Of all the causes which conspire to blind
> Man's erring judgment, and misguide the mind,
> What the weak head with strongest bias rules
> Is pride, the never-failing vice of fools. . . .
> If once right reason drives that cloud away,
> Truth breaks upon us with resistless day.
>
> (201–12)

Seen in this light, a psychologized reality must be a morally confused misperception. The cure for pride is reason, and the basis of reason is truth.

---

19. Gilbert Wakefield, *Observations on Pope* (1796), p. 83 (signed with an "S" as a contribution by George Steevens). "I received this narrative from one of the Doctor's grand-daughters, who is still alive; and remembers that this line of Pope was always supposed to have reference to this story."

20. See David B. Morris, *Alexander Pope: The Genius of Sense* (Cambridge, Mass.: Harvard University Press, 1984), ch. 10.

In later years Pope grew less sanguine about the inevitability of "resistless day," but he was more confident than ever about the coherence of the psychological system. Balanced opposites are fundamental to everything in Pope's conception, from the couplet to the cosmos, and when pride is redefined as self-love it turns out to be the very "spring of action" that Montaigne was looking for:

> Two principles in human nature reign;
> Self-love, to urge, and reason, to restrain. . . .
> Self-love, the spring of motion, acts the soul;
> Reason's comparing balance rules the whole.
> (*Essay on Man* II.53–54, 59–60)

As with the checks and balances of eighteenth-century political thought, reason is "formed but to check, delib'rate, and advise" (II.70). "Modes of self-love the passions we may call" (II.93), and the six principal passions interact in a *concordia discors* analogous to that of a work of art.

> Love, hope, and joy, fair pleasure's smiling train,
> Hate, fear, and grief, the family of pain;
> These mixed with art, and to due bounds confined,
> Make and maintain the balance of the mind:
> The lights and shades, whose well accorded strife
> Gives all the strength and colour of our life.
> (II.117–22)

Reason does not so much preside over this activity as furnish a compass card by which to steer:

> On life's vast ocean diversely we sail,
> Reason the card, but passion is the gale.
> (107–8)

But if passion supplies the energy and reason only restrains, we find a paradoxical situation in which the highest faculty is strangely recessive, a moderator rather than a commander.[21] Pope later laments that unless reason can give us weapons as well as rules, she can only

21. See Douglas H. White, *Pope and the Context of Controversy: The Manipulation of Ideas in "An Essay on Man"* (Chicago: University of Chicago Press, 1970), ch. 4.

teach us to mourn our Nature, not to mend,
A sharp accuser, but a helpless friend!
                    (II.153–54)

Indeed, the relations between reason and passion in the *Essay on Man* are hopelessly murky, with reason now dominant, now impotent, depending on the polemical position Pope finds himself in.[22]

Pope thought that his own special contribution was the theory of a ruling passion that controls every aspect of a person's life, and this makes matters more paradoxical still. Etymologically it was passion that was passive, as in Johnson's first *Dictionary* definition: "Any effect caused by external agency." Johnson next defines passion as "violent commotion of the mind,"[23] and we need to remember that in classical psychology, with its emphasis on balance and temperance, a ruling passion was seen as an unmitigated disaster. According to Plato a "master passion" (*Eros*) is like a great winged drone that implants "the sting of a longing that cannot be satisfied" and permanently deforms the soul, and this is identical with tyranny of the mob in the political realm. "If the individual, then, is analogous to the state, we shall find the same order of things in him: a soul labouring under the meanest servitude, the best elements in it being enslaved, while a small part, which is also the most frenzied and corrupt, plays the master."[24] Pope is certainly not prepared to let the mob govern society, but he accepts the passions, and beyond them the ruling passion, as the source of human action.

To Cobham begins with the lines already quoted about the whirls and eddies of the mind. The great value of the ruling passion theory, Pope declares in that poem, is that it can account for even the most contradictory behavior just as Newton's physics does.

22. See Nuttall's unsparing analysis, *Pope's "Essay on Man,"* pp. 87–98.
23. Samuel Johnson, *A Dictionary of the English Language* (1755).
24. *The Republic of Plato,* tr. Francis M. Cornford (Oxford: Clarendon, 1941), pp. 291, 297 (IX.572, 577).

> Nature well known, no prodigies remain,
> Comets are regular, and Wharton plain.
> (208–9)

But the ruling passion accounts for behavior from the outside, without implying control. Pope writes ironically of Newton in the *Essay on Man,*

> Could he, whose rules the rapid comet bind,
> Describe or fix one movement of his mind?
> (II.35–36)

Warburton comments on the lines in *To Cobham,*

> This illustration has an exquisite beauty, arising from the exactness of the analogy: for, as the appearance of irregularity, in a comet's motion, is occasioned by the greatness of the force which pushes it round a very eccentric orb [i.e., orbit]; so it is the *violence* of the ruling passion that, impatient for its object, in the impetuosity of its course towards it, is frequently hurried to an immense distance from it, which occasions all that puzzling inconsistency of conduct we observe in it.[25]

A kind of determinism creeps in, and in proportion as a person is psychologically explicable, he or she becomes morally unreliable if not reprehensible.

Fearing determinism, Pope keeps veering away from his own grimmer insights:

> Thus nature gives us (let it check our pride)
> The virtue nearest to our vice allied;
> Reason the bias turns to good from ill,
> And Nero reigns a Titus, if he will.
> (*Essay on Man* II.195–98)

"But he won't, he didn't," Thomas Edwards comments.[26] At best a "bias"—the metaphor derives from the off-center weight of the ball in lawn bowling—implies an unavoidable deviation from a straight line, just as in the elliptical orbits of

---

25. Warburton's edition of Pope's *Works* (1751), III, 188.
26. "Visible Poetry: Pope and Modern Criticism," in *Twentieth-Century Literature in Retrospect*, ed. Reuben A. Brower (Cambridge, Mass.: Harvard University Press, 1971), p. 311.

comets. The Restoration playwright Shadwell wrote, in the humor tradition of Jonson,

> A humor is the bias of the mind,
> By which with violence 'tis one way inclined:
> It makes our actions lean on one side still,
> And in all changes that way bends the will.[27]

Dryden, mocking in *Mac Flecknoe* Shadwell's claim to be the true Son of Ben, transformed the image into a critique of Shadwell's literary ineptness:

> This is that boasted bias of thy mind,
> By which one way, to dullness, 'tis inclined.
> Which makes thy writings lean on one side still,
> And in all changes that way bends thy will.
>   (189–92)

More than ever one realizes how deeply Pope's terms are those of satire, superbly suited to exposing folly from a position of assumed superiority, but less apt for analysis of the insoluble dilemmas of the human condition.

It was probably for this reason that Cobham himself, reading *To Cobham* in advance of publication, urged Pope to confine his account to unnatural passions rather than natural ones.

> I like your lecher better now 'tis shorter and the glutton is a very good epigram, but they are both appetites that from nature we indulge as well for her ends as our pleasure. . . . I mean that a passion or habit that has not a natural foundation falls in better with your subject than any of our natural wants which in some degree we cannot avoid pursuing to the last, and if a man has spirits or appetite enough to take a bit of either kind at parting you may condemn him but you would be proud to imitate him.
>   (*Corr.* III, 393)

Cobham's criticism assumes a stable and conventional view of the ruling passion, and if Pope at times encourages this, at other times he seems to be groping for something stranger

---

27. Thomas Shadwell, Epilogue to *The Humorists*.

and more pessimistic. In a remarkable passage in the *Essay
on Man* he compares the ruling passion to a wasting and in-
curable disease:

> As man, perhaps, the moment of his breath,
> Receives the lurking principle of death;
> The young disease, that must subdue at length,
> Grows with his growth, and strengthens with his strength:
> So, cast and mingled with his very frame,
> The mind's disease, its ruling passion came.
>
> (II.133–38)

The metaphor is strikingly relevant to the poet for whom illness was an inseparable companion in "this long disease, my
life" (*To Arbuthnot*, 132). One can strive to make a virtue of a
defect, but all the same a fatal disease is hardly an encouraging basis for health.

In *To Cobham* Pope emphasizes that the ruling passion is
not a mode of behavior that one can choose or alter, but
an irreducible core of individuality that endures even when
everything else has eroded away.

> Time, that on all things lays his lenient hand,
> Yet tames not this; it sticks to our last sand.
>
> (224–25)

Cobham's own ruling passion, Pope flatteringly suggests, is
that specialized form of love known as patriotism, which in
"godlike Hector" was "his principal passion, and the motive
of all his actions."[28]

> And you! brave Cobham, to the latest breath
> Shall feel your ruling passion strong in death:
> Such in those moments as in all the past,
> "Oh, save my country, heav'n!" shall be your last.
>
> (262–65)

It is either distressing or gratifying, depending on one's temperament, to learn that what Cobham would have called a
natural passion operated at his own deathbed. "In his last

---

28. *Iliad* III.53 and Pope's note (*TE* VII, 191).

moments, not being able to carry a glass of jelly to his mouth, he was in such a passion, that he threw the jelly, glass and all in the face of his niece, Hester Grenville, and expired" (*TE* III–ii, 38n).

No doubt the Age of Reason is the wrong term for the eighteenth century, if by that we mean system-building reason in the seventeenth-century sense, but it is just as misleading to call it (as Kenneth MacLean once proposed) the Age of Passion.[29] What people like Pope wanted was a dynamic balance, passion prompting and reason guiding, that could oppose every impulse with a counterimpulse. The "though deep, yet clear" model is always waiting to be applied, and a minor writer can cheerfully let rhetoric do the work of argument, as in Aaron Hill's advice to actors wishing to portray love:

> Love is intense desire, by rev'rence checked;
> 'Tis hope's hot transport, streaked with fear's respect. . . .
> 'Tis passion's every soul-felt power, *disjoined*,
> Tis all th' assembled train's whole force, *combined*.[30]

A writer of genius like Pope cannot be satisfied with these easy harmonies, and his forays into psychology represent a never-ending struggle to find harmony without misrepresenting human experience.

Passion without destructive consequences is unimaginable, at least outside an unfallen paradise, and even there Milton sees in passion the seeds of disaster. Flowers and birdsong work no change in the mind, Adam tells Raphael, but Eve affects him very differently:

> Far otherwise, transported I behold,
> Transported touch; here passion first I felt,
> Commotion strange, in all enjoyments else
> Superior and unmoved, here only weak
> Against the charm of beauty's powerful glance.

29. *John Locke and English Literature of the Eighteenth Century* (New Haven: Yale University Press, 1936), p. 38.

30. *The Art of Acting*, in *The Works of the Late Aaron Hill* (1753), III, 403.

The angel replies with contracted brow, "Accuse not nature, she hath done her part; / Do thou but thine," and goes on to explain, "In loving thou dost well, in passion not, / Wherein true love consists not."[31] Swift's Houyhnhnms manage to love without passion, but human readers have always regarded them as inhuman. What is at stake finally is the dilemma of any hierarchical psychology that tries to enthrone "reason" above "passion" while admitting that passion is the source of energy. It is a rare thinker who, like Blake, tries to imagine a dynamic equilibrium of energies, with reason not exalted over passion or even different in kind from it. But Blake's system has plenty of paradoxes of its own. We are confronted with the dilemmas of human nature itself, not of one or another theoretical system.

Beyond psychology, if one may so express it, Pope seeks character, a determinate structure on the analogy of "characters" in printing. Johnson defines the word as "a mark; a stamp; a representation" and as "a letter used in writing or printing," goes on to "a representation of any man as to his personal qualities," and only afterward gives "the person with his assemblage of qualities." Recent scholars have been strongly attracted to the freewheeling improvisation of Renaissance self-fashioning, but Pope and his contemporaries were not. Weary of instability, they wanted a stable self in a stable world. Above all they saw character as socially determined and constrained. Again it is a matter of seeing oneself as others do; in Hume's words, "By our continual and earnest pursuit of a character, a name, a reputation in the world, we bring our own deportment and conduct frequently in review and consider how they appear in the eyes of those who approach and regard us."[32]

Pondering the vulnerability of tyrants in Hobbesian terms, Pope asks in the *Essay on Man,*

---

31. John Milton, *Paradise Lost* VIII.525–33, 561–62, 588–89.
32. David Hume, *An Inquiry concerning the Principles of Morals* (1751), ed. Charles W. Hendel (Indianapolis: Bobbs-Merrill, Library of the Liberal Arts, 1957), conclusion, p. 96.

> How shall he keep, what, sleeping or awake,
> A weaker may surprise, a stronger take?
> His safety must his liberty restrain:
> All join to guard what each desires to gain.
>
> (III.275–78)

"The last line," Martin Price comments, "is built of intense rhetorical oppositions: *all* against *each*, *join* against *desires*, *guard* against *gain*. In each opposition, the thrust of selfishness becomes transformed to the embrace of confederation."[33] Moreover, the confederation is made up of a host of individuals.

In Locke the abyss of consciousness is avoided by the multiple connections of social existence:

> One single man may at once be concerned in, and sustain all these following relations, and many more, viz. father, brother, son, grandfather, grandson, father-in-law, son-in-law, husband, friend, enemy, subject, general, judge, patron, client, professor, European, Englishman, islander, servant, master, possessor, captain, superior, inferior, bigger, less, older, younger, contemporary, like, unlike, etc., to an almost infinite number.[34]

Pope sees himself not as an isolated self but as son, friend, possessor; he is younger than Swift, inferior to Bolingbroke, and smaller than everybody. Ronald Paulson, remarking on the ubiquity of a motivating "other" in Pope's works, proposes that "Pope has at every stage to prove his own position to himself by provoking it from something existent; as if without the actual presence of another person or object, the sense of his own identity lacks firmness."[35] Paulson relates this to Pope's temperament and to eighteenth-century epistemology. But isn't it true of all of us? Surely the fantasy of self-

33. *To the Palace of Wisdom: Studies in Order and Energy from Dryden to Blake* (New York: Doubleday, Anchor, 1965), p. 131.

34. John Locke, *Essay*, II.xxv.7.

35. "Satire, and Poetry, and Pope," in *English Satire: Papers Read at a Clark Library Seminar* (Los Angeles: William Andrews Clark Memorial Library, 1972), p. 101.

sufficiency, whether in *Robinson Crusoe* or the *Prelude*, is what needs justification.

Character for Pope is defined by comparison, not by absolute definition, as in the individuality of "the characters of his persons" that he admires in Homer.

> Every one has something so singularly his own, that no painter could have distinguished them more by their features, than the poet has by their manners. . . . The single quality of courage is wonderfully diversified in the several characters of the *Iliad*. That of Achilles is furious and intractable; that of Diomede forward, yet listening to advice and subject to command: that of Ajax is heavy and self-confiding; of Hector, active and vigilant: the courage of Agamemnon is inspirited by love of empire and ambition, that of Menelaus mixed with softness and tenderness for his people: we find in Idomeneus a plain direct soldier, in Sarpedon a gallant and generous one.
>
> (*TE* VII, 7)

This is almost the reverse of what we mean by personality; it is the stamp of some general quality in a particular proportion. Virgil is inferior to Homer in this respect, Pope says, for "many of his persons have no apparent characters" (p. 8).

So also with the notorious beginning of *To a Lady*, "Most women have no characters at all" (2). The thought comes quite directly from La Bruyère: "*La plûpart des femmes n'ont guère de principes, elles se conduisent par le coeur.*"[36] Rather than having a single fixed character as they ought, women play a series of roles and have *too many* characters, which amounts to having none in particular.

> How many pictures of one nymph we view,
> All how unlike each other, all how true!
> Arcadia's countess, here, in ermined pride,
> Is there, Pastora by a fountain side:
> Here Fannia, leering on her own good man,
> Is there, a naked Leda with a swan.
>
> (5–10)

---

36. Quoted by Benjamin Boyce, *The Character-Sketches in Pope's Poems* (Durham, N.C.: Duke University Press, 1962), p. 120. La Bruyère remarks that most men lack "certain characters" too.

The poet's job, like the artist's, is to capture these shifting posturings before they vanish:

> Come then, the colours and the ground prepare!
> Dip in the rainbow, trick her off in air,
> Choose a firm cloud, before it fall, and in it
> Catch, ere she change, the Cynthia of this minute.
>
> (17–20)

These chameleonic ladies are like dancers at a masquerade. It is not that they lack a central self, but rather that they prefer not to stabilize it, and enjoy an endless role-playing calculated entirely for its effect on others. Playing at being many things, they are no single definite thing. One can also be characterless, of course, by simple indistinctness, as Johnson remarks, applying Pope's lines to both sexes: "The greater part of mankind 'have no character at all,' have little that distinguishes them from others equally good or bad, and therefore nothing can be said of them which may not be applied with equal propriety to a thousand more."[37] But there is nothing indistinct about the women in *To a Lady*.

A thoughtful person will still play roles, but can choose to concentrate on appropriate ones, as Pope himself strove to do. Even if one's roles sometimes conflict, they are watched over by an intelligence that knows exactly what is going on. So Eloisa describes her surrender to passionate fantasy:

> When at the close of each sad, sorrowing day,
> Fancy restores what vengeance snatched away,
> Then conscience sleeps, and leaving nature free,
> All my loose soul unbounded springs to thee.
>
> (*Eloisa to Abelard*, 225–28)

Eloisa deliberately gives herself to the pleasures of reverie; she chooses to let herself go, and afterward she chooses to describe where she has been. Everything in her epistle to Abelard is calculated, including the desperate emotionalism.

---

37. Examination of Pope's *Epitaphs*, appended to Samuel Johnson, *Life of Pope*, in *Lives of the English Poets*, ed. G. B. Hill (Oxford: Clarendon, 1905), III, 263–64.

Descent into the self is an indulgence, not an existential plunge. Pope describes the psychotic Atossa as "sick of herself through very selfishness" (*To a Lady*, 146). A later era might see her as tragically trapped in her selfhood; Pope sees her condition as merely selfish.

In a rich essay S. L. Goldberg suggests that integrity of character can be thought of in three overlapping but distinct senses: moral consistency based on firm principles ("a man of character"); psychological consistency ("most women have no characters at all"); and authenticity or fully realized identity, which may be as evident in a "bad" person as in a "good" one. Goldberg argues that in practice if not in theory Pope was greatly interested in the third category, though he had no name for it.[38] That may be true, but the theory is not irrelevant, because Pope very badly wanted the first two categories. Goldberg talks about the Romantics' Shakespeare, the chameleon poet who enjoys his imagined persons in all their fullness. Pope may at times do this, but he always draws back to "place" them and to assert his own integrity in the first two of Goldberg's senses.

Pope's concept of artistic creation, and of the poet's self-revelation, is so remote from post-Romantic assumptions that the gulf between them deserves to be emphasized. Here is Julia Kristeva on the two "brinks" on which any speaking person hesitates, for instance a patient in analysis:

> On the one hand, there is pain—but it also makes one secure—caused as one recognizes oneself as subject of (others') discourse, hence tributary of a universal Law. On the other, there is pleasure—but it kills—at finding oneself different, irreducible, for one is borne by a simply singular speech, not merging with the others, but then exposed to the black thrusts of a desire that borders on idiolect and aphasia.[39]

38. "Integrity and Life in Pope's Poetry," in *Studies in the Eighteenth Century III*, ed. R. F. Brissenden and J. C. Eade (Toronto: University of Toronto Press, 1976), pp. 185–207.

39. *Desire in Language: A Semiotic Approach to Literature and Art*, tr. Thomas Gora, Alice Jardine, and Leon S. Roudiez (New York: Columbia University Press, 1980), p. x.

The strenuous syntax and excited metaphors of modern theory are appropriate to a poet like Blake, who does indeed feel pain at merging with the discourse of others, and pleasure in a singularity that leads to an ever-deepening isolation. Pope, very differently, is concerned to minimize the ways in which he differs from others, and to forge a language that will let him speak confidently for the group.

There must be many reasons why the lyric did not flourish in Pope's lifetime, but one surely is a suspicion of the subjective. The hatred these writers felt for Puritan "enthusiasm" reflects a fear of the chaos they thought it led to: inwardly, the arrogantly private conscience that Swift satirized in *A Tale of a Tub*, and outwardly, the disorder into which the Puritans plunged English society. The answer was to emphasize the uniformity of human nature even in its eccentricities ("Comets are regular, and Wharton plain") and to excoriate individualism as aberrant and immoral. Swift's *Mechanical Operation of the Spirit* turns subjectivism on its head, seeking to show that private mental experience is physiologically caused and is a kind of disease. Like the politics of the so-called Augustans, this was a psychology of nostalgia, a repudiation of everything that had been developing since the Renaissance. Subjectivism would eventually be welcomed and put on plausible theoretical foundations. Meanwhile Pope and Swift conducted their energetic rearguard action, and if in the end it was erecting a fence against a glacier, they devoted great skill and intelligence to the construction of the fence.

6

Religion and Metaphysics

If Pope had never written the *Essay on Man*, an extended review of his philosophical ideas might not readily suggest itself. And the *Essay on Man* itself is more a problem than a solution, a reflection of Pope's deep wish to make sense of experience rather than a successful feat of metaphysical argument. Let us begin by considering what the poem is and is not, and then try to understand why he handled it as he did.

The best approach is not necessarily to locate the poem in the context of contemporary philosophical thought. As in the closely related case of psychology, the central project of eighteenth-century empiricism was very remote from Pope's interests. In Richard Rorty's critique, "The Cartesian change from mind-as-reason to mind-as-inner-arena was . . . the triumph of the quest for certainty over the quest for wisdom."[1] Pope consistently appeals to reason, shows little interest in the notion that experiential data are filtered and recombined inside the mind, and constantly inveighs against claims to certainty. Wisdom in the classical sense is exactly what he aspires to. Rorty later addresses a favorite problem of post-Lockean British philosophy, the difficulty of knowing other minds, and states its primary axiom as, "We know our minds better than we know anything else" (p. 107). Pope (and Swift and Fielding and Johnson) would regard this as absurd, and the "problem" of other minds as virtually irrelevant.

1. *Philosophy and the Mirror of Nature* (Princeton: Princeton University Press, 1979), p. 61.

More generally, it is hard to see that Pope participates in the great empiricist move from ontology to epistemology. Insofar as he addresses either concern—and "ontology" is a higher-order abstraction than the "wisdom" he seeks—an emphasis on epistemology is certainly unattractive to him. John Richetti's summary of post-Lockean psychologizing helps us to see that it is not just remote from Pope's style and interests, but antithetical to them:

> The modern philosopher-writer is a man alone, a sort of voluntary Robinson Crusoe or self-appointed philosophical Adam whose thought tends to represent itself as a new beginning rather than a continuation and modification of older thought. . . . Such [traditional] thought has visible social location as well as overt ethical and political concerns. The radical epistemologizing of thought after, say, Descartes requires the denial or at least the functional dismissal of context. Society and its concerns become effects of consciousness rather than its cause or accompaniment.[2]

As Richetti observes, many eighteenth-century writers attacked this tendency energetically, asserting instead a tradition in which "the self is limited to certain roles and rhetoric expresses a cultural and moral order" (p. 30). And they attacked it in richly metaphorical language that directly opposed the "understatement" and "plainness" espoused by Locke (p. 16). Pope is among the attackers, not among the epistemologists.

At the deepest level, Pope's religious yearnings are for ethical harmony rather than dogmatic certainty, and the *Essay on Man* is an attempt to establish just as much belief as will adequately ground ethics. Pope is a conservative of the type Oakeshott describes, who wants the moral life to be "a habit of affection and behavior" rather than of thought, but who is obliged to defend a code of belief since Western morality— whether classical or Christian—is a "moral ideology" based

2. *Philosophical Writing: Locke, Berkeley, Hume* (Cambridge, Mass.: Harvard University Press, 1983), p. 7.

on a system of abstract ideals.[3] *An Essay on Man* is a picture of man as fitted into his cosmic and social worlds, as the sequence of Epistles urges:

I.   Of the Nature and State of Man, with respect to the UNIVERSE.

II. Of the Nature and State of Man, with respect to Himself, as an Individual.

III. Of the Nature and State of Man, with respect to Society.

IV. Of the Nature and State of Man, with respect to Happiness.[4]

The moment of greatest danger comes in the leap from I to II, which so often, from the middle of the seventeenth century onward, meant a leap into monadic individualism. All of the arguing and hectoring in the *Essay on Man* is intended to render speculation unnecessary, to reverse the course of Western experience, and to turn moral ideology back into moral habit.

Pope got his philosophical ideas very much secondhand, principally from Bolingbroke. Bathurst told Warton that "he had read the whole scheme of the *Essay on Man*, in the handwriting of Bolingbroke, and drawn up in a series of propositions, which Pope was to versify and illustrate."[5] To this Johnson objected that "the poetical imagery, which makes a great part of the poem, was Pope's own."[6] But matters are only complicated further when one person "versifies" another's ideas with "poetical imagery." In an essay of 1755 entitled *Pope Ein Metaphysiker!*, Lessing precedes his analysis of Pope's

3. Michael Oakeshott, *Rationalism in Politics and Other Essays* (New York: Basic, 1962), pp. 61, 78.

4. Pope's prose Arguments to the four Epistles.

5. Joseph Warton, *An Essay on the Genius and Writings of Pope* (1782), II, 62.

6. James Boswell, *Life of Samuel Johnson*, ed. G. B. Hill, rev. L. F. Powell (Oxford: Clarendon, 1934), III, 403 (10 Oct. 1779). Johnson was commenting on Hugh Blair's version of Bathurst's story.

argument with some trenchant remarks on the use of language in a work like the *Essay on Man*:

> What must the metaphysician do above all? He must define [*erklären*] the words he wants to use; he must never use them in other senses; he must not confuse them with words that appear synonymous. What does the poet obey of all this? None of it. Melodious sound is in itself a sufficient motive to exchange one expression for another, and for him the variation of synonymous words is a source of beauty.[7]

It follows that when a poet draws upon philosophy he translates it into his own imaginative structure, in which forcible images are more important than connected arguments, and in which obscurity is never acceptable even if a full presentation of the reasoning would necessarily be obscure. It is often claimed that the elegances of poetry blur the sharp distinctions of philosophy, but given the subtlety and depth of the ideas Pope tries to cast into his patterned couplets, one might well argue the reverse. As Auden remarks, "The danger of argument in verse—Pope's *Essay on Man* is an example—is that the verse makes the ideas *too* clear and distinct, more Cartesian than they really are."[8]

Lessing concludes,

> The philosopher who wants to ascend Parnassus, and the poet who wants to descend to the valleys of solemn and tranquil wisdom, meet each other at the halfway point, where they (so to speak) exchange clothes and then go back. Each brings home with him the other's form [*Gestalt*], but nothing more than the form. The poet has become a philosophical poet, and the philosopher a poetic philosopher.

(p. 234)

In this passage the philosopher is first called *Philosoph*, a word rich with Enlightenment connotations, but after the exchange of clothes *Weltweise*, the wise man who knows the world.

7. Gotthold Ephraim Lessing, *Gesammelte Werke* (Aufbau-Verlag Berlin, 1956), VII, 233. Moses Mendelssohn collaborated on the essay, but the editors believe that this section is mainly the work of Lessing (p. 864).

8. W. H. Auden, *The Dyer's Hand and Other Essays* (New York: Vintage, 1968), p. 26.

Pope himself, in the *Design* that precedes the *Essay on Man*, betrays some uneasiness about the union of philosophy and poetry. "I was unable to treat this part of my subject more in detail, without becoming dry and tedious; or more *poetically*, without sacrificing perspicuity to ornament, without wandering from the precision, or breaking the chain of reasoning" (*TE* III–i, 8). But a chain of reasoning was precisely what many intelligent readers found wanting in a poem whose ornaments were its principal recommendation.

> Having exalted himself into the chair of wisdom he tells us much that every man knows, and much that he does not know himself. . . . Surely a man of no very comprehensive search may venture to say that he has heard all this before, but it was never till now recommended by such a blaze of embellishment or such sweetness of melody. The vigorous contraction of some thoughts, the luxuriant amplification of others, the incidental illustrations, and sometimes the dignity, sometimes the softness of the verses, enchain philosophy, suspend criticism, and oppress judgment by overpowering pleasure.[9]

It is perhaps because the *Essay on Man* no longer gives overpowering pleasure that modern scholars have sought to prove its integrity as philosophy.

Why did Pope want to write this ambitious and hazardous poem? Not, surely, in a spirit of abstract system building. Bolingbroke, like Swift, had nothing but contempt for formal metaphysics. "I profess no system of philosophy whatever," he wrote to Pope, "for I know none which has not been pushed beyond [the bounds] of nature and of truth" (*Corr.* II, 220). At the end of the *Essay on Man* Pope praises Bolingbroke's conversational brilliance, which moves easily between moods and topics:

> Come then, my friend, my genius, come along,
> Oh master of the poet, and the song! . . .
> Formed by thy converse, happily to steer
> From grave to gay, from lively to severe;

9. Samuel Johnson, *Life of Pope*, in *Lives of the English Poets*, ed. G. B. Hill (Oxford: Clarendon, 1905), III, 243–44.

> Correct with spirit, eloquent with ease,
> Intent to reason, or polite to please.
> (IV.373–82)

Bolingbroke's own mood at this time, as his letters to Swift show, was very much a willed *contemptus mundi*, trying to put a life of ambition and intrigue behind him.

> What hurt does age do us in subduing what we toil to subdue all our lives? It is now six in the morning. I recall the time, and am glad it is over, when about this hour I used to be going to bed, surfeited with pleasure, or jaded with business, my head often full of schemes, and my heart as often full of anxiety. Is it a misfortune, think you, that I rise at this hour; refreshed, serene, and calm? That the past, and even the present affairs of life stand like objects at a distance from me?
>
> (*Corr.* III, 184)

This pose was deeply attractive to Pope, offering both a Horatian detachment from the world and an Olympian elevation from which to look down upon it. If his poetry in general seeks to make a virtue of limitation, then the *Essay on Man* allows him to do so on the scale of the entire universe. Pope will "vindicate the ways of God to man" (I.16) and show that "whatever is, is RIGHT" (I.294), which as Lessing observes is very different from showing that "Whatever is, is good."[10] It might seem paradoxical that Pope, a mordant satirist, should insist so strenuously that whatever is is right, playing Pangloss to his own Voltaire. Pretty clearly the argument of the *Essay on Man* reflects a deep emotional need, and in any case "philosophical optimism" is not all that optimistic by ordinary standards. As Robert M. Adams defines it, "This is the best of all possible worlds, and everything in it is a necessary evil."[11]

The poem suggests itself as the conceptual center of an

---

10. The Berlin Academy had proposed an essay competition on the theme "*Que tout ce qui est, est bien.*" Lessing points out that the correct translation of *right* is not *gut* but *recht* (*Pope Ein Metaphysiker!*, p. 247).

11. "Putting Pope in His Place," *New York Review of Books*, 13 Mar. 1986, p. 29.

immense "*Opus Magnum*," as Pope liked to call it, into which all of his fragments of wisdom—the *Epistles to Several Persons,* the sketch on education that ended up in *Dunciad* IV, and so on—might be organized into something structured and complete.[12] However much he may have told himself that the *Essay on Man* formed a coherent system, what he was really doing was drawing on all sorts of sources and analogues, in the spirit of eighteenth-century comprehensiveness. "If I could flatter myself that this Essay has any merit," he wrote in *The Design* that introduces it, "it is in steering betwixt the extremes of doctrines seemingly opposite" (*TE* III–i, 7). This is not dialectic but compromise. That "seemingly" is telling: reading the *Essay on Man*, one sometimes wonders if any two ideas, however antithetical, can escape being united in the dance of Pope's harmonious couplets.

> For modes of faith, let graceless zealots fight;
> His can't be wrong whose life is in the right.
>
> (III.305–6)

Dissenters anxiously looked for symptoms of divine grace; Pope sarcastically reduces them to social gracelessness, the opposite of Horatian politeness.

At this point we need to ponder the religious implications of the *Essay on Man*. For Pope and his contemporaries philosophy and religion were inseparable, or were supposed to be, but formal philosophy was relegating religion to a marginal place, and formal theology was giving way to ethical homily. First, however, we need to assess the importance of Pope's Catholicism. He did not belong to an ancient Catholic family; one of his grandfathers was an Anglican priest, and his father was a convert to the Catholic faith.[13] The consequence of conversion was membership in a tiny minority, something like

---

12. Pope's evolving, and finally abandoned, hopes for this project are examined by Miriam Leranbaum, *Alexander Pope's "Opus Magnum," 1729–1744* (Oxford: Clarendon, 1977).

13. See George Sherburn, *The Early Career of Alexander Pope* (Oxford: Clarendon, 1934), pp. 27 ff.

60,000 persons in a nation of 6 million,[14] with very serious financial, legal, and political implications.[15] Edward Blount wrote to Pope, "Ambition is a vice that is timely mortified in us poor Papists" (*Corr.* I, 248). Pope often had to worry about protecting his property and investments from confiscation, and there were graver threats too. In 1723 he edited the works of the late duke of Buckingham and was alarmed to find them seized by the government for possible Jacobite tendencies. Then his close friend Bishop Atterbury was arrested for Jacobite plotting, and Pope was forced to appear as a character witness at the trial; Atterbury was exiled for life and his associate executed.[16]

Beyond these practical anxieties, Catholicism must have entailed more general psychological ones. For if culture, in Edward Said's formulation, is not only "something that one possesses" but also a boundary defining what is excluded,[17] then Pope was constantly reminded of his status as an outsider. It looks as if his allegiance to the Church was a matter of loyalty to an embattled social group, rather than commitment to theological arguments as it had been for Dryden. When Atterbury was urging him to convert to Anglicanism, Pope stressed the pain that this would give his mother, and went on,

> Whether the change would be to my spiritual advantage, God only knows: this I know, that I mean as well in the religion I now profess, as I can possibly ever do in another. Can a man who thinks so, justify a change, even if he thought both equally good? To such an one, the part of *joining* with any one

14. This is the figure given for 1710 by W. A. Speck, *Stability and Strife: England, 1714–1760* (Cambridge, Mass.: Harvard University Press, 1977), p. 102.

15. The fullest survey is that of John M. Aden, *Pope's Once and Future Kings: Satire and Politics in the Early Career* (Knoxville: University of Tennessee Press, 1978).

16. See Maynard Mack's excellent account of the episode, *Alexander Pope: A Life* (New York: Norton, 1985), pp. 392–402.

17. *The World, the Text, and the Critic* (Cambridge, Mass.: Harvard University Press, 1983), p. 9.

> body of Christians might perhaps be easy, but I think it would
> not be so to *renounce* the other.
>
> (*Corr.* I, 453–54)

We have already noted that the civil war left a deep distrust
of "enthusiasm," which Pope locates in tyrannies of every
kind: "Zeal then, not charity, became the guide" (*Essay on
Man* III.261). Charity could be exercised as well in one church
as another, and conversion would be a sign either of improper
zeal or (more likely) of selfish surrender to worldly advantage. Without doubt Pope cares about his religion, but it
seems to operate for him chiefly as a mode of ethical and
social accommodation, and as Thomas Edwards remarks,
"His religious moments usually sound like rhetorical devices."[18] The social aspect is complicated by Pope's simultaneous membership in two groups, the embattled Catholic minority and the group of right-thinking Tory intellectuals that
included Dean Swift, Bishop Atterbury, and the deist Bolingbroke.

Like Swift criticizing "nominal Christianity,"[19] Pope saw
empty forms everywhere among his contemporaries.

> To rest, the cushion and soft dean invite,
> Who never mentions hell to ears polite.
>
> (*To Burlington* 149–50)

But Pope himself, though certainly not soft like the cushion
and the dean, never mentions hell either, and professes a
moderation in which even the favorite apostle of the predes-
tinarian Puritans is made to participate.

> But ask not, to what doctors I apply?
> Sworn to no master, of no sect am I:
> As drives the storm, at any door I knock,
> And house with Montaigne now, or now with Locke. . . .

---

18. "Visible Poetry: Pope and Modern Criticism," in *Twentieth-Century Literature in Retrospect,* ed. Reuben A. Brower (Cambridge, Mass.: Harvard University Press, 1971), p. 320.

19. Jonathan Swift, *An Argument to Prove That the Abolishing of Christianity
in England, May As Things Now Stand, Be Attended with Some Inconveniencies,
and Perhaps Not Produce Those Many Good Effects Proposed Thereby* (1708).

> Sometimes, with Aristippus, or St. Paul,
> Indulge my candor, and grow all to all;
> Back to my native moderation slide,
> And win my way by yielding to the tide.
> (*Epistle* I.i.23–35)

St. Paul wanted to be "all things to all men" (1 Cor. 9:22), but nonetheless this is strange company to find him in. "There is an impropriety and indecorum," Warton objects, "in joining the name of the most profligate parasite in the court of Dionysius with that of an apostle."[20] In fact the passage is closely grounded in Pope's relation to Bolingbroke, whose friends liked to call him Aristippus in allusion to that philosopher's love of pleasure. Bolingbroke thought Locke too gullible in accepting Christian theology and Montaigne too skeptical about natural law.[21] Pope may well have had some disagreements with his friend's judgments, but the list at any rate is Bolingbrokean, a set of opposing "masters" that frees Pope from allegiance to any master at all, not counting Bolingbroke of course.

Why, in any case, is Bolingbroke the sponsor of the *Essay on Man*? Johnson defines *irony* in his dictionary as "a mode of speech in which the meaning is contrary to the words: as, *Bolingbroke was a holy man.*" And a modern summary of the views of Aristippus (a friend of Socrates, none of whose writings survive) is strikingly applicable to Bolingbroke:

> Since all acts were indifferent except in their capacity to provide immediate pleasure, the science of life was displayed in a calculated adaptation of self to circumstances, combined with the ability to use people and situations for self-gratification. The key to this philosophy was the character of Aristippus himself, which superimposed on a Socratic freedom from desires an uninhibited capacity for enjoyment. Anecdotes tell how he could revel in luxury or be content with the simplest needs, choosing each as he saw fit and as the circum-

---

20. *Essay on . . . Pope*, II, 320.
21. See Brean S. Hammond, *Pope and Bolingbroke: A Study of Friendship and Influence* (Columbia: University of Missouri Press, 1984), pp. 121–22.

stances demanded. His successors, however, found it more difficult to reconcile the two main elements in his teaching.[22]

After complaining that Pope links Aristippus with St. Paul, Warton adds, "I know not why he omitted a strong sentiment that follows immediately, *Et mihi res, non me rebus subjungere conor.* Which line Corneille took for his motto."[23] Bolingbroke, like Aristippus, sought to bend the world to himself, but for Pope moderation meant submission to the current, winning his way "by yielding to the tide."

In planning the *Essay on Man,* Bolingbroke and Pope united in the desire to simplify and clarify religious philosophy, leaving revelation intact perhaps on a higher plane—Pope at least believed they were doing that—but enforcing acceptance of things as they are by means of plain arguments and striking illustrations. In a long letter to Swift about the then-unfinished *Essay,* Bolingbroke wrote very interestingly about the folly of traditional theodicy:

> 'Tis a noble subject. He [Pope] pleads the cause of God, I use Seneca's expression, against that famous charge which atheists in all ages have brought, the supposed unequal dispensations of providence, a charge which I cannot heartily forgive you divines for admitting. You admit it indeed for an extreme good purpose, and you build on this admission the necessity of a future state of rewards and punishments. But what if you should find that this future state will not account for God's justice, in the present state, which you give up, in opposition to the atheist? Would it not have been better to defend God's justice in this world against these daring men by irrefragable reasons, and to have rested the proof of the other point on revelation? . . . You will not understand by what I have said that Pope will go so deep into the argument, or carry it so far, as I have hinted.
>
> (*Corr.* III, 214)

Bolingbroke here participates in the widespread eighteenth-century attraction to deism and natural religion, in which

22. I. G. Kidd, "Aristippus of Cyrene," in *The Encyclopedia of Philosophy,* ed. Paul Edwards (New York: Macmillan, 1967), I, 148.

23. *Essay on . . . Pope,* II, 320–21. On Horace, see p. 28 above.

revelation is only called in when philosophy breaks down, and in which philosophy thinks it necessary to deduce religion from the world we see around us. A more traditional believer could well join hands with an extreme skeptic, as Hume makes the pious Demea join with the ironic Philo in *Dialogues concerning Natural Religion*, and declare that life as we know it is profoundly unsatisfactory. Johnson, indeed, believed this recognition to be a strong proof of a future life, since a good God would not have made us suffer so dreadfully without eventual reparation. But of course one could also argue, as Hume's Philo does, that a God who could make a world like ours is not obviously good, or even especially competent.[24]

It was a wise instinct that inhibited Pope from carrying the argument as far as Bolingbroke might have wished. But he certainly agreed with his mentor that the central tenets of Christianity were not directly involved in the *Essay on Man*. As he told Spence years afterward,

> Some wonder why I did not take in the fall of man in my *Essay*, and others how the immortality of the soul came to be omitted. The reason is plain. They both lay out of my subject, which was only to consider man as he is, in his present state, not in his past or future.[25]

This accords exactly with Bolingbroke's views, and so does Pope's further remark about refusing to speculate about what cannot be known:

> The rule laid down in the beginning of the *Essay on Man* of reasoning only from what we know is certainly a right one, and will go a great way toward destroying all the school metaphysics. As the church-writers have introduced so much of those metaphysics into their systems, it will destroy a great deal of what is advanced by them too.[26]

24. David Hume, *Dialogues concerning Natural Religion*, begun ca. 1751–1755, published posthumously 1779. Samuel Johnson, *Adventurer* 120.

25. Joseph Spence, *Observations, Anecdotes, and Characters of Books and Men*, ed. James M. Osborn (Oxford: Clarendon, 1966), I, 136.

26. Ibid., I, 134.

Similarly Christ cannot be mentioned, Pope tells Caryll, "with any congruity to [my] confined and strictly philosophical subject" (*Corr.* III, 390).

What is really involved is a powerful impulse, shared by many in the eighteenth century, to avoid the thorns of theology while continuing to affirm some of the beliefs that theology had evolved to try to make sense of. Locke declares in *The Reasonableness of Christianity,*

> It is enough to justify the fitness of any thing to be done, by resolving it into the "wisdom of God," who has done it; though our short views, and narrow understandings, may utterly incapacitate us to see that wisdom, and to judge rightly of it. . . . And we shall take too much upon us, if we shall call God's wisdom or providence to account, and pertly condemn for needless, all that our weak and perhaps biased understanding cannot account for.[27]

Locke's position led straight to the deism of Toland's *Christianity Not Mysterious* and Tindal's *Christianity As Old As the Creation, or the Gospel a Republication of the Religion of Nature.* But that was a conclusion which many people were not eager to admit. However orthodox Pope's modern interpreters sometimes make him seem, Leslie Stephen, who knew the eighteenth-century controversies intimately, was surely right to say, "The deist whose creed was varnished with Christian phrases was often bitter against the deist who rejected the varnish; and Pope put Toland and Tindal into the *Dunciad* as scandalous assailants of all religion."[28] It would certainly be wrong to say that Pope "was" a deist, if by that one means a person who dismisses revelation and thinks that reason is competent to deduce all religious truth.[29] All the same, Pope chooses to leave revelation out of the *Essay on Man,* and he tends to talk about error rather than sin.

It should be emphasized that more orthodox attitudes

27. John Locke, *The Reasonableness of Christianity,* ed. and abr. I. T. Ramsey (Stanford: Stanford University Press, 1958), p. 56.

28. *Alexander Pope* (New York: Harper, 1902), p. 174.

29. See G. Douglas Atkins, "Pope and Deism: A New Analysis," *Huntington Library Quarterly,* 35 (1972), 257–78.

were not confined to pedants and Puritans. Elijah Fenton, Pope's collaborator on the *Odyssey*, is at once Platonist and Augustinian in lines that Pope would never have written:

> While in the womb we forming lie,
> While yet the lamp of life displays
> A doubtful dawn with feeble rays,
> New issuing from non-entity,
> The shell of flesh pollutes with sin
> Its gem, the soul, just entered in;
> And, by transmitted vice defiled,
> The fiend commences with the child.[30]

Johnson says of this ode, "As the sentiments are pious, they cannot easily be new."[31]

Bolingbroke's God, as he states explicitly in *The Idea of a Patriot King*, governs very much like a king of England, bound by rules that must not be violated. "With reverence be it spoken, God is a monarch, yet not an arbitrary but a limited monarch, limited by the rule which infinite wisdom prescribes to infinite power."[32] So also with Pope, who rebukes mortals for imagining (as the Puritans certainly did) that God is free to alter his own dispensations. A strong king knows how to obey the rules:

> Think we, like some weak prince, th' eternal cause
> Prone for his fav'rites to reverse his laws?
>
> (IV.121–22)

This is a God more of reason rather than of love (though he "loves from whole to parts," IV.361), an unmoved mover who beholds his handiwork from afar:

> Who sees with equal eye, as God of all,
> A hero perish, or a sparrow fall,
> Atoms or systems into ruin hurled,
> And now a bubble burst, and now a world.
>
> (I.87–90)

---

30. *An Ode*, in *Poems on Several Occasions* (1717), p. 31.

31. Samuel Johnson, *Life of Fenton*, *Lives*, II, 263.

32. Henry St. John, Viscount Bolingbroke, *The Idea of a Patriot King*, ed. Sydney W. Jackman (Indianapolis: Bobbs-Merrill, 1965), p. 18.

Divine equanimity looks almost like indifference here, and the fallen sparrow has very different implications here than in the Biblical source:[33]

> Are not two sparrows sold for a farthing? and one of them shall not fall on the ground without your Father. But the very hairs of your head are all numbered. Fear ye not therefore, ye are of more value than many sparrows.
>
> (Matthew 10: 29–31)

Pope's way of vindicating the ways of God to man is to proclaim divine logic. The *Essay on Man* is built upon two axioms: (1) the best possible universe has been formed by divine wisdom; (2) "best" implies an unbroken continuity and hierarchy.

> Of systems possible, if 'tis confest
> That Wisdom infinite must form the best,
> Where all must full or not coherent be,
> And all that rises, rise in due degree.
>
> (I.43–46)

Douglas White comments, "A great deal is 'confest' in these lines."[34] The entire poem, in fact, is a series of deductions from these axioms, whose plausibility is never subjected to scrutiny. Objections soon arose; one critic called the *Essay on Man* "reason rarify'd to smoke."[35]

Pope undoubtedly thought his poem orthodox and was shocked when it was attacked. There is real pathos in his gratitude to Warburton, who wrote in its defense and received Pope's thanks before they had yet met:

> You have made my system as clear as I ought to have done and could not. It is indeed the same system as mine, but illustrated with a ray of your own, as they say our natural body is

33. As A. D. Nuttall has commented: *Pope's "Essay on Man"* (London: Allen & Unwin, 1984), pp. 67–68.

34. *Pope and the Context of Controversy: The Manipulation of Ideas in "An Essay on Man"* (Chicago: University of Chicago Press, 1970), p. 13; and see ch. 2.

35. *Mr. P-PE's Picture in Miniature* (1743), p. 5.

the same still, when it is glorified. I am sure I like it better than
I did before, and so will every man else. I know I meant just
what you explain, but I did not explain my own meaning so
well as you: you understand me as well as I do myself, but
you express me better than I could express myself.

(Corr. IV, 171–72)

The poet who aspired to say "What oft was thought, but ne'er
so well expressed" (*Essay on Criticism,* 298) was reduced
to thanking a clerical controversialist for expressing his
thoughts better than himself. As Johnson dryly puts it,
"Pope, who probably began to doubt the tendency of his own
work, was glad that the positions of which he perceived himself not to know the full meaning could by any mode of
interpretation be made to mean well."[36] Henry Brooke flatteringly gave Pope credit for creating the system which Warburton elucidated, "the Newton of your system, which he
illustrates by sharpening and assisting our sight" (*Corr.* IV,
213). But Johnson, hearing it said that Pope had made Warburton a bishop, replied, "Warburton did more for Pope; he
made him a Christian."[37] And Warton long afterward commented tartly, "Surely the attempt to reconcile the doctrines
of the *Essay on Man* to the doctrines of Revelation, is the rash-
est adventure in which ever critic yet engaged. This is, in
truth, to divine, rather than to explain an author's meaning."[38]

More interesting today, when the extent of Pope's orthodoxy is no longer a pressing concern, is his eagerness to deny
that evil is really evil. In *Common Sense a Common Delusion*
(1751), a writer masquerading as "Almonides a Believing
Heathen" argues that Pope's brand of common sense is contradictory to the best of pagan morality as well as to Christianity. Quoting the lines "Respecting man, whatever wrong
we call, / May, must be right, as relative to all" (*Essay on Man*

36. *Lives,* III, 168.
37. Boswell, *Life of Samuel Johnson,* II, 37n.
38. Joseph Warton's edition of Pope's *Works* (1797), I, 174.

I.51–52), this writer comments, "That is to say, the perfection of the whole creation taken together consists in a due mixture of good and evil. . . . From whence it plainly follows, that if all men were virtuous, or only less vicious than they are, this world of ours at least, would go to ruin."[39] The mistake lies in confusing moral with natural order, and in taking too literally the metaphor of the universe as a smoothly running machine:

> It is this absurd notion then of the Creation's being a machine, and the confounding of moral with natural order, which makes men of *common sense* fancy, that whatever is must be right; and indeed granting them these premises . . . every thing in the Creation would have its own proper place and use, and the most notorious villains, such as parricides and traitors to their king and their country, perfidious and perjured wretches, and such as trample upon all laws, and blaspheme every thing that is sacred, and deny the being of the gods, which naturally subverts all truth and virtue, would be eternally as necessary parts of this imaginary machine, as men of the greatest talents, virtue, and probity could possibly be: and the destruction of these destroyers of the world would be the destruction of the universe.
>
> (pp. 33–34)

Obviously Pope did not exactly intend these implications, but he found them pressing in upon him.

> If plagues or earthquakes break not Heav'n's design,
> Why then a Borgia, or a Catiline?
> Who knows but he, whose hand the light'ning forms,
> Who heaves old ocean, and who wings the storms,
> Pours fierce ambition in a Caesar's mind,
> Or turns young Ammon loose to scourge mankind?
> (I.155–60)

Pope knows that he has no explanation, and claims that he is content not to have one: "To reason right is to submit" (164).

---

39. *Common Sense a Common Delusion: Or, The Generally-Received Notions of Natural Causes, Deity, Religion, Virtue, &c. As exhibited in Mr. Pope's Essay on Man, Proved Ridiculous, Impious, and the Effect of Infatuation . . . By Almonides a Believing Heathen* (1751), p. 9.

Johnson, trampling an imitator of Pope's system, trenchantly satirized the consolations proposed by the poem and indicated that it ratifies the social order in which Pope occupied so comfortable a place.

> Life must be seen before it can be known. This author and Pope, perhaps, never saw the miseries which they imagine thus easy to be borne. The poor, indeed, are insensible of many little vexations, which sometimes imbitter the possessions and pollute the enjoyments of the rich. They are not pained by casual incivility, or mortified by the mutilation of a compliment; but this happiness is like that of a malefactor, who ceases to feel the cords that bind him, when the pincers are tearing his flesh.[40]

One might add that cosmologies tend to reflect the societies that project them, and that Pope's imaginative universe is one in which both his physical handicaps and his material and social advantages are justified and explained. Suffering must be borne because in the last analysis it is not suffering at all, while good things can be freely accepted since they come to each of us in the immense context of the chain of being. Barbara Lewalski observes that reason in Milton implies choice, in Pope submission, and that hierarchy in *Paradise Lost* is involved in dynamic change while in Pope it is "absolute, fixed, static, immutable."[41] *Paradise Lost* is a mighty narrative that offers a temporal account of the ruinous human condition. In *An Essay on Man* things are as they must be, and are going to stay like that. Pope inhabits a profoundly non-narrative universe.

Contrasting the two works, Leslie Stephen comments, "For a revelation was substituted a demonstration."[42] An instance of the demonstration comes at the end of Epistle I, shortly before "Whatever is, is RIGHT":

---

40. Review in *The Literary Magazine* (1757) of Soame Jenyns's *A Free Inquiry into the Nature and Origin of Evil;* in *The Works of Samuel Johnson* (Oxford, 1825), VI, 54–55.

41. "On Looking into Pope's Milton," *Études Anglaises,* 27 (1974), 491. The whole of this essay is of great interest in pondering the differences between Milton's theodicy and Pope's.

42. *Alexander Pope,* p. 161.

> Cease then, nor ORDER imperfection name:
> Our proper bliss depends on what we blame.
> Know thy own point: this kind, this due degree
> Of blindness, weakness, heav'n bestows on thee.
>
> (281–84)

Maynard Mack comments in a footnote, "*Paradise Lost*, VIII 167–84, is the best commentary on this passage, and comes close to summarizing the argument of this Epistle" (*TE* III–i, 49n). But the passage in Milton has very different connotations:

> Solicit not thy thoughts with matters hid. . . .
> Wherever placed, let him dispose; joy thou
> In what he gives to thee, this Paradise
> And thy fair Eve: heav'n is for thee too high
> To know what passes there; be lowly wise.

Adam, before the Fall, is instructed by an angel not to seek hidden knowledge that angels possess. Milton, though a (fallen) man, can put angelic words into an angel's mouth. Pope, a man like Milton, is less convincing when he commands the reader in his own person not to seek forbidden knowledge. Moreover, Raphael urges Adam to accept a position that is filled with joy, and will remain so unless he himself should ruin it. Pope's reader is urged simply to believe that "blindness" and "weakness" are corollaries of universal "ORDER." Seventeenth-century religious poetry could still engage mystery, because mystery was not felt to threaten belief; indeed, it formed an essential part of it. By the eighteenth century, every form of ambiguity, from "false wit" in poetry to paradox in theology, is felt to be dangerous. Pope's God, unlike Milton's, does not send messengers to man. He just *is*, and man's responsibility is to accept that fact and to get on with life accordingly.

Pretty clearly the Fall is omitted from the *Essay on Man* not only because it is too doctrinal for the poem, but also because Pope finds it deeply unattractive. It survives as a metaphor for man's perennial failures, rather than as a theological account of how the world went wrong.

> The gen'ral ORDER, since the whole began,
> Is kept in nature, and is kept in man.
>
> (I.171–72)

As Warton says, "How this opinion is any way reconcileable with the orthodox doctrine of the lapsed condition of man, the chief foundation of the Christian revelation, it is difficult to say."[43] It has been suggested that Pope's metaphorizing of the Fall implies a further leap of faith, beyond the limits of metaphor, that brings him back round to Pascal.[44] The leap is highly inexplicit, and at best is an implication or consequence of the *Essay on Man*, not its deliberate message. One might rather say that Pope participates in the widespread eighteenth-century movement away from doctrine, even while he wants to believe that his poem remains consistent with doctrine. "To speak of secularization," Peter Gay says, "is to speak of a subtle shift of attention: religious institutions and religious explanations of events were slowly being displaced from the center of life to its periphery."[45]

For some eighteenth-century people, God remained a presence in emotional experience. For others, God was mainly a necessary hypothesis to restrain individualism from its logical conclusion. As Locke expressed it,

> A dependent intelligent being is under the power and direc-
> tion of him on whom he depends and must be for the ends
> appointed him by that superior being. If man were indepen-
> dent he could have no law but his own will, no end but him-
> self. He would be a god to himself and the satisfaction of his
> own will the sole measure and end of all his actions.[46]

In cultural hindsight, one can say that a great deal is being held at bay here. John Dunn comments, "What gave Locke the nerve to be a reductive egoistic liberal . . . was a some-

43. *Essay on . . . Pope*, II, 70.
44. See Douglas Canfield, "The Fate of the Fall in Pope's *Essay on Man*," *The Eighteenth Century*, 23 (1982), 134–50.
45. *The Enlightenment: An Interpretation*, I, *The Rise of Modern Paganism* (New York: Knopf, 1966), p. 338.
46. John Locke, Manuscript *Ethica B*, in John Dunn, *The Political Thought of Locke* (Cambridge: Cambridge University Press, 1969), p. 40.

what supine religious conviction, which if it had been effectively threatened would have left him not a solid spokesman of bourgeois capitalist social achievements but a morally anarchic exponent of individual self-creation, a somewhat doleful Nietzschean, way before his time."[47]

Pascal too was haunted by the disenchanted universe, as Goldmann eloquently shows in his study of the tragic vision of Pascal and Racine.[48] But the Jansenist Pascal imagines a very different universe from that of the English latitudinarian Papist. Pope's is invoked in highly structured couplets, in which ignorance is pacified with rhetorical control:

> Placed on this isthmus of a middle state,
> A being darkly wise, and rudely great. . . .
> Chaos of thought and passion, all confused;
> Still by himself abused, or disabused;
> Created half to rise, and half to fall,
> Great lord of all things, yet a prey to all. . . .
> Sole judge of truth, in endless error hurled,
> The glory, jest, and riddle of the world!
>
> (II.3–18)

Pope's source in Pascal is drastically different in tone, jolting from contradiction to contradiction rather than displaying alternatives in patterned pairs:[49]

What a chimera then is man! What a novelty! What a monster, what a chaos, what a contradiction, what a prodigy! Judge of all things, imbecile worm of the earth; depositary of truth, a sink of uncertainty and error; the pride and refuse of the universe![50]

Pope and Pascal both assert human ignorance, but Pascal's assertion is far bleaker:

47. *Western Political Theory in the Face of the Future* (Cambridge: Cambridge University Press, 1979), p. 40.

48. Lucien Goldmann, *Le Dieu Caché: Étude sur la Vision Tragique dans les Pensées de Pascal et dans le Théâtre de Racine* (Paris: Gallimard, 1959).

49. See Nuttall on the "note of deliberate levity" in Pope's introduction of the word *jest*, possibly owing to a misreading of Pascal's *rebut* ("trash") as *butt* (Pope's *"Essay on Man,"* p. 82).

50. Blaise Pascal, *Pensées*, tr. W. F. Trotter (New York: Modern Library, 1941), no. 434, p. 143.

> When I see the blindness and the wretchedness of man, when
> I regard the whole silent universe, and man without light, left
> to himself, and, as it were, lost in this corner of the universe,
> without knowing who has put him there, what he has come
> to do, what will become of him at death, and incapable of all
> knowledge, I become terrified, like a man who should be car-
> ried in his sleep to a dreadful desert island, and should awake
> without knowing where he is, and without means of escape.[51]

Pope characteristically adapts his sources to imply a
greater confidence and security; Nuttall contrasts his "isthmus of a middle state" with Cowley's more disturbing "Vain
weak-built isthmus, which does proudly rise / Up betwixt two
eternities."[52] One might imagine that this is simply a contrast
between the seventeenth century and the eighteenth, but
really it is a question of temperament as much as of historical
position. And it needs to be added that Pope himself, when
pondering human behavior instead of the rightness of the
universe, expresses paradoxes that are far more turbulent
and unresolvable:

> Wise wretch! with pleasures too refined to please,
> With too much spirit to be e'er at ease,
> With too much quickness ever to be taught,
> With too much thinking to have common thought:
> Who purchase pain with all that joy can give,
> And die of nothing but a rage to live.
> (*To a Lady,* 95–100)

The tone of the *Essay on Man*, as both admirers and de-
tractors agree, is confident and even hectoring, in the style
that Dryden developed for ethical controversy:

> Vain, wretched creature, how art thou misled
> To think thy wit these god-like notions bred!
>
> Dar'st thou, poor worm, offend Infinity?
> And must the terms of peace be given by thee?[53]

51. Ibid., no. 692, p. 234.
52. Abraham Cowley, *Life and Fame*; Nuttall, *Pope's "Essay on Man,"* p. 81.
53. John Dryden, *Religio Laici*, 64–65, 93–94.

Dryden's *Religio Laici* is squarely based on revealed religion, while Pope, with his uneasy relation to doctrine, seeks to persuade with an exclamatory tone. Martin Price sums up the result well: "The aesthetic vision is essentially a comic pattern in which man stumbles into a greater success than he can plan; the moral vision is largely a satiric pattern in which the failure of man is shown to be contemptibly foolish."[54] One might say that for Pascal the aesthetic and moral visions are both tragic; Christianity may ultimately embody a divine comedy, but there is nothing comic about the origin and continuance of suffering and evil. "I now must change / These notes to tragic," Milton says in introducing the narrative of the Fall.[55] Very differently, Pope is committed, like the eighteenth century generally, to avoiding or neutralizing tragedy. Certainly his view of sin is that of a satirist, in the spirit of a writer like G. K. Chesterton (himself a Catholic):

> As for sin, let us call it folly and have done with it. . . . The conception of sin flatters us grossly. There is something grandiose in it that cannot but appeal to the child in every man. That we infinitesimal creatures, scrambling like ants over the face of this minor planet in pursuit of our personal aims—that we have it in our power to affront the majesty of the universe is a most preposterous, delightful fancy.[56]

Sociologists distinguish between knowledge and ideas—between what people "know" in their everyday experience, and the "ideas" with which they reflect on their experience and try to explain it.[57] Literary scholars tend to treat *An Essay on Man* as an exercise in the history of ideas, when in fact it works the other way round: the poem attempts to show that the received knowledge of Pope's culture can be defended

54. *To the Palace of Wisdom: Studies in Order and Energy from Dryden to Blake* (New York: Doubleday, Anchor, 1965), p. 143.

55. John Milton, *Paradise Lost* IX.5–6.

56. Quoted by Owen Barfield, *History in English Words* (London: Faber & Faber, 1954), p. 158.

57. See, e.g., Peter L. Berger and Thomas Luckmann, *The Social Construction of Reality* (New York: Doubleday, Anchor, 1967), p. 15.

against various modernist threats by recourse to ideas that are supposed to underlie it. Johnson says sarcastically,

> He tells us much that every man knows, and much that he does not know himself. . . . The reader feels his mind full, though he learns nothing; and when he meets it in its new array no longer knows the talk of his mother and his nurse. . . . Surely a man of no very comprehensive search may venture to say that he has heard all this before.[58]

Pope may indeed have fancied himself a philosopher, but the force of the *Essay on Man* depends upon a retailing of commonplaces, with the constant suggestion, justified or not, that they are somehow "philosophical." And the commonplaces, in turn, are desired so strongly because they stave off fears of a hostile or meaningless universe. It is precisely because God is felt to be fading that Pope's generation keeps defending him with such vehement (if abstract) language. By placing the emphasis differently, one might say that Milton undertakes to "justify the *ways* of God to men," and Pope to "vindicate the ways of *God* to man."[59] The generalization from "men" to "man" is also deeply revealing.

An important goal of the *Essay on Man* is to show that a living spirit energizes the world.

> All are but parts of one stupendous whole,
> Whose body nature is, and God the soul;
> That, changed through all, and yet in all the same,
> Great in the earth, as in th' etherial frame,
> Warms in the sun, refreshes in the breeze,
> Glows in the stars, and blossoms in the trees,
> Lives through all life, extends through all extent,
> Spreads undivided, operates unspent. . . .
>
> (I.267–74)

This passage is filled with analogies whose relations are passionately desired: the distant sun and the nearby breeze both give physical pleasure; as stars are to the firmament, so blos-

58. *Lives*, III, 243–44.
59. *Paradise Lost* I.26; *Essay on Man* I.16.

soms are to trees. Warburton wrote a long indignant footnote
defending Pope here from the charge of Spinozan pantheism.[60] The reason Pope flirted with something like it was that
he badly wanted God's goodness to pervade existence, for if
God were only a remote artificer, one could argue as skeptics
did that the machine had begun to malfunction in his absence.[61] Spinozan or Newtonian, this imaginative pantheism
is very different from orthodox apologetics. Traditional theodicy did indeed leap from man's helplessness to God's
power, urging the Christian solution because one came to see
that it was true. Pope urges it because we *cannot* see, or at
least "'tis but a part we see, and not a whole" (I.60). Mack
cites I Cor. 13:12, "For now we see through a glass, darkly,
but then face to face; now I know in part, but then shall I
know even as also I am known" (*TE* III–i, 20n). But Pope does
not say that we will someday see face to face, and he certainly
does not say that we will know even as we are known.

Pope's God orders our existence as "first almighty cause"
(I.145), "wisdom infinite" (I.44), and "directing mind of all"
(I.266). But this is not a God whom one can love, and man
must get on as best he can in the disenchanted world.

> The soul, uneasy and confined at home,
> Rests and expatiates in a life to come.
> (I.97–98)

As Mack comments (*TE* III–i, p. 27n), "at home" might seem
to imply a disbelief in immortality, and Pope revised the line
in 1743 (at Warburton's prompting) to read "confined *from*
home." But the original version is probably closer to existence
as he actually perceived it, however piously he sometimes
talked in his letters. As with so much eighteenth-century literature, the *Essay on Man* teeters on the very brink of unbelief:
not the atheism that fears and rejects a potent God, but the
unbelief that has no real place for God anymore, even if his

---

60. Warburton's edition of Pope's *Works* (1751), III, 31–33. Lessing points
out that Spinoza would never distinguish as Pope does between nature as
body and God as soul (*Pope Ein Metaphysiker!*, p. 261).
61. See White, *Pope and the Context of Controversy*, ch. 3.

existence is still asserted. The Christian narrative of the Fall has given way to a rueful acceptance of civilization and its discontents; "wit oblique" shatters the clear vision in which God was distinct from his works and was still a loving father:

> The worker from the work distinct was known,
> And simple reason never sought but one:
> Ere wit oblique had broke that steady light,
> Man, like his Maker, saw that all was right,
> To virtue, in the paths of pleasure, trod,
> And owned a father when he owned a God.
>   (*Essay on Man* III.229–34)

Behind all of the philosophizing of the *Essay on Man* is a longing to rise above the poignancy of individual experience, with its continual disappointments, by recognizing the endless mutability in which individuals are immersed.

> See dying vegetables life sustain,
> See life dissolving vegetate again:
> All forms that perish other forms supply,
> (By turns we catch the vital breath, and die)
> Like bubbles on the sea of matter born,
> They rise, they break, and to that sea return.
>   (III.15–20)

Here as everywhere Pope struggles with the burden of self-hood. He wants the integrity and nobility of a separate and private existence, but he also wants to merge himself in "nature" and to avoid the suspicion that his experience is merely psychologically conditioned.

But what if nature should turn out to be as incomprehensible as nature's God?

> Know, God and nature only are the same:
> In man, the judgment shoots at flying game,
> A bird of passage! gone as soon as found,
> Now in the moon perhaps, now under ground.
>   (154–57)

Warton comments on the first of these lines, "It is not very clear what is precisely meant by Nature in this passage."[62]

62. Warton's edition of Pope's *Works* (1797), III, 190.

Part of Pope's meaning is surely that human imaginations transform the nature that they perceive. For Blake or Wordsworth this would be a happy truism; for Pope it is a symptom of disturbed fantasy and error, as with Eloisa, who projects her feelings upon

> the dying gales that pant upon the trees,
> The lakes that quiver to the curling breeze.
> (*Eloisa to Abelard*, 159–60)

It is interesting, incidentally, to reflect on the difference between Eloisa's desperate yearnings and the conventional order that Pope tries to impose on his own conception—"the struggles of grace and nature, virtue and passion."[63]

Despite the charm of Pope's pantheistic flights, he wants nature to be a stable structure in which man takes his assigned place, not a stream of experience that carries the individual along. Wordsworth's "I wandered lonely as a cloud" is an inconceivable sentiment for an Augustan poet, who is likely to see the movement of clouds as analogous to the instability of the political mob. Thus Dryden (with internal rhyme for emphasis):

> The crowd, to restless motion still enclined,
> Are clouds, that rack according to the wind.[64]

Concordia discors, of course, is the approved means of defining stability, in nature as in the state. Denham's *Cooper's Hill*, an extended analogy between the two, seems to have originated the cloud-crowd analogy with its vision of the far-off city

> whose state and wealth, the business and the crowd,
> Seems at this distance but a darker cloud.
> (27–28)

And Pope gladly takes up the notion that natural and political order emerges from disorder:

63. "The Argument" preceding *Eloisa to Abelard*, TE II, 318.
64. John Dryden, *Prologue to His Royal Highness upon His First Appearance at the Duke's Theatre since His Return from Scotland*, 32–33.

> Till jarring int'rests of themselves create
> Th' according music of a well-mixed state.
> Such is the world's great harmony, that springs
> From order, union, full consent of things!
> > (*Essay on Man* III, 293–96)

The term *concordia discors* comes from Horace,[65] and unlike the Romantic dialectic of contraries, it begins rather than ends with the reconciled "mean." The aphorism "All discord, harmony, not understood" (I.291) is notoriously unclear. David Morris shows that it might mean any of the following: (1) There isn't really any discord at all, only harmony. (2) Discord does exist, but as a necessary element in a larger harmony. (3) Discord *is* harmony, on the analogy of musical notes that combine to make a single harmonious sound. Pope thus moves from saying "Black is white" to the equally mysterious, if less openly illogical, "Black is an unknown shade of white."[66] In the third of these instances, it is hard to see that the concept of "discord" retains much meaning, and in all of them Pope fails to distinguish between elements that are genuinely opposed to each other and those that are merely different.[67] One might say that his metaphors, many of which are highly seductive, tend to illustrate difference while claiming to prove connection.

Like any passionately held ideal of order, Pope's reflects a deep anxiety about disorder, and at many points his art confesses the precariousness of the ideal. Consider the famous lines in *Windsor-Forest* describing the emblematic rural scene:

> Not chaos-like together crushed and bruised,
> But as the world, harmoniously confused.
> > (13–14)

Though the first line begins with *not*, negating what follows, its effect is still to emphasize the pain of chaos: the jarring

65. *Epistle* I.xii.19.
66. *Alexander Pope: The Genius of Sense* (Cambridge, Mass.: Harvard University Press, 1984), p. 171.
67. As Frederick M. Keener comments in *An Essay on Pope* (New York: Columbia University Press, 1974), p. 30n.

atoms of Lucretius that Dryden often invoked, and the physical anguish of crushing and bruising. In the second line, "the world," image of completed order, is contrasted with chaos. Next comes "harmoniously"; all is fine so far. But the line ends with "confused." (Johnson's *Dictionary* definitions for *confuse* are "1. To disorder; to disperse irregularly; 2. To mix, not separate; 3. To perplex, not distinguish; to obscure.") To call this an oxymoron is only to name it rhetorically, just as to invoke *concordia discors* is to invoke an oxymoronic formula. Pope gives eloquent expression to the discords as much as the concord, even while asserting that they are fully harmonized. His source in Waller, incidentally, lacks the crucial emphasis on harmony:

> As in old chaos heaven with earth confused,
> And stars with rocks, together crushed and bruised.[68]

George Eliot complained that Young's *Night Thoughts* promoted a religion of "the remote, the vague, and the unknown"—"You see at what a telescopic distance he stands from mother earth and simple human joys."[69] Pope, very differently, fills his poems with unforgettable images deployed by unforgettable rhetoric, and he longs very deeply for "the soul's calm sun-shine, and the heart-felt joy" (*Essay on Man* IV.168), a release from the blustery "April weather in the mind" (*Corr.* I, 185) of which he often complained. Happiness is the goal of Pope's carefully crafted life, but it is a goal that can only be achieved in the face of pain:

> Oh happiness! our being's end and aim!
> Good, pleasure, ease, content! whate'er thy name:
> That something still which prompts th' eternal sigh,
> For which we bear to live, or dare to die.
>
> (IV.1–4)

Critics often quote the apparently complacent lines

68. Edmund Waller, *Of Her Passing through a Crowd of People*, cited in *TE* I, 149n.
69. "Worldliness and Other-Worldliness: The Poet Young," in *The Writings of George Eliot* (Boston, 1908, rept. New York: AMS, 1970), XXI, 67, 49.

> Why has not man a microscopic eye?
> For this plain reason, man is not a fly.
> Say what the use, were finer optics giv'n,
> T' inspect a mite, not comprehend the heav'n?
>
> (I.193–96)

The comparisons are filled with rhetorical scorn for those who would deny the human condition, and the scorn is supported by syllogistic logic in the Aristotelian figure that a seventeenth-century logician defines:

> In a demonstration that showeth what a thing is, sometimes also the medium is placed without the extremes, as when we say, why doth not the wall breathe? We answer, because it is not a living creature; and these syllogisms are always made in the second figure, after this sort: Whatsoever doth breathe, is a living creature: But the wall is not a living creature. Therefore a wall doth not breathe.[70]

But the definition serves to remind us why empiricism fought so strenuously against syllogistic reasoning, which works by internal logic rather than responding to the complexities of experience. Pope's couplet conceals an ambiguity in the word *why*, making logic do the work of metaphysics. In the syllogism, *why* simply answers the question "How do we distinguish men from flies?" But Pope implies that it can also answer the question "For what reason has God withheld certain advantages from human beings?"

At its best, however, the *Essay on Man* is not an exercise in syllogism, notwithstanding Pope's fondness for "the pleasures of the conclusive and the ship-shape."[71] Pope no doubt regards it as a series of arguments which are supported by illustrations, but in fact the illustrations *are* the argument. As is evident from the criticisms of Warton, Johnson, and others—not to mention Crousaz, the Swiss antagonist against

---

70. Thomas Spencer, *The Art of Logick* (1628), p. 287, quoted in connection with the Pope couplet by Douglas Lane Patey, *Probability and Literary Form: Philosophic Theory and Literary Practice in the Augustan Age* (Cambridge: Cambridge University Press, 1984), p. 12.

71. Claude Rawson, *Order from Confusion Sprung: Studies in Eighteenth-Century Literature from Swift to Cowper* (London: Allen & Unwin, 1985), p. 224.

whom Warburton defended Pope—a strong intelligence can easily take the poem apart, and no amount of Renaissance parallels can conceal the dissonance between rhetorical procedure and metaphysical claims. Wakefield points out that the "microscopic eye" analogy is taken from Locke, and Locke's Victorian idealist editor comments gravely on that passage, "Why an organism and organs are the established conditions of perception in man is really the mystery."[72] It is either a mystery or too obvious to deserve discussion, as Johnson might have said when he kicked the stone.

Whatever Pope may argue when he reasons about life, he *feels* it so keenly that the thought of a still keener life can excite a kind of horror in him. The famous lines that follow the "microscopic eye," on the implications of heightened senses, express this acuity of sensation unforgettably:

> Or touch, if tremblingly alive all o'er,
> To smart and agonize at ev'ry pore?
> Or quick effluvia darting through the brain,
> Die of a rose in aromatic pain?
> If nature thundered in his op'ning ears,
> And stunned him with the music of the spheres,
> How would he wish that heav'n had left him still
> The whisp'ring zephyr, and the purling rill?
> (197–204)

It is after all as a poet that Pope is great. Lessing is right: a philosophic poet is still not a philosopher, and his strength lies in those very ambiguities that a philosopher seeks to dispel. Pope's vision of hierarchy, similarly (though this may seem a retrograde New Critical response), is most powerful when it is imaginatively felt rather than argued:

> Far as creation's ample range extends,
> The scale of sensual, mental pow'rs ascends:
> Mark how it mounts, to man's imperial race,
> From the green myriads in the peopled grass;

---

72. John Locke, *An Essay concerning Human Understanding*, ed. Alexander Fraser (New York: Dover, 1959), I, 191 (the passage in question is *Essay* II.ix.10–15).

> What modes of sight betwixt each wide extreme,
> The mole's dim curtain, and the lynx's beam;
> Of smell, the headlong lioness between,
> And hound sagacious on the tainted green;
> Of hearing, from the life that fills the flood,
> To that which warbles through the vernal wood;
> The spider's touch, how exquisitely fine!
> Feels at each thread, and lives along the line.
>   (I.207–18)

The *Essay on Man* is a tremendous attempt to believe in harmony, in the face of those human failings which Pope acknowledges—in very Johnsonian terms—at moments when he descends from the pulpit of omniscience:

> Each want of happiness by hope supplied,
> And each vacuity of sense by pride:
> These build as fast as knowledge can destroy;
> In folly's cup still laughs the bubble, joy.
>   (II.285–88)

The labor of binding metaphor down to "truth" left Pope weary and disillusioned. He wrote movingly to Swift at the end of 1734, the year in which he published *To Cobham* and the fourth Epistle of the *Essay on Man*,

> I am almost at the end of my morals, as I've been, long ago, of my wit; my system is a short one, and my circle narrow. Imagination has no limits, and that is a sphere in which you may move on to eternity; but where one is confined to truth (or to speak more like a human creature, to the appearances of truth) we soon find the shortness of our tether. Indeed by the help of a metaphysical chain of ideas, one may extend the circulation, go round and round for ever, without making any progress beyond the point to which providence has pinned us.
>
> *(Corr.* IV, 445)

The *Essay on Man* is full of great poetry but never quite becomes a great poem. The *Opus Magnum* was never completed. Pope's achievement rests finally on the local brilliance and depth of his verse, and the concluding section of this book will consider the ways in which that verse gives life as well as formal shape to his lifelong preoccupations.

PART THREE

ART

7

The Descent to Truth

Pope's short preface to his 1717 *Works* is full of gracefully deprecated anxieties, beginning by regretting that readers expect a writer to sacrifice his whole life to their entertainment, and ending by confessing that this early bid for completeness (he was not yet thirty) might turn out to be an elegy rather than a manifesto. "In this office of collecting my pieces, I am altogether uncertain whether to look upon myself as a man building a monument, or burying the dead" (*TE* I, 9). Throughout the preface Pope agonizes over the intimate affinities between great writers and dreadful ones. Readers ought to pardon bad writers who don't realize that they are bad, for how can one find out except by risking publication? Even the good writer begins to publish without being sure he is good, "all the while trembling with the fear of being ridiculous," and if he meets with success he is then condemned to endless flattery, and "must expect to hear no more truth than if he were a prince, or a beauty" (p. 5). And of course to be interested in reputation is to commit oneself to a ceaseless and potentially degrading struggle. "The life of a wit is a warfare upon earth" (p. 6).

Most interesting of all is Pope's frank assessment of his own gifts. "One may be ashamed," he says with a humility that is not entirely feigned, "to consume half one's days in bringing sense and rhyme together" (p. 8). *Consume* is a strong verb, suggesting an obsession that usurps other pleasures and interests, and there is a sense of exhausting labor in endlessly uniting two elements (sense and rhyme) that always tend to separate. But it is not enough just to bring them together, for as Johnson was to declare in his account of metaphysical wit, many things can be yoked together that ought not to be. Pope's famous desire for "correctness"[1] certainly reflects a deep need to control—if not at times to repress—his own imaginative energies. Just as guilt internalizes the censorship of a moral value system, so Pope's "judgment" is forever on guard to rebuke the anarchic pleasures of "wit," to which it is ambiguously joined in an ironic spousal metaphor:

> For wit and judgment often are at strife,
> Though meant each other's aid, like man and wife.
>
> (*Essay on Criticism* 82–83)

Most important of all, Pope's achievements are measured against an ideal which they cannot possibly satisfy, since it is the ideal of perfection. "They have always fallen short not only of what I read of others, but even of my own ideas of poetry" (*Preface*, p. 6). This is the Pope whom Johnson admires:

> Of his intellectual character the constituent and fundamental principle was good sense, a prompt and intuitive perception of consonance and propriety. He saw immediately, of his own conceptions, what was to be chosen, and what to be rejected; and in the works of others, what was to be shunned, and what was to be copied.
>
> But good sense alone is a sedate and quiescent quality, which manages its possessions well, but does not increase them; it collects few materials for its own operations, and preserves safety, but never gains supremacy. Pope had likewise genius; a mind active, ambitious, and adventurous, always investigating, always aspiring; in its widest searches still longing to go forward, in its highest flights still wishing to be higher; always imagining something greater than it knows, always endeavouring more than it can do.[2]

1. "About fifteen, I got acquainted with Mr. Walsh. He encouraged me much, and used to tell me that there was one way left of excelling, for though we had had several great poets, we never had any one great poet that was correct—and he desired me to make that my study and aim." Joseph Spence, *Observations, Anecdotes, and Characters of Books and Men*, ed. James M. Osborn (Oxford: Clarendon, 1966), I, 32.

2. Samuel Johnson, *Life of Pope*, in *Lives of the English Poets*, ed. G. B. Hill (Oxford: Clarendon, 1905), III, 216–17.

This account seems both accurate and paradoxical. For here is a writer who aspires immensely—Johnson makes him sound almost like Milton—and yet whose fundamental character is a sense of propriety and an ability to choose, reject, and copy judiciously. Pope himself certainly hoped to effect this difficult union of sense and genius.[3] But by his own confession, "I believe no one qualification is so likely to make a good writer, as the power of rejecting his own thoughts; and it must be this (if any thing) that can give me a chance to be one" (*Preface*, p. 8).

Our theme in the final section of this book will be the scope and implications of Pope's art. His mastery of certain kinds of technique has long been praised and analyzed, and need not be reviewed here. What will concern us rather are the motives and implications that lie behind technique, and the significance of the rejection of all forms of untruth, whether political or aesthetic:

> Not proud, nor servile, be one poet's praise
> That, if he pleased, he pleased by manly ways;
> That flatt'ry, ev'n to kings, he held a shame,
> And thought a lie in verse or prose the same:
> That not in fancy's maze he wandered long,
> But stooped to truth, and moralized his song.
> (*To Arbuthnot* 336–41)

In a real sense, the 1717 *Works* are a monument, bidding farewell to older modes of writing. Before the edition came out Pope wrote Parnell that it would contain "all I ever intend to give" (*Corr.* I, 396), and it is indeed a kind of ending.

The term *wit* was notoriously polysemantic in Pope's time, and he rings the changes on it throughout the *Essay on Criticism*.[4] Ideally it ought to cooperate with the "good sense" Johnson speaks of, or even merge in it. As Leslie Stephen

3. See David B. Morris's "Conclusion: The Poet as Man of Sense," in *Alexander Pope: The Genius of Sense* (Cambridge, Mass.: Harvard University Press, 1984), pp. 296–321.

4. See William Empson's classic essay "Wit in the Essay on Criticism," ch. 3 in *The Structure of Complex Words* (New York: New Directions, 1951).

says, "Wit and sense are but different avatars of the same spirit; wit was the form in which it showed itself in coffee-houses, and sense that in which it appeared in the pulpit or parliament."[5] But there were also temptations in wit that a witty man like Pope had to fear, especially since its Restoration prestige was rapidly dwindling. Wycherley, a veteran wit of the former period, wrote in a volume which Pope revised and edited for him,

> The jovial or conversable man thinks much prating, noise and laughter to be wit; the confident, open courtier thinks lying invention, and much babbling, much wit. . . . Wit in the city is craft, where they call cozening, cheating, or betraying a man, outwitting him; amongst lawyers, wit is having the last word in any dispute, right or wrong; so with them, 'tis impudence and lying, which are the supports of their reputation; amongst little courtiers, 'tis called address, which is fraud and flattery; amongst men of honour and the great, 'tis policy, which is treachery and villainy amongst the poor, and little men.[6]

Wit is not just an accomplishment or sign of inner quickness, but a weapon used (or misused) in an endless range of social contexts, all too often synonymous with lying. As the years went by, Pope continued to deploy the weapon when appropriate, but he renounced wit as a way of life. Rereading his early letters at about the time of the first *Dunciad*, he wrote to Swift, "It was not unentertaining to my self to observe, how and by what degrees I ceased to be a witty writer; as either my experience grew on the one hand, or my affection to my correspondents on the other" (*Corr.* III, 79).

Sense became wit's proper successor. Pope had written in the *Essay on Criticism*, "Fools admire, but men of sense approve" (391), borrowing the thought and the words from La Bruyère (*TE* I, 284n). The ultimate source was Horace's famous *nil admirari*, which Pope later imitated with a wry parenthesis:

5. *Alexander Pope* (New York: Harper, 1902), p. 29.
6. William Wycherley, *Miscellany Poems* (1704), Preface, pp. xv–xvi.

> "Not to admire, is all the art I know,
> To make men happy, and to keep them so."
> (Plain truth, dear Murray, needs no flow'rs of speech,
> So take it in the very words of Creech.)
>
> *(Epistle* I.vi.1–4)

The superbly uncharming rhyme on "Creech" confirms the willed prosiness of the new poetry of sense. Horace speaks of his prosaic muse, *musa pedestri,* and Pope (contributing to a version by Swift) asks for the ability to "compose / Something in verse as true as prose."[7] In another Horatian imitation he speaks of

> my head and heart thus flowing through my quill,
> Verse-man or prose-man, term me which you will.
> *(Satire* II.i.63–64)

The same idea had occurred to Fenton many years before Pope turned Horatian:

> So dull to Horace did the moments glide,
> Till his free muse her sprightly force employed
> To combat vice, and follies to expose,
> In easy numbers near allied to prose. . . .
> Suffice it me, that (having spent my prime
> In picking epithets, and yoking rhyme)
> To steadier rule my thoughts I now compose,
> And prize ideas clad in honest prose.[8]

In 1736, writing to Swift about the projected *Opus Magnum,* Pope concludes with what seem genuine sentiments enough:

But alas! the task is great, and *non sum qualis eram!* My understanding indeed, such as it is, is extended rather than diminished: I see things more in the whole, more consistent, and more clearly deduced from, and related to, each other. But what I gain on the side of philosophy, I lose on the side of poetry: the flowers are gone, when the fruits begin to ripen, and the fruits perhaps will never ripen perfectly. The climate

---

7. *Satire* II.vi.26 (line 17 in the Horatian original).
8. Elijah Fenton, *An Epistle to Thomas Lambard, Esq.,* in *Poems on Several Occasions* (1717), pp. 198–99.

(under our heaven of a court) is but cold and uncertain: the winds rise, and the winter comes on.

(*Corr.* IV, 5)

The parenthesis glances at the hostile political environment of the 1730s, but the burden of the passage is about aging. In the language of the *Essay on Criticism*, as judgment ripens wit must correspondingly decline.

From a less gloomy point of view, however, the lost flowers of fancy were perhaps not so important after all. Addressing his close friend Delany, Swift indicates that prosy verse is really a compliment to the reader:

> To you the muse this verse bestows,
> Which might as well have been in prose;
> No thought, no fancy, no sublime,
> But simple topics told in rhyme.[9]

In another poem Swift's profound affection for Stella is couched in a refusal of conventional love poetry, which is said to belong only to the inexperienced young:

> No poet ever sweetly sung,
> Unless he were like Phoebus, young;
> Nor ever nymph inspired to rhyme,
> Unless, like Venus, in her prime.
> At fifty-six, if this be true,
> Am I a poet fit for you?
> Or at the age of forty-three,
> Are you a subject fit for me?
> Adieu bright wit, and radiant eyes;
> You must be grave, and I be wise.
> Our fate in vain we would oppose,
> But I'll be still your friend in prose.[10]

Like Swift, Pope bids farewell to fancy, sublimity, and conventional ornaments. He rarely permits himself this sort of rattling doggerel, and his pentameter couplets retain a highly charged density of implication. Still his is a poetry that de-

---

9. Jonathan Swift, *To Mr. Delany*, 9–12.
10. Jonathan Swift, *Stella's Birthday (1725)*, 19–30.

clines poeticalness and aspires to the virtues of good prose, even if it is prose sublimated. A great nineteenth-century poet might write,

> I dwell in Possibility—
> A fairer House than Prose.[11]

Pope dwells in probability and aspires to actuality.

Only in an incompetent writer would verse and prose actually be identical, as Pope writes witheringly to Hervey: "I take your Lordship's verse to be as much prose as this letter."[12] Hervey is the "Fanny" with whom Pope ironically compares himself when he recalls his early career:

> Soft were my numbers, who could take offence
> While pure description held the place of sense?
> Like gentle Fanny's was my flow'ry theme,
> A painted mistress, or a purling stream.
>
> (*To Arbuthnot*, 147–50)

The painted mistress presumably was Belinda in *The Rape of the Lock*, and the purling stream the Thames in *Windsor-Forest*; Pope raised both to the level of art. Hervey's slender verses purl like their shallow subjects, and his mistresses (like himself) wear real paint.

But if Pope has relinquished the flowers of fancy and descended to prosy sense, why does he represent "description" as the antithesis of sense? The answer is that he understands description in a specialized way: not a comprehensive image of familiar "reality," but a carefully managed version of it, purified of ugliness and indecency, and expressed in language and images inherited from previous describers. Neoclassical art makes a point of leaving things out. In his *Discourse on Pastoral Poetry*, which he claims was "written at sixteen years of age" (*TE* I, 23n), Pope follows Rapin in saying that pastoral was invented when rustics were not at all like

11. Emily Dickinson, No. 657, in *The Complete Poems of Emily Dickinson,* ed. Thomas H. Johnson (Boston: Little, Brown, 1957), p. 327.

12. *A Letter to a Noble Lord*, in Warburton's edition of Pope's *Works* (1751), VIII, 254.

modern ones: "So that we are not to describe our shepherds as shepherds at this day really are, but as they may be conceived then to have been, when the best of men followed the employment" (p. 25). We describe shepherds, but not as shepherds are. It follows that what is "natural" should conform to ideal nature, not to actuality. "We must therefore use some illusion to render a pastoral delightful; and this consists in exposing the best side only of a shepherd's life, and in concealing its miseries" (p. 27).

In *Windsor-Forest* as in the pastorals, Pope constantly sought to raise the familiar to a level of beautiful artifice. The 1712 version of that poem has the line "The silver eel in slimy volumes rolled." "Happily for the reader, if not for the ichthyologist," Brower comments complacently, "Pope changed the line to 'The silver eel in shining volumes rolled.'"[13] Pure description, then, means description purified of coarse and unpleasant associations. Eels shine, but we forget the slime that makes them shiny. *Windsor-Forest* offers a systematically "poetic" world, committed to allegorizing the darker human passions in a painterly harmony, using a compound of classical allusion and pictorial hints based on the landscape tradition of Claude Lorrain and others.[14] But *The Rape of the Lock*, dating from exactly the same period, is far more circumstantial about everyday phenomena, and much of the pleasure is in seeing the surprising periphrases with which Pope can describe what everybody knows. The ombre game is significantly translated into the language of heroic combat, but as scholars have shown it is technically accurate; Warton says, "I question whether Hoyle could have played it better than Belinda."[15] Here we approach the point where mock-epic topples over into mockery of epic, permitting (sometimes inadvertently) familiar experience to cut the stilts out from

13. *Windsor-Forest*, 143; Reuben A. Brower, *Alexander Pope: The Poetry of Allusion* (Oxford: Clarendon, 1959), p. 54.
14. See Morris R. Brownell, *Alexander Pope and the Arts of Georgian England* (Oxford: Clarendon, 1978), pp. 74–78.
15. Joseph Warton, *An Essay on the Genius and Writings of Pope* (1756, 1782), I, 233.

under the epic elevation. As Johnson says of Gay's *Shepherd's Week*, "The effect of reality and truth became conspicuous, even when the intention was to show them groveling and degraded. These pastorals became popular, and were read with delight, as just representations of rural manners and occupations."[16]

Stooping to truth and rejecting "pure description" implies repudiation of the ideal perfections that neoclassical art aspired to. Addison writes of his travels in Italy,

> Sometimes, misguided by the tuneful throng,
> I look for streams immortalized in song,
> That lost in silence and oblivion lie,
> (Dumb are their fountains and their channels dry)
> Yet run for ever by the muse's skill,
> And in the smooth description murmur still.[17]

The streams really did flow in classical times, and they still murmur in Latin verse because the murmuring verse has outlived the streams. But that is all that "smooth description" can do; it is unequal to the reality of Italy when Addison finally gets there. And despite the survival of Latin in the schools, people were beginning to sense that classical civilization was drying up along with its streams.

The descriptions in *Windsor-Forest* depend upon a dual commitment, to the ideal beauty of the British countryside and also to the ideal beauty of classicizing imagery. Even while composing the poem, Pope could write playfully to Caryll about the contrast between imagined ideal and experienced reality:

> These are the scenes the season presents to me, and what can be more ridiculous than that in the midst of this bleak prospect that sets my very imagination a-shivering, I am endeavouring to raise up round about me a painted scene of woods and forests in verdure and beauty, trees springing, fields flowering, nature laughing. I am wandering through bowers and

16. Samuel Johnson, *Life of Gay*, in *Lives*, II, 269.
17. Joseph Addison, *A Letter from Italy*, in *The Works of . . . Joseph Addison* (1721), I, 45–47.

grottos in conceit, and while my trembling body is cowering o'er a fire, my mind is expatiating in an open sunshine.

> —Videor pios errare per lucos, amoenae
> Quos et aquae subeunt et aurae.

(Corr. I, 168)

In the ode from which Pope quotes, Horace asks Calliope to play or sing a melody, and exclaims, "Methinks I hear her and am straying through hallowed groves, where pleasant waters steal and breezes stir." But the "methinks" (*videor*) is operative here, and the line immediately before asks, *Auditis, an me ludit amabilis / insania?* "Do ye hear? Or does some fond illusion mock me?"[18]

Windsor-Forest was the product of a particular historical moment, in which the Tories could hope for a genuinely constructive European peace, as well as of a particular moment in Pope's poetic development. Its harmonies are an act of faith, or perhaps of wish fulfillment, rather than a fully elaborated picture of the world as Pope perceives it. And others might perceive that world very differently. Some commendatory verses on *Windsor-Forest*, printed in the 1717 edition of Pope's *Works*, bitterly contrast the west of Ireland with Windsor, and reject Denham's "O let me flow like thee" model even while invoking it. This is a nature that inspires the *wrong* language of description:

> I in a cold, and in a barren clime,
> Cold as my thought, and barren as my rhyme,
> Here on the western beach attempt to chime!
> O joyless flood! O rough tempestuous main!
> Bordered with weeds, and solitudes obscene!
> Let me ne'er flow like thee! nor make thy stream
> My sad example or my wretched theme.
> Like bombast now thy raging billows roar,
> And vainly dash themselves against the shore:
> About like quibbles now thy froth is thrown,
> And all extremes are in a moment shown.[19]

18. *Odes* III.iv.1–8, as translated by C. E. Bennett in *Horace: The Odes and Epodes*, Loeb Classical Library (London: Heinemann, 1927), p. 187.

19. F. Knapp, *To Mr. Pope on His Windsor-Forest, Killola in the County of Mayo in Ireland, June 7, 1715* (printed in vol. I of the 1717 *Works*).

Language and nature present a chaos of extremes to this writer, not the *concordia discors* of Denham and Pope.

A poem by Pope's collaborator Broome, praising the verisimilitude of Jervas's paintings, stresses artifice so heavily that it threatens to become unreality instead of heightened reality:

> If life be drawn responsive to the thought,
> The breathing figures live throughout the draught;
> The mimic bird in skies fictitious moves,
> Or fancied beasts in imitated groves.[20]

Mimic, fictitious, fancied, and *imitated* suggest a disturbing weight of artificiality. Pope's own *Epistle to Jervas* ends with an admission of the limits of art:

> Alas! how little from the grave we claim?
> Thou but preserv'st a face and I a name.
>   (77–78)

It is only paint and words after all; Pope would have little use for an aestheticism that values these more than their living subjects. And by naming a contemporary painter who was also his friend, Pope invites rude comments from outsiders like Welsted, who was not pleased to find himself in the *Dunciad*:

> J[ervas]! who so refined a rake is reckoned,
> He breaks all Sinai's laws, except the second.

In a footnote Welsted quotes the second commandment to drive the point home: "Thou shalt not make the likeness of any thing in heaven above, or on the earth beneath, or the waters under the earth."[21] Jervas's pictures are unobjectionable because they are not likenesses.

---

20. William Broome, *To . . . Lady Elizabeth Townshend, Now Lady Cornwallis, on Her Picture, Drawn by Mr. Jervas,* in *Poems on Several Occasions* (1717), p. 92. Broome was chaplain to Lord Cornwallis.

21. Leonard Welsted, *One Epistle to Mr. A. Pope* (1730), facsimile edited by J. V. Guerinot (Los Angeles: University of California Press, 1965), pp. 17, 23. This hoary sarcasm was also applied to Jervas by Kneller, and Pope playfully applied it to himself; see Maynard Mack, *Alexander Pope: A Life* (New York: Norton, 1985), pp. 227, 229.

Even while scholars were industriously uncovering a wealth of details about the people in Pope's poems, critics used to maintain that the details were finally trivial. "In the character of Sporus," Tillotson declares, "the reader's mind is kept so busy merely taking in the baroque zigzag of beauty and nastiness that Hervey is forgotten." According to Mack, the Sporus portrait is an exemplum that begins with the historical Hervey but rises rhetorically to describe "the fundamental attributes of the invader in every garden."[22] Certainly the portrait is unforgettable, and that could not be so, presumably, if it were limited to the accidental characteristics of a minor figure in the court of George II. But is the invader in every garden sexually ambivalent (Sporus was a beautiful youth whom Nero castrated and then married), and heavily painted, and witty yet absurd, and fond of asses' milk as a health cure ("Sporus, that mere white curd of ass's milk," 306)? It is hard not to feel that the historical Lord John Hervey is inseparable from the portrait, and that however brilliant it is rhetorically, Johnson is right to say that "the meanest passage is the satire upon Sporus."[23] The rhetoric may rise, but the subject is "low" and so is Pope's attack. His bitterness and disgust are excited by the kind of person he believed to be corrupting England, not by an abstract notion of the Satanic, and the portrait is effective in proportion as it is felt to be true. This is gossip raised to the level of art: just as tragedy can never forget its roots in melodrama, so satire never forgets its roots in gossip.

Moreover, the attack on Sporus is extorted from the speaker by the objection of his friend (presumably Arbuthnot himself) that Hervey is not worth so much fuss:

> Satire or sense alas! can Sporus feel?
> Who breaks a butterfly upon a wheel?
> (307–8)

22. Geoffrey Tillotson, *On the Poetry of Pope* (Oxford: Clarendon, 1950), p. 156; Maynard Mack, "The Muse of Satire," *Yale Review*, 41 (1951), 92.
23. *Lives*, III, 246.

Pope does. He thus represents himself as being spurred into wrath not by his own malice but by a cynical friend whose cynicism is too easy. Familiarity may at first breed contempt, but in time it will breed tolerance and even sympathy. As Pope puts it in the *Essay on Man*,

> Vice is a monster of so frightful mien,
> As, to be hated, needs but to be seen;
> Yet seen too oft, familiar with her face,
> We first endure, then pity, then embrace.
>
> (II.217–20)

Whatever else the *Epistle to Arbuthnot* may be, it is not impersonal. Rather it is a satiric catharsis, as Arbuthnot's casual contempt is corrected by Pope's deeper contempt for what Hervey is and for a society that condones or even admires him.

The apogee of the higher gossip occurs in the *Dunciad*, in which one could be awarded a "place" with real consequences in the world outside the poem. "Ralph, who, unnecessarily interposing in the quarrel, got a place in a subsequent edition, complained that for a time he was in danger of starving, as the booksellers had no longer any confidence in his capacity."[24] For readers today, a figure like Ralph remains shadowy even when editors have done their best. To some extent, of course, that was true in Pope's time too. Swift wrote to him when the first edition appeared, "The notes I could wish to be very large, in what relates to the persons concerned; for I have long observed that twenty miles from London nobody understands hints, initial letters, or town-facts and passages; and in a few years not even those who live in London." The answer, according to Swift, was more specificity rather than less: "Again I insist, you must have your asterisks filled up with some real names of real Dunces" (*Corr.* II, 504–5). But readers also took pleasure in puzzle solving. It happens that Ralph himself wrote in the same year,

---

24. Ibid., 146. On Ralph see pp. 123–25 in this volume.

Some politicians, informers, reformers, and small wits may be very inquisitive about my half blanks, whole blanks, or mutilated sentences. . . . I am sensible most people love to meet with such gaps, in order to fill them up. If every thing was set down plain, and at full length in any work; no words to be guessed at or no obscurity in the sense; it would be thought only proper for the perusal of a schoolboy, and argue an author's assurance, in his giving no fair play to a reader's penetration.[25]

That account could almost have been written by Wolfgang Iser, modern theorist of gaps,[26] except that Ralph invites the insertion of names from the world outside the poem, not an imaginative completion of a self-contained internal world.

Even if the reader (or some readers) might get pleasure from this kind of gap filling, it was always possible to object that the victims were too trivial to deserve such treatment. Boileau, Pope's master in many aspects of satire, asks himself what the little writers have done to justify placing them in a hundred "niches":

Que vous ont fait Perrin, Bardin, Pradon, Hainaut,
Colletet, Pelletier, Titreville, Quinault,
Dont les noms en cent lieux, placés comme en leurs niches,
Vont de vos vers malins remplir les hémistiches?[27]

What have Perrin (etc.) done to you, whose names, positioned in a hundred places as if in their niches, have filled up the half-lines of your malicious verses?

Boileau's reply is that a satirist, of all people, cannot be expected to stay quiet when folly is rampant:

Et je serai le seul qui ne pourrai rien dire!
On sera ridicule, et je n'oserai rire!
(p. 63)

---

25. James Ralph, *The Touch-Stone: or, Historical, Critical, Political, Philosophical, and Theological Essays on the Reigning Diversions of the Town* (1728), quoted by Vincent Carretta, *The Snarling Muse: Verbal and Visual Political Satire from Pope to Churchill* (Philadelphia: University of Pennsylvania Press, 1983), p. 42.

26. *The Act of Reading: A Theory of Aesthetic Response* (Baltimore: Johns Hopkins University Press, 1978).

27. Nicolas Boileau-Despréaux, *Satire IX*, in *Oeuvres*, ed. Georges Mongrédien (Paris: Garnier, 1961), p. 61.

And I am to be the only one who can't say anything! People
will be ridiculous, and I won't dare to laugh!

Pope similarly claims that his victims force themselves on
him: "Fools rush into my head, and so I write" (*Satire* II.i.14).
Fools would therefore be well advised to keep clear of Pope:

> Who-e'er offends, at some unlucky time
> Slides into verse, and hitches in a rhyme.
> Sacred to ridicule! his whole life long,
> And the sad burthen of some merry song.
>   (77–80)

Poetry is power and satire a sharp weapon.

A chance encounter with Pope may confer a horrible kind
of immortality, as Richardson comments: "After all, Mr. Pope
is (even in his *Dunciad* methinks) much more worthily employed than Domitian was, since it is nobler to immortalize
flies than to destroy them."[28] Or to turn them into flies before
immortalizing them:

> Yet let me flap this bug with gilded wings,
> This painted child of dirt that stinks and stings.
>   (*To Arbuthnot*, 309–10)

An ancient topos compares works of art to the drops of amber
that transform tiny creatures into gems, as in Martial's epigram (in an eighteenth-century translation):

> A drop of amber, from a poplar plant,
> Fell, unexpected, and embalmed an ant:
> The little insect we so much contemn
> Is from a worthless ant become a gem.[29]

Pope runs the analogy the other way. In amber or not, a bug
is still a bug.

> Pretty! in amber to observe the forms
> Of hairs, or straws, or dirt, or grubs, or worms;

28. Samuel Richardson, Letter to George Cheyne, 21 Jan. 1743, in *Selected
Letters of Samuel Richardson*, ed. John Carroll (Oxford: Clarendon, 1964), p. 57.
29. Anonymous translation of Martial VI.xv, in *The Flower-Piece: A Collection of Miscellany Poems* (1731), p. 170.

> The things, we know, are neither rich nor rare,
> But wonder how the devil they got there?
> >   (*To Arbuthnot*, 169–72)

They got there because Pope put them there.

It is well to admit that even when we are able to fill in the blanks, they remain essentially blank. When "auspicious Health" appears at the end of Garth's *Dispensary* (the mock-epic that immediately suggested *The Rape of the Lock*),

> A charm she takes from each excelling fair,
> And borrows C——ll's shape, and G——ton's air.
> Her eyes like R——agh's their beams dispense,
> With Ch——ill's bloom, and B——kley's innocence.

The clues seem relatively transparent, and in a copy of the poem at the Folger Shakespeare Library a contemporary hand has inserted the names *Cecill's*, *Gayton's*, *Ranelagh's*, *Churchill's*, and *Bulkley's*.[30] But that leaves us little the wiser. Even if we could dig up biographical information for all of these women, we have no way of knowing what was arresting about Cecill's shape, let alone Gayton's air. For us the names might just as well be Chloris and Sylvia. But this would have been equally true for a provincial reader in Garth's time, whose knowledge of London celebrities could only have been vague. Later editions of *The Dispensary* in fact filled in the blanks, and not always as the owner of the Folger copy guessed: Carlisle for Cecill, Grafton for Gayton. The poem excludes us to some extent, whether we are twentieth-century readers or eighteenth-century ones, not by hiding in Kermode's parabolic "secrecy,"[31] but by a simple recognition that the real world is prior to the fictive. By naming Cecill (or Carlisle?) Garth grounds his poem in the world from which it sprang.

When the gaps are successfully filled, literary pleasure can still result, and sometimes the name alone is enough. In a

---

30. Samuel Garth, *The Dispensary*, 3rd ed. (1699), Canto VI, p. 75.
31. Frank Kermode, *The Genesis of Secrecy: On the Interpretation of Narrative* (Cambridge, Mass.: Harvard University Press, 1979).

manuscript draft of *To Arbuthnot* Pope wrote, "Is there a parson mad or steeped in beer."[32] Perhaps he already had the
Rev. Laurence Eusden in mind, or else a happy coincidence
of sounds brought him there. At any rate he deleted "mad or
steeped" and produced the immortal line "Is there a parson,
much be-mused in beer" (*To Arbuthnot,* 15). Anyone with a
name so fortunate becomes a welcome companion, and Pope
bids him a genial farewell in the final *Dunciad:*

> Know, Eusden thirsts no more for sack or praise;
> He sleeps among the dull of ancient days;
> Safe, where no critics damn, no duns molest,
> Where wretched Withers, Ward, and Gildon rest.
> (I.293–96)

But one critic does damn, of course, forever.

A number of scholars have admired the assertion of fictiveness in the "poet's form" that Dulness constructs:

> All as a partridge plump, full-fed, and fair,
> She formed this image of well-bodied air. . . .
> Never was dashed out, at one lucky hit,
> A fool, so just a copy of a wit;
> So like, that critics said, and courtiers swore,
> A wit it was, and called the phantom More.
> (*Dunciad* II.41–50)

Pope's immensely detailed footnote recounts the plagiarisms
of James Moore Smith and concludes, "It appears from hence
that this is not the name of a real person, but fictitious; *More*
from *morós, stultus, moría, stultitia,* to represent the folly of a
plagiary. Thus Erasmus . . ." (*TE* V, 101–3). The phantom author Moore Smith serves to reincarnate Erasmus's old joke on
the name of Thomas More. But one should not press the fictiveness of Moore/More too far. Just as with Swift's satires
against Partridge, the joke depends upon the existence of a
real person whom the fictional one is said to supersede. "But

---

32. Quoted by Maynard Mack, *The Last and Greatest Art: Some Unpublished
Political Manuscripts of Alexander Pope* (Newark: University of Delaware Press,
1984), p. 430.

now, if an uninformed carcass walks still about, and is pleased to call itself Partridge, Mr. Bickerstaff does not think himself anyway answerable for that."[33] Like the grub in amber, Partridge and Moore will survive on the page long after their bodies really have ceased to exist. In a curious way they are assimilated to the fate of the poet, whose own death haunts the ending of so many of Pope's poems: "The muse forgot, and thou belov'd no more" (*Unfortunate Lady,* 82). More is no more, and no more is Pope, but they both live in Pope's verse. This kind of immortality is better than none, and it is therefore an immense compliment, if a backward one, to be elected to the *Dunciad.* If Pope can exalt Belinda's lock to the heavens, he can also resurrect hack writers with his negative panegyric.

The so-called dunces, naturally, were not pleased with their fate, and some of them mounted effective counterattacks. Cibber's major reply begins with fine understatement, "You have for several years past (particularly in your poetical works) mentioned my name, without my desiring it."[34] Having refrained from answering until now, Cibber admits the fear "that a disgrace from such a pen, might stick upon me to posterity" (p. 7), as indeed it has. His tactic is to profess good humor, shrewdly noting Pope's tendency to be "a self-tormentor" (p. 6), and to acknowledge cheerfully the very point on which Pope tirelessly harps. "I wrote more to be fed, than be famous, and since my writings still give me a dinner, do you rhyme me out of my stomach if you can" (p. 9). Pope strives to keep the controversy at an exalted level of good writing versus bad; Cibber, with considerable humor, narrates anecdotes in which Pope was personally involved— "his lips pale and his voice trembling" when he protested a joke against the Scriblerian comedy *Three Hours after Marriage* (p. 19), and his alleged visit with Cibber and an unnamed

33. Jonathan Swift, *A Vindication of Isaac Bickerstaff, Esq.,* in *Gulliver's Travels and Other Writings,* ed. Louis A. Landa (Boston: Houghton Mifflin, 1960), p. 394.

34. Colley Cibber, *A Letter from Mr. Cibber, to Mr. Pope* (1742), p. 5.

nobleman to a whorehouse "where I found this little hasty hero, like a terrible Tom Tit, pertly perching upon the mount of love" (p. 48).

Pope's poems depend upon their real-life context but claim to fictionalize or fantasize it, and their brilliance derives from their success in controlling context. Cibber's attack works in the other direction, replacing Pope in context more firmly than he would like. There is no question that attacks like Cibber's disturbed Pope deeply. In a sequel two years later, after finding himself the new hero of the *Dunciad*, Cibber reports with satisfaction that the earlier pamphlet "(as everybody tells me) made you as uneasy as a rat in a hot kettle for a twelvemonth together."[35] Cibber cleverly goes on to accuse Pope's commentator Warburton of being one of the figments himself: "Being, at first, in some doubt whether Mr. *W.W.* really existed, or might be some phantom of Mr. Pope's own forming . . ." (p. 27). Time has proved Cibber right. Like Moore Smith—and like Cibber—Warburton exists today only as a fossilized object in the lower strata of Pope's poems.

Pope's contemporaries, despite the lip service they frequently paid to Aristotelian generality, had an insatiable appetite for "real" persons and events, and this preference needs to be stressed when we consider the status of fiction in their time. In 1756 Warton asserted that the *Elegy to the Memory of an Unfortunate Lady* was excellent because "the occasion of it was real; for it is certainly an indisputable maxim, 'That nature is more powerful than fancy; that we can always feel more than we can imagine; and that the most artful fiction must give way to truth.'"[36] Warton's examples are surprising, to say the least:

> If we briefly cast our eyes over the most interesting and affecting stories, ancient or modern, we shall find that they are such, as however adorned and a little diversified, are yet grounded on true history, and on real matters of fact. Such,

35. Colley Cibber, *Another Occasional Letter from Mr. Cibber to Mr. Pope* (1744), p. 15.
36. *Essay on . . . Pope*, I, 253.

for instance, among the ancients, are the stories of Joseph, of Oedipus, the Trojan war and its consequences, of Virginia and the Horatii; such, among the moderns, are the stories of King Lear, the Cid, Romeo and Juliet, and Oronooko.

(p. 254)

This is an age that wants its legends to resolve into facts. Repeating his "maxim" forty years later, Warton triumphantly reports that he has identified the Unfortunate Lady: "After many and wide enquiries, I have been informed that her name was Wainsbury; and that (which is a singular circumstance) she was as ill-shaped and deformed as our author."[37] Presumably modern critics are right when they say that the Lady was a composite of several unfortunates, or even that Pope's *Elegy* "is the product of his imagination working upon his reading."[38] Still, if Warton's or some other identification could be proved correct, it would be hard not to take it into account. And one can surely appreciate Horace Walpole's pleasure at recalling the dramatis personae of Pope's imaginative world: "I was standing at my window after dinner, in summer, in Arlington Street, and saw *Patty Blount* (after Pope's death), with nothing remaining of her immortal charms but her *blue eyes*, trudging on foot with her petticoats pinned up, for it rained, to visit *blameless Bethel*, who was sick at the end of the street."[39]

In the *Essay on Criticism* Pope had soared into a stratosphere of Platonic idealism:

> Unerring nature, still divinely bright,
> One clear, unchanged, and universal light.
> (70–71)

37. Joseph Warton's edition of Pope's *Works* (1797), I, 336.

38. Ian Jack, "The Elegy as Exorcism: Pope's 'Verses to the Memory of an Unfortunate Lady,'" *Augustan Worlds*, ed. J. C. Hilson et al. (Leicester: Leicester University Press, 1978), p. 75. Jack surveys the many futile attempts to identify the Lady, which seem to have been encouraged by the poet himself in a "mischievous footnote" (p. 81).

39. Letter to the countess of Upper Ossory, 27 Jan. 1786, quoted in *TE*, III–ii, 73n.

His later career is a deliberate descent from that altitude, down from the Renaissance to the modern world. The real is now Aristotelian rather than Platonic: not the ideal norm radiant with eternal light, but rather the sum total of life's experiences. The more you see of the complexity of things, the more you are able to recognize the common patterns that recur; universality in art is also specificity. "Every single character in Shakespeare," Pope says, "is as much an individual as those in life itself."[40] The corollary to "What oft was thought, but ne'er so well expressed" (*Essay on Criticism,* 298) is that a memorable expression gives new meaning to lived experience, not just to art. As A. D. Nuttall puts it in his attempt to rescue mimesis from its current theoretical disgrace, "Rembrandt in his self-portraits profoundly enhances our knowledge of a possible face, but he does more than that. When we leave the gallery we look with greater insight into the first face we encounter. He thereby directly deepens our experiential knowledge of the real human face."[41] Hervey and Bolingbroke, Cibber and Bethel, Lady Mary and Martha Blount are all gathered up into the world of Pope's poems, and more than those of any other great English poet, these poems stubbornly insist on the world from which they grew.

40. Pope's Preface to the *Works of Shakespeare* (1725), in *Literary Criticism of Alexander Pope,* ed. Bertrand A. Goldgar (Lincoln: University of Nebraska Press, 1965), p. 162.
41. *A New Mimesis: Shakespeare and the Representation of Reality* (London: Methuen, 1983), p. 76.

8

Art as Mirror, Art as Technique

Let us consider again the lovely passage in *Windsor-Forest*, added in a late revision,[1] in which when Lodona has metamorphosed into the river Loddon she becomes a mirror of art:

> Oft in her glass the musing shepherd spies
> The headlong mountains and the downward skies,
> The watry landskip of the pendant woods,
> And absent trees that tremble in the floods;
> In the clear azure gleam the flocks are seen,
> And floating forests paint the waves with green.
>
> (211–16)

Pope's source here is no longer Ovid, but Ausonius's very detailed poem about life along the Moselle. In this passage Ausonius stresses the deceptive merging of reflection and reality:

> The waters of the stream seem to bear leaves and the flood to be all o'ergrown with shoots of vines. . . . Whole hills float on the shivering ripples; here quivers the far-off [*tremit absens*] tendril of the vine, here in the glassy flood swells the full cluster. The deluded boatman tells o'er the green vines—the boatman whose skiff of bark floats on the watery floor out on midstream, where the pictured hill blends with the river [*qua sese amni confundit imago / collis*] and where the river joins with the edges of the shadows.[2]

1. Lines 211–16 are not in the 1712 manuscript, which survives in Pope's hand. See the reproduction and transcription by Robert M. Schmitz, *Pope's Windsor Forest 1712* (St. Louis: Washington University, 1952), p. 32.
2. *Mosella* 189–99, in *Ausonius*, ed. and tr. H. G. E. White, Loeb Classical Library (London: Heinemann, 1919), I, 238–39.

Pope is less interested in illusion than Ausonius is. For him the mirror is manifestly a mirror, confirming absence rather than mimicking presence, and the trembling of what is absent (*tremit absens*) reinforces the difference between image and reality. Art is always a representation of one thing by another, so the forests "paint" the waves with green and exhibit an inverted image to the musing shepherd.

In *Summer* Pope had fancied that art might recover its lost Orphic power over nature:

> But would you sing, and rival Orpheus' strain,
> The wond'ring forests soon should dance again,
> The moving mountains hear the pow'rful call,
> And headlong streams hang list'ning in their fall!
>   (81–84)

But even in the pastorals the hope is conditional only, and Alexis's song is a bitter one. In *Windsor-Forest* art changes nothing, merely making a reflection of the external world available to contemplation. A passive construction declares the passive nature of perception—"the flocks are seen"—and the mind is free to reflect on the reflection. The mental component is important, of course; Johnson defines *reflect* both as "to throw back light" and as "to throw back thoughts upon the past or on themselves."[3] But the metaphor of the mirror, as Abrams has shown in detail, presumes an identifiable and stable reality *out there*, which the various arts seek to represent. Hagstrum points out that the *ut pictura poesis* equation was increasingly invoked when theorists began to emphasize the objects of imitation rather than the artistic means.[4]

The mirror image, then, cannot be identical with the thing mirrored, but it is generated by the "real" object and permits the viewer or reader to recreate it. The intensely pictorial mode of Pope's early work is characterized not by circum-

3. Samuel Johnson, *A Dictionary of the English Language* (1755).
4. M. H. Abrams, *The Mirror and the Lamp: Romantic Theory and the Critical Tradition* (New York: Norton, 1958), pp. 31–42; J. H. Hagstrum, *The Sister Arts: The Tradition of Literary Pictorialism and English Poetry from Dryden to Gray* (Chicago: University of Chicago Press, 1958), p. 7.

stantial detail but by conventional triggers for the reader's visualization, of the kind that Eric Rothstein analyzes in a masterly article.[5] The absent presence of Pope's woods can be paralleled in the much-derided Blackmore: "a true and bright idea" (that is, a mental image) gives so strong a verbal impression "that the absent object seems in some sort present to the admiring reader." Ambrose Philips goes so far as to suggest that the experience of reading overwhelms all consciousness of artifice: "Words, in [the poet's] disposal, are things: and the deception proves so strong, that the reader forgets he is perusing a piece of writing."[6] Pope would never have accepted that, particularly with respect to Philips's own pedestrian poetry, but the focus on what we would now call reader response helps to explain why "pure description held the place of sense" (*To Arbuthnot*, 148) before Pope stooped to truth. If description worked by conventional associations to invite the reader to create the poem, then it could hardly be wedded to the actual world in the way that "sense" requires.

At the end of *Windsor-Forest* Pope declares,

> My humble muse, in unambitious strains,
> Paints the green forests and the flow'ry plains.
> (427–28)

In his later verse he drops the mask of humility, and he paints no more. If a river continues to reflect mental visions, it does so in a localized and domesticated way, as in one of his rare imitations of the lyric Horace:

> His house, embosomed in the grove,
> Sacred to social life and social love,
>   Shall glitter o'er the pendent green,
> Where Thames reflects the visionary scene.
> (*Ode* IV.i.21–24)

---

5. "'Ideal Presence' and the 'Non Finito' in Eighteenth-Century Aesthetics," *Eighteenth-Century Studies*, 9 (1976), 307–32.

6. Richard Blackmore, *Essays upon Several Subjects* (1716), p. 136; Philips, *The Free-Thinker* (1722), No. 63; both quoted by Rothstein, "'Ideal Presence,'" p. 311.

This is the ode that begins with the proverbial *non sum qualis eram*, which Pope adapts to refer to the period of *The Rape of the Lock* and *Windsor-Forest*:

> I am not now, alas! the man
> As in the gentle reign of my Queen Anne.
> (3–4)

Even if the mirror reflects reality accurately, it does so by highly artificial means, and consciousness of artifice is a principal source of pleasure. When one shuts the door of his grotto, Pope reports, "it becomes on the instant, from a luminous room, a *camera obscura;* on the walls of which all the objects of the river, hills, woods, and boats, are forming a moving picture in their visible radiations" (*Corr.* II, 296). If the picture were wholly identical with the reality, there would be no point in closing the door: one could simply look at the river directly. The pleasure is in seeing the familiar made strange, and thereby made new. But all the same the picture is continuously connected to the reality beyond.

In his later verse Pope no longer uses the image of the mirror, emblem of a perfect fit between art and life. Instead he tends to emphasize the artificiality of the devices by which reality is not presented but re-presented, just as Addison had done in writing of Italian sculpture:

> Still to new scenes my wand'ring muse retires,
> And the dumb show of breathing rocks admires;
> Where the smooth chisel all its force has shown,
> And softened into flesh the rugged stone.[7]

Marble is an extremely hard stone; Addison emphasizes the "force" that is needed to make it seem soft and breathing, and also the gap that must remain between this "dumb show" and life. So also Pope, remembering the art of the Restoration:

---

7. Joseph Addison, *A Letter from Italy,* in *The Works of . . . Joseph Addison* (1721), I, 49.

> Then marble softened into life grew warm,
> And yielding metal flowed to human form.
> Lely on animated canvas stole
> The sleepy eye, that spoke the melting soul.
> (*Epistle* II.i.147–50)

The sexual warmth of Charles II's court finds its expression in stone and paint, but only because human artists know how to translate life into art.

The term *creation* was sometimes used for art in the eighteenth century, in explicit analogy to the divine creation, but the usual term was *invention*. This ambiguous word, as Johnson's definitions show, hesitated between its root meaning of finding out (Latin *invenio*) and its modern meaning of "fiction" or "excogitation; act of producing something new." It would be misleading to impose a Renaissance meaning too firmly on the eighteenth century, as Wasserman does in his magisterial book: "Neoclassic art is not the art of creating, but of inventing, or finding—the art of pursuing with perfect and unstrained consistency a system of similitudes inherent in the given materials."[8] Pope probably did aspire to something like that in the early *Windsor-Forest*, which Wasserman examines exhaustively, but the terms *perfect*, *unstrained*, *system*, and *inherent* all point to assumptions which Pope's later art rejects. In Pope's time *image* was coming to mean a picture in the imagination, and was well on its way to becoming (as it still was for the New Critics) a synonym for *metaphor*.[9] But the picture was expected to correspond to an external reality, and artistic devices were means to that end, not ends in themselves.

Just as the poet's visualized "idea" should conjure up a corresponding one in the reader's mind, so too should his thoughts in their widest sense.

> True wit is nature to advantage dressed,
> What oft was thought, but ne'er so well expressed,

8. Earl R. Wasserman, *The Subtler Language: Critical Readings of Neoclassic and Romantic Poems* (Baltimore: Johns Hopkins University Press, 1959), p. 123.

9. See Roy Frazer, "The Origin of the Term 'Image,'" *Journal of English Literary History*, 27 (1960), 149–61.

> Something, whose truth convinced at sight we find,
> That gives us back the image of our mind.
>
>   (*Essay on Criticism*, 297–300)

The function of expression is to make us see more clearly the thing expressed:

> But true expression, like th' unchanging sun,
> Clears, and improves whate'er it shines upon,
> It gilds all objects, but it alters none.
>
>   (315–17)

Later theorists might think of expression as the ex-pressing of inner feelings; a turn to expressivism in that sense was central to poetry in the generation following Pope. But Johnson's definitions in 1755 still conform to the older practice. His first three definitions of the verb *express* are as follows:

> To copy; to resemble; to represent.
> To represent by any of the imitative arts: as poetry, sculpture, painting.
> To represent in words; to exhibit by language; to utter; to declare.

A skillful artist, accordingly, can represent convincingly because his techniques call forth the appropriate thoughts and images. Aaron Hill, writing to Pope in 1738, objects to "nature to advantage dressed" and revises accordingly:

> I believe the idea must have been *shape* (not *dress*) of *thought;* dress, however an ornament, being a *concealment,* or *covering;* whereas expression is manifestation and *exposure.*
>
> Expression is the *birth* of thought—*grows* round,
> Limbs the loose soul, and shapes it into sound.
>
>   (*Corr.* IV, 96)

Hill's version perhaps anticipates an organic notion of poetry, in which language and meaning are identical, but it ignores the way in which Pope *wants* language to conceal as well as exhibit. It is easy to imagine that Pope, more than most people, would not care to expose nakedness, and Dryden has a similar thought when he says of Kneller's paintings,

> Likeness is ever there; but still the best,
> Like proper thoughts in lofty language dressed.[10]

Dryden says elsewhere that nakedness is less alluring than attractive clothing:

> Our author [Du Fresnoy] calls colouring *lena sororis;* in plain English, the bawd of her sister, the design or drawing: she clothes, she dresses her up, she paints her, she makes her appear more lovely than naturally she is, she procures for the design, and makes lovers for her. For the design of itself is only so many naked lines. Thus in poetry, the expression is that which charms the reader, and beautifies the design.[11]

To the lines about the sun gilding but not altering, Pope adds,

> Expression is the dress of thought, and still
> Appears more decent as more suitable;
> A vile conceit in pompous words expressed
> Is like a clown in regal purple dressed;
> For diff'rent styles with diff'rent subjects sort,
> As several garbs with country, town, and court.
>
> (318–23)

As so often with Pope, the analogy is drawn from an overtly social context, and reminds us of the social basis of language itself. The "clown" is of course a rustic, not a jester, who is unacceptable in polite society even if disguised in elegant dress. In keeping with the notion of "propriety," different garbs suit different circumstances, and the best ones are the most "decent," which still has its Latin meaning of "suitable." Johnson illustrates *decent* from Dryden: "Since there must be ornaments both in painting and poetry, if they are not necessary, they must at least be decent; that is, in their due place, and but moderately used."[12]

In our own age of linguistic freedom, it is hard to grasp

10. John Dryden, *To Sir Godfrey Kneller,* 67–68.
11. John Dryden, *A Parallel betwixt Poetry and Painting,* in *Of Dramatic Poesy and Other Critical Essays,* ed. George Watson, Everyman's Library (London: Dent, 1962), II, 203.
12. The quoted passage comes from ibid., p. 196.

the intensity with which people once reacted against in-
decorous diction, particularly if it seemed indecent and not
just "low." "Realism," as is well known, is always conventional, but even the most conventional realism faces difficulties when some things cannot be described at all. Spence cites
with disgust the drunken cyclops in Pope's *Odyssey*—

> There belched the mingled streams of wine and blood,
> And human flesh, his indigested food—

and comments that "every description that is just, is *poetically
good;* but then I fancy 'tis as true that a description poetically
good, may be the more improper to be inserted, on that very
account. This will be readily allowed in all cases of obscenity;
the *best description* in such points is certainly the most *improper.*" [13] Only in burlesque can a poet use "low" language
freely, as Swift does in his mock-Virgilian *Description of a City
Shower:*

> Sweepings from butchers' stalls, dung, guts and blood,
> Drowned puppies, stinking sprats, all drenched in mud,
> Dead cats and turnip-tops come tumbling down the flood.

But linguistic hypersensitivity is not limited to the indecent, as is evident from Warton's praise of *The Rape of the Lock:*
"It is doubtless as hard to make a coffee-pot shine in poetry
as a plough: yet Pope has succeeded in giving elegance to so
familiar an object, as well as Virgil." In a footnote Warton
adds, "Observe the many periphrasis's and uncommon ap-
pelations Pope has used for *scissors,* which would sound too
vulgar—'fatal engine,' 'forfex,' 'shears,' 'meeting-points,'
&c." [14] A modern reader (perhaps rightly) is likely to see these
descriptions as playfully mocking; Warton sees them simply
as poetically heightening. But it should be added that in any
age, *some* words are bound to seem inappropriate in some

13. *Odyssey* IX.443–44 (this is one of the books translated by Pope, not
his collaborators); Spence, *An Essay on Pope's Odyssey* (1726), II, 147–48.
14. Joseph Warton, *An Essay on the Writings and Genius of Pope* (1756, 1782),
I, 234, 235n.

contexts. One can still smile at most of the examples in *Peri Bathous:*

> Sometimes a single word will familiarize a poetical idea, as where a ship set on fire owes all the spirit of the Bathos to one choice word that ends the line:

> And his scorched ribs the hot contagion *fried.*[15]

In Blackmore's original, however, the "ribs" belong to Arthur's Saxon enemy King Octa, and not, as Pope implies, to his burning ship. It is quite possible that Blackmore wanted *fried* to suggest satiric scorn.

In his youth Pope hoped that classical "rules" could help him to dress nature decently:

> Those rules of old discovered, not devised,
> Are nature still, but nature methodized.
> (*Essay on Criticism*, 88–89)

Rules are desired because art needs structure, and the poet longs to be "led by some rule, that guides, but not constrains" (*To Mr. Jervas*, 67). This is a matter of practical techniques, not of idealized law. Quintilian says of rhetorical examples, "These are weapons [*arma*] which we should always have stored in our armoury ready for immediate use as occasion may demand."[16] Pope's expanded version likewise emphasizes utility rather than aesthetic theory:

> In grave Quintilian's copious work we find
> The justest rules, and clearest method joined;
> Thus useful arms in magazines we place,
> All ranged in order, and disposed with grace,
> But less to please the eye, than arm the hand,
> Still fit for use, and ready at command.
> (*Essay on Criticism*, 669–74)

15. *Peri Bathous: Of the Art of Sinking in Poetry* (1728), in *Literary Criticism of Alexander Pope*, ed. Bertrand A. Goldgar (Lincoln: University of Nebraska Press, 1965), p. 74. The line is quoted from Blackmore's *Prince Arthur.*

16. *Institutes* II.i.12, tr. H. E. Butler (London: Loeb Classical Library, 1921), I, 209.

Beyond rules lies the real world, which rules help poets to imitate. If invention can range freely through the whole field of memory, what is to keep the result from being "one glaring chaos and wild heap of wit" (*Essay on Criticism*, 292)? Ideally that would be a principle of order inherent both in the external world and in the art that mirrors it, as Virgil is supposed to have found when he studied Homer:

> But when t' examine ev'ry part he came,
> Nature and Homer were, he found, the same. . . .
> Learn hence for ancient rules a just esteem;
> To copy nature is to copy them.
>
> (134–40)

But this was very much a youthful fantasy, and should not be allowed to govern our impression of Pope's mature art, particularly since he never worked in the two main genres (epic and tragedy) from which the rules were derived. The Restoration mood of French-influenced neoclassicism was still prevalent, among critics if not poets, when Pope was starting out and worrying about critical censure. After *The Rape of the Lock* he knew he had nothing to fear, and knew also that he could confidently develop his poems in his own way (Addison, probably with good intentions, had urged him not to revise the *Rape* to include the sylphs). But if he no longer feared critics, he still labored with critics in mind, and as Johnson says he took care to protect himself at every point: "He did not court the candour, but dared the judgment of his reader, and, expecting no indulgence from others, he showed none to himself. He examined lines and words with minute and punctilious observation, and retouched every part with indefatigable diligence, till he had left nothing to be forgiven."[17]

Pope's diligence, it might seem, was devoted to the parts rather than the whole, in a way characteristic of a period when neoclassical formalism gave way to a literature of ex-

17. Samuel Johnson, *Life of Pope*, in *Lives of the English Poets*, ed. G. B. Hill (Oxford: Clarendon, 1905), III, 221.

perience. One aspect of this evolution was a total breakdown of the traditional genres. Another was a conception of poems not as unities but as built-up collections of parts, whose connections were established by psychological association rather than logical coherence, and whose accretive nature was justified by appeal to an external world, which was itself infinitely various.[18] Tillotson puts it very well: Pope's "idea of form was not that of the centre with its nimbus of radiations, but that of growth along a line."[19] If the ideal Romantic poem is *Kubla Khan* or the *Ode to a Nightingale*, composed in a sudden access of imaginative power, the ideal Augustan poem is a slow accumulation. Pope wrote to Fortescue, who was arranging to have the drafts of the *Essay on Man* transcribed, "I employ myself . . . in casting my eye upon the great heap of fragments and hints before me, for my large and almost boundless work" (*Corr.* III, 271). Swift has left a playful but accurate account of Pope's method of composing:

> Now backs of letters, though designed
>   For those who more will need 'em,
> Are filled with hints, and interlined,
>   Himself can hardly read 'em.
>
> Each atom by some other struck,
>   All turns and motions tries;
> Till in a lump together stuck,
>   Behold a poem rise![20]

A Lucretian stuck-together lump is no Romantic metaphor for a poem. Its sticking together and rising suggest, perhaps, the solidity and nourishing qualities of a loaf of bread.

In practical terms, Pope's method (like Jonson's and Racine's) was to begin with prose paragraphs, turn these into verse, revise the verse, and seek to combine the parts into a

18. See Ralph Cohen, "The Augustan Mode in English Poetry," *Eighteenth-Century Studies*, 1 (1967), 3–32, and C. R. Kropf, "Unity and the Study of Eighteenth-Century Literature," *The Eighteenth Century*, 21 (1980), 25–40.

19. Geoffrey Tillotson, *On the Poetry of Pope* (Oxford: Clarendon, 1950), p. 44.

20. Jonathan Swift, *Dr. Swift to Mr. Pope, While He Was Writing the "Dunciad,"* 9–16.

persuasive whole.[21] More specifically, he would reserve the left-hand side of the page for a provisional draft, and add revisions on the right-hand side until the text was so ravaged that it had to be begun anew.[22] The revisions are almost invariably improvements, both in detail and in general; it is startling to read a draft version of a familiar poem and to notice how many of the finest passages do not yet exist. Pope wrote to Caryll in 1730, when he was well launched on the *Essay on Man*, "I have many fragments which I am beginning to put together, but nothing perfect, nor finished" (*Corr.* III, 155). The challenge then was to weld the fragments (or knead the loaf) until the result was indeed finished and perfect. Pope usually succeeded. The *Epistle to Arbuthnot*, Johnson rightly says, consists of "many fragments wrought into one design."[23]

"One design," in such a case, implies a convincing connection of parts rather than an organic unity of the whole. Transitions are all-important, as Pope implied when Wycherley, whose works he was helping to revise, grew nettled at the liberties Pope was taking:

> I must take some notice of what you say, of "My pains to make your dulness methodical;" and of your hint, that "The sprightliness of wit despises method." This is true enough, if by *wit* you mean no more than *fancy* or *conceit;* but in the better notion of *wit*, considered as propriety, surely *method* is not only necessary for perspicuity and harmony of parts, but gives beauty even to the minute and particular thoughts, which receive an additional advantage from those which precede or follow in their due place.
>
> (*Corr.* I, 34)

It needs to be emphasized that there is nothing inevitable about the final disposition of parts. Modern editors reject

21. See George Sherburn, "Pope at Work," in *Essays on the Eighteenth Century Presented to David Nichol Smith*, ed. James Sutherland and F. P. Wilson (Oxford, 1945, rept. New York: Russell and Russell, 1963), pp. 49–64.

22. See Maynard Mack's description of Pope's method of composition in *The Last and Greatest Art: Some Unpublished Poetical Manuscripts of Alexander Pope* (Newark: University of Delaware Press, 1984), p. 5.

23. *Lives*, III, 246.

Warburton's rearrangement of the poems which he renamed the *Moral Essays,* and have labored to show their imaginative coherence. But Warburton claims that Pope himself was impressed by the criticism that his "fine observations" were at first "so jumbled and confounded in one another, as if the several parts of a regular poem had been rolled up in tickets, drawn at random, and then set down as they arose."[24]

Pope's characteristic mode is the essayistic one, which Rosalie Colie describes so well in Locke's predecessors, a pose of direct conversation with the reader that could move freely between rambling frankness and formulaic conciseness. "There was . . . a screen of formality conventionally thin between the essayist and his readers, so that vernacular language and syntax could alternate with passages of remarkable balance and aphoristic detachment."[25] Just so in Pope; there is always a screen of formality, and its very thinness is a convention, whether carefully preserved as in the early *Essay on Criticism,* or breached frequently by colloquialisms as in the Horatian poems. Pope would never say with Locke, "I am not nice about phrases."[26] Phrases are the one thing that Pope is invariably nice about, and his aim is always to make them seem both striking and effortless. Thus he writes to Broome that his preliminary *Odyssey* translations are "sometimes too figurative and constrained," and that he is revising them accordingly: "I correct daily, and make them seem less corrected, that is, more easy, more fluent, more natural" (*Corr.* II, 320).

Pope tended to think of life itself as an aesthetic object, shaped by the same strife of opposites that informs everything in the universe:

> The lights and shades, whose well accorded strife
> Gives all the strength and colour of our life.
> (*Essay on Man* II.121–22)

24. Pope's *Works* (1751), III, 163.
25. "The Essayist in His *Essay,*" in *John Locke: Problems and Perspectives,* ed. John W. Yolton (Cambridge: Cambridge University Press, 1969), p. 238.
26. John Locke, *Essay concerning Human Understanding,* II.xxi.73.

In such a world, nothing could be less attractive than an art of rigid structure. Pope remarks in *Peri Bathous,* "Seldom are we without geniuses for still life, which they can work up and stiffen with incredible accuracy."[27] But nature by itself tends to produce random wildness, and the Augustan ideal is nature directed and shaped by art. "A work of this kind seems like a mighty tree which rises from the most vigorous seed, is improved with industry, flourishes, and produces the finest fruit; nature and art conspire to raise it; pleasure and profit join to make it valuable."[28] What is true of art as nature is equally true of nature as art, as Pope proclaims in his homage to Lord Burlington's estate:

> Still follow sense, of ev'ry art the soul,
> Parts answ'ring parts shall slide into a whole,
> Spontaneous beauties all around advance,
> Start ev'n from difficulty, strike from chance;
> Nature shall join you, time shall make it grow
> A work to wonder at—perhaps a Stowe.
>
> (*To Burlington* 65–70)

An art that derives from sense has room in it for spontaneity, for chance, and for growth over time. The result is not a fixed object but a living world through which one can wander. As Horace Walpole said of the progressive experience of Pope's garden: "The passing through the gloom from the grotto to the opening day, the retiring and again assembling shades, the dusky groves, the larger lawn, and the solemnity of the termination at the cypresses that lead up to his mother's tomb, are managed with exquisite judgment." Warton, who quotes this, names some famous gardens as "fine examples of practical poetry."[29]

Pope's poems, then, are collections of parts, joined together with skill but still distinct, and the fundamental unit

27. *Peri Bathous,* p. 53.
28. Preface to the *Iliad, TE* VII, 17.
29. Horace Walpole, *A History of the Modern Taste in Gardening* (1780), reprinted by Isabel W. V. Chase, *Horace Walpole: Gardenist* (Princeton: Princeton University Press, 1943), pp. 28–29; Warton, *Essay on . . . Pope,* II, 180–81, 186.

is the self-contained couplet. Even in his teens Pope was a master of the style that distributes the elements of experience into structured pattern. Reading Chaucer he found these lines:

> A wyf is Goddes yifte verraily;
> Alle othere manere yiftes hardily,
> As londes, rentes, pasture, or commune,
> Or moebles, alle been yiftes of Fortune,
> That passen as a shadwe upon a wal.
> But drede nat, if pleynly speke I shal,
> A wyf wol laste, and in thyn hous endure,
> Wel lenger than thee list, paraventure.[30]

The garrulity of Chaucer's narrator is antipathetic to Pope, particularly in a throwaway word like *paraventure* (made worse because it bears the rhyme). The list of fortune's gifts is needlessly circumstantial for his purpose. And the contrast between God and fortune needs to be not only sharpened, but also turned around to make the progression logical. So Pope adapts as follows:

> All other goods by fortune's hand are giv'n,
> A wife is the peculiar gift of heav'n:
> Vain fortune's favours, never at a stay,
> Like empty shadows, pass, and glide away;
> One solid comfort, our eternal wife,
> Abundantly supplies us all our life:
> This blessing lasts (if those who try, say true)
> As long as heart can wish—and longer too.
> *(January and May* 51–58)

Pope has seized here upon the haunting image of the shadow and made it rhetorically climactic (completing a couplet instead of beginning one), and he has dropped Chaucer's vivid "upon a wal" in preference for a phrase that emphasizes transitoriness, "and glide away." The rest of his changes are intended to bring out the wit, sometimes too nudgingly no

---

30. *The Merchant's Tale* 1311–18, in *The Works of Geoffrey Chaucer*, ed. F. N. Robinson (Boston: Houghton Mifflin, 1957), p. 116.

doubt: "peculiar gift," "eternal wife," "If those who try, say true," and the triumphant "and longer too."

This is very early Pope. Later on he would leave more to the reader's imagination. But this example shows how fully he had mastered Dryden's epigrammatic mode, which does not actually condense the thought, but rather expands it in clearly charted directions. Chaucer writes of Chaunticleer,

> But swich a joye was it to here hem synge,
> Whan that the brighte sonne gan to sprynge,
> In sweete accord, "My lief is faren in londe!"
> For thilke tyme, as I have understonde,
> Beestes and briddes koude speke and synge.[31]

Dryden keeps the (almost inevitable) rhyme on *sing* and *spring*, but generalizes "the brighte sonne" to "the day," adds a fine line that describes Chaunticleer's singing, and ends with Augustan whimsy:

> But oh! what joy it was to hear him sing
> In summer, when the day began to spring,
> Stretching his neck, and warbling in his throat,
> *Solus cum sola*, then was all his note.
> For in the days of yore, the birds of parts
> Were bred to speak, and sing, and learn the lib'ral arts.[32]

As there are men of parts, so also birds of parts, and then the rhyme on "lib'ral arts" readily suggests itself. Chaucer's beast fable has been turned into a Restoration *jeu d'esprit*, with added material that insists on the Restoration mood:

> Ardent in love, outrageous in his play,
> He feathered her a hundred times a day.
>   (69–70)

This is no fowl, but Rochester or Charles II in avian disguise.

As he developed his own style Pope retained this kind of

31. Geoffrey Chaucer, *The Nun's Priest's Tale* 2877–81, p. 200 in Robinson's edition.

32. *The Cock and the Fox: or, The Tale of the Nun's Priest, from Chaucer,* 87–92.

wit, but he regularly—one might say obsessively—shaped the thought to fit not only into the paired lines, but also into balanced half-lines. There is usually a marked caesura at the middle of the line, and enjambment almost never carries the syntax from one line to the next. For as Dryden said, "The excellence and dignity of [rhyme] were never fully known till Mr. Waller taught it; he first made writing easily an art; first showed us to conclude the sense most commonly in distichs; which, in the verse of those before him, runs on for so many lines together that the reader is out of breath to overtake it."[33] On the very rare occasions when these rules are violated, the reader is meant to be surprised by an expressive effect:

> One tide of glory, one unclouded blaze,
> O'erflow thy courts: the LIGHT HIMSELF shall shine
> Revealed; and God's eternal day be thine!
> > *(Messiah* 102–4)

> Chariots on chariots roll; the clashing spokes
> Shock; while the maddening steeds break short their yokes.
> > *(Iliad* XVI.444–45)

Whatever variations may occur within a couplet, the second line is invariably a true conclusion; Pope never allows the thought to spill from one couplet into the next, as Chaucer and Donne regularly do.

More often than is usually recognized, the couplet works to suppress or modify the kind of "poeticalness" that other eras have sought. By themselves, lines like these are startling in their energy and metrical freedom:

> And the pale ghosts start at the flash of day!

> The sick'ning stars fade off th' ethereal plain.

Put back into their couplets, they are still memorable lines, but firmly tied down and, as it were, surrounded:

---

33. John Dryden, "To Roger, Earl of Orrery," prefixed to *The Rival Ladies* (1664), in *Of Dramatic Poesy and Other Critical Essays*, ed. George Watson (London: Everyman, 1962), I, 7.

Earth shakes her nodding tow'rs, the ground gives way;
And the pale ghosts start at the flash of day!
                              (*Rape of the Lock* V.51–52)

As one by one, at dread Medea's strain,
The sick'ning stars fade off th' ethereal plain.
                              (*Dunciad* IV.635–36)

One may be surprised to find Pope saying that a great poet should "tear my heart," but replaced in context the phrase seems almost routine:

Enrage, compose, with more than magic art,
With pity, and with terror, tear my heart.
                              (*Epistle* II.i.344–45)

An admirer in 1731, recalling Pope's advent on the literary scene "with all the fire of youth and strength of years," emphasized especially the regularity of his art:

How just the turns! how regular the draught!
How smooth the language! how refined the thought![34]

The half-lines here are more mechanical than Pope's could ever be, but they do reflect the norm of Popean versification as he and his readers understood it.

Pope's fondness for making the sound echo the sense has always been admired. Very possibly he did seek in poetry a doubling of "signification," in which the meaning is corroborated by the sound.[35] But in fact sound effects aren't usually noticed one way or the other unless the context expressly calls attention to them. Daniel Webb in 1762 quotes from the *Essay on Man*—

Is it for thee the lark ascends and sings?
Joy tunes his voice, joy elevates his wings—

---

34. An anonymous *Progress of Poetry,* in *The Flower-Piece: A Collection of Miscellany Poems* (1731), p. 139. A poem in answer to this one refers to the author as an "ingenious Lady" (p. 141).

35. See Dean T. Mace, "The Doctrine of Sound and Sense in Augustan Poetic Theory," *Review of English Studies,* n.s. 2 (1951), 129–39.

and notices that there are five *s* sounds in the first line and six in the second: "Here, instead of the melting warble of a lark, we have the dissonant hissing of a serpent."[36] But surely no one hears the serpent. Apart from occasional set pieces in which rocks crash and waves murmur, the goal seems to be musical grace rather than literal mimicry. Pope quotes Catullus in a letter and remarks, "One sees the ancients are often content with saying a very plain thing, if it be but very natural. The last of these lines [*Desideratoque acquiescimus lecto*] has a lazy indolent flow of languishing numbers, that perfectly corresponds with the weariness and sense of repose described in it" (*Corr.* II, 289).

Particularly in the early poems, Pope spares no effort to intensify alliterative pleasure. In "The silver eel, in shining volumes rolled" (*Windsor-Forest* 143), not only is the *l* sound repeated four times, but each time in an accented syllable, and with a progression of increasingly open vowels: *il, eel, ol, oll.* Whatever it may imply about meaning, alliteration works to tie the line together. In "Fields ever fresh, and groves for ever green" (*Winter* 72), there is obvious alliteration in *fields, fresh* and *groves, green,* and also the *v* in *ever, groves, ever* that unifies the two half-lines. But these are only devices. What gives the line its life is the shifting stress on *ever,* which suddenly gets the main emphasis: "Fíelds ever frésh, and gróves for éver gréen." So also in "Thin trees arise that shun each other's shade" (*Windsor-Forest* 22), the sequence *thin, shun, shade* has consonance and then alliteration, as the echo moves from the final consonant to the initial one.[37] This is not really a matter to be intellectualized; the reader simply feels the joining in separation that the line describes. It was for this kind of mastery that Johnson declared, "Sir, a thousand years

36. *Essay on Man* III.31–32; Webb, *Remarks on the Beauties of Poetry* (1762), p. 28.

37. This line and many others are analyzed by Percy G. Adams, *Graces of Harmony: Alliteration, Assonance, and Consonance in Eighteenth-Century British Poetry* (Athens: University of Georgia Press, 1977), ch. 3.

may elapse before there shall appear another man with a power of versification equal to that of Pope."[38]

If *concordia discors* is to be a persuasive ideal, it has to work at a deeper level than the conceptual one where scholars usually locate it. In a long note at the beginning of *Odyssey* XIV discussing Homer's mastery of "numbers," Pope makes an interesting comment on Denham's famous couplet:

> I will conclude this note with observing what Mr. Dryden says of these two lines from *Cooper's Hill*,
>
> > Though deep, yet clear, though gentle, yet not dull,
> > Strong without rage, without o'erflowing full.
>
> "There are few (says he) who make verses, that have observed the sweetness of these lines, and fewer who can find the reason of it." . . . I doubt not but the chief sweetness arises from the judicious and harmonious pauses of the several periods of the verses; not to mention the happy choice of the words, in which there is scarce one rough consonant, many liquids, and those liquids softened with a multitude of vowels.
>
> (*TE* X, 34)

Not least among the effects of poetry is sensory pleasure. One might say that Denham and Pope take as a norm what for later poets, Elizabeth Bishop for instance, can only be a passing conceit: "The waves are running in verses this fine morning."[39]

There are some things that this superbly structured form cannot do. It cannot present a loose, rambling narrative, and it cannot convey the incoherent way in which much of life is in fact experienced. Everything comes to us preformed, arranged as Wimsatt says "with atomic care."[40] In a travel book

---

38. James Boswell, *Life of Samuel Johnson*, ed. G. B. Hill, rev. L. F. Powell (Oxford: Clarendon, 1934), IV, 46 (under 1781).

39. *Invitation to Miss Marianne Moore*, in Elizabeth Bishop, *The Complete Poems, 1927–1979* (New York: Farrar, Straus and Giroux, 1983), p. 82.

40. W. K. Wimsatt, Jr., "Rhetoric and Poems: The Example of Swift," in *The Author in His Work*, ed. Louis L. Martz and Aubrey Williams (New Haven:

Pope found the following description of Nova Zembla in the Arctic:

> Near to the land . . . some greater ice-mountains are seen . . . that stand firm on the shore, and never melt at bottom, but increase every year higher and higher, by reason of the snow that falls on them, and then rain that freezes and then snow again alternately; and after this manner the icy-hills increase yearly, and are never melted by the heat of the sun at the top. . . . The true rocks looked fiery, and the sun shined pale upon them, the snow giving the air a bright reflection. . . . Where the ice is fixed upon the sea, you see a snow-white brightness in the skies, as if the sun shined, for the snow is reflected by the air.[41]

Pope was evidently strongly drawn to this description, and he directly borrows the gradual increase of snow, the pale sun, the bright sky, and the "lightnings" elsewhere described. But in his version everything is stabilized and, as it were, pre-interpreted:

> So Zembla's rocks (the beauteous work of frost)
> Rise white in air, and glitter o'er the coast;
> Pale suns, unfelt, at distance roll away,
> And on th' impassive ice the lightnings play:
> Eternal snows the growing mass supply,
> Till the bright mountains prop th' incumbent sky:
> As Atlas fixed, each hoary pile appears,
> The gathered winter of a thousand years.
>   (*The Temple of Fame* 53–60)

One reason why Thomson chose blank verse for his *Seasons* was surely to recover a sense of process as opposed to completion.[42]

To say that a poetic passage is structured is not to say that

---

Yale University Press, 1978), p. 233. Wimsatt contrasts with Pope Swift's short couplets, "pieces of stock language laid together in bundles, clattering parallels" (p. 235).

41. F. Marten's *Observations Made in Greenland and Other Northern Countries,* in a 1711 book of voyages; quoted in *TE* II, 411.

42. See Ralph Cohen, *The Unfolding of "The Seasons": A Study of James Thomson's Poem* (Baltimore: Johns Hopkins University Press, 1970).

it lacks vividness and energy, or that a series of couplets may not display, in A. D. Nuttall's fine expression, "a springing order endlessly branching into new life."[43] Vividness and energy, in fact, were precisely what the notorious poetic diction was supposed to contribute. Leaving aside specialized cases like "fleecy care,"[44] what Pope meant by poetic diction was condensed metaphor, as he explained in his preface to Homer:

> We acknowledge him the father of poetical diction, the first who taught that language of the gods to men. His expression is like the colouring of some great masters, which discovers itself to be laid on boldly, and executed with rapidity. It is indeed the strongest and most glowing imaginable, and touched with the greatest spirit. Aristotle had reason to say, he was the only poet who had found out living words; there are in him more daring figures and metaphors than in any good author whatever.
>
> (*TE* VII, 9–10)

Pope goes on to talk about Homer's epithets as able to conjure up pictures, and "in some measure to thicken the images." This thickening is as much a matter of verbal density as of pictorial; Patricia Meyer Spacks rightly says that Pope is "a poet of imagery without being primarily a poet of the visual."[45]

Pope's contemporaries relished these effects. Wakefield greatly admires the way in which Pope packs his lines with energy, and sometimes proposes turning up the volume still further:

> And break upon thee in a flood of day.

43. *Pope's "Essay on Man"* (London: Allen & Unwin, 1984), p. 28.

44. In such cases Pope is usually invoking a Latin root to broaden the range of meaning; in this instance, *care* derives from the Latin *cura*, which greatly extends its implications. See Tillotson, *On the Poetry of Pope*, p. 74, and more generally the same author's *Augustan Poetic Diction* (London: Athlone, 1964).

45. *An Argument of Images: The Poetry of Alexander Pope* (Cambridge, Mass.: Harvard University Press, 1971), p. 11.

A magnificent verse; but susceptible of improvement, perhaps by the substitution of a more forcible expression:

And *burst* upon thee in a flood of day.[46]

Spence's commentary on Pope's *Odyssey* is full of praise for the epithets, and Warton gives revealing praise to some lines in the *Essay on Man* that might seem unremarkable to a modern reader:

> He from the wond'ring furrow called the food,
> Taught to command the fire, control the flood,
> Draw forth the monsters of th' abyss profound,
> Or fetch th' aerial eagle to the ground.
> (III.219–22)

A finer example can perhaps scarce be given of a compact and comprehensive style. The manner in which the four elements were subdued is comprised in these four lines alone. . . . There is not an useless word in this passage; there are but three epithets, *wondering, profound, aerial;* and they are placed precisely with the very substantive that is of most consequence: if there had been epithets joined with the other substantives, it would have weakened the nervousness of the sentence. This was a secret of versification Pope well understood, and hath often practised with peculiar success.[47]

The purpose of the well-chosen epithet is the same as that of the well-structured couplet: using suggestive conciseness to stimulate the reader's ideas. In Walter Harte's words,

> Transitions must be quick, and yet designed,
> Not made to fill, but just retain the mind:
> And similes, like meteors of the night,
> Just give one flash of momentary light.[48]

Pope's ability to compress a thought was proverbial; Swift said wryly that he could "in one couplet fix / More sense than

---

46. Gilbert Wakefield, *Observations on Pope* (1796), p. 22, quoting *Messiah* 98.

47. *Essay on . . . Pope*, II, 106.

48. *An Essay on Satire, Particularly on the Dunciad* (1730), p. 9.

I can do in six."[49] Pope always obeys the rule to "show no mercy to an empty line" (*Epistle* II.ii.175), and his contemporaries admired conciseness so much that they praise lines that look very ordinary today.

> There is no greater symptom of weakness in a writer, than his being apt to say *a little in a great deal;* as nothing is more strong and emphatical, than to say *a great deal in a little.* Hence the force and emphasis of this line of Mr. Pope.
>
>> Oh every sacred name in one, my friend!
>
> And of this,
>
>> The great, the good; your father and your king.[50]

Some of Pope's lines have literally become proverbs, few users of which have any idea that they are Pope's or even that they are verse: "Hope springs eternal in the human breast" (*Essay on Man* I.95), "The proper study of mankind is man" (II.2), "An honest man's the noblest work of God" (IV.248), "A little learning is a dang'rous thing" (*Essay on Criticism* 215), "To err is human, to forgive, divine" (525), "Fools rush in where angels fear to tread" (625). These are indeed instances of what oft was thought but ne'er so well expressed, as is obvious in a distinguished historian's misquotation: "He cannot attempt to master the field, and should not be intimidated by that most idiotic of proverbs that a little knowledge is a dangerous thing."[51] Pope's objection is not to knowledge, of which a little is better than none, but to learning, which can certainly be dangerous when misconceived and misapplied.

The real significance of a proverblike line is in the context that it brings into focus, not the detachable aphorism. Consider the context of "Hope springs eternal":

49. Jonathan Swift, *Verses on the Death of Dr. Swift,* 49–50. Johnson contradicted this view of Pope (Boswell's *Journal of a Tour to the Hebrides,* 23 Oct. 1773), but he was probably thinking of "sense" as logical exposition rather than as condensed imagery.

50. Spence, *Essay on Pope's Odyssey,* II, 112–13, citing *Odyssey* XXII.226 and II.54.

51. Lawrence Stone, *The Past and the Present* (Boston: Routledge & Kegan Paul, 1981), p. 20.

> Hope humbly then; with trembling pinions soar;
> Wait the great teacher Death, and God adore!
> What future bliss, he gives thee not to know,
> But gives that hope to be thy blessing now.
> Hope springs eternal in the human breast:
> Man never is, but always to be blest:
> The soul, uneasy and confined from home,
> Rests and expatiates in a life to come.
>
> (*Essay on Man* I.91–98)

Hope works to make the future seem more open than it really is. If you knew what was going to happen you might not be able to bear it. So hope is inseparable from ignorance; it springs eternal, but not with the greeting-card optimism that familiarity has made of Pope's line. We hope for what we don't know because we can't bear what we do know. As a passage a few lines earlier chillingly puts it, heaven hides the book of fate because otherwise no one could "suffer Being here below":

> The lamb thy riot dooms to bleed today,
> Had he thy reason, would he skip and play?
> Pleased to the last, he crops the flow'ry food,
> And licks the hand just raised to shed his blood.
>
> (81–84)

Augustan morality and empiricist philosophy both insist that we must learn from experience. But the point about hope is that it refuses to do so, and that we would be miserable (perhaps even suicidal) if it did. Much that happens in human life represents, in Johnson's phrase, the triumph of hope over experience. Considered in this light, hope is necessarily humble (the meter stresses *humbly,* not *hope,* in "Hope humbly then") and must tremble as well as soar. Death is the great teacher because once we are dead, we will at last know what the future holds, or rather, distinctions between present and future will cease to matter.

Reflections like these take us a long way from the blithe *concordia* and seductive melody of the early Pope. Even considered merely as technique, his melody had become so familiar as to be no longer his. As Warton saw it in 1756,

Upon the whole, the principal merit of the Pastorals of Pope consists in their correct and musical versification; musical, to a degree of which rhyme could hardly be thought capable: and in giving the first specimen of that harmony in English verse, which is now become indispensably necessary; and which has so forcibly and universally influenced the public ear, as to have rendered every moderate rhymer melodious.[52]

Alliteration and elevated imagery were the stock in trade of journeymen like Blackmore and Budgell, often made more despicable by political sycophancy.

> What? like Sir Richard, rumbling, rough and fierce,
> With ARMS, and GEORGE, and BRUNSWICK crowd the
>   verse?
> Rend with tremendous sound your ears asunder,
> With gun, drum, trumpet, blunderbuss and thunder?
> Or nobly wild, with Budgell's fire and force,
> Paint angels trembling round his falling horse?
>   (*Satire* II.i.23–28)

Likewise the "liquids" that Pope praised in *Cooper's Hill* had learned to grovel in a princess's service: "Lull with Amelia's liquid name the nine" (31). Pastoral diction becomes mere diction, as it is for the Grub Street poet "lulled by soft zephyrs through the broken pane" (*To Arbuthnot* 42).

The heroic couplet was "heroic" because of its past history, particularly in its affinity with the French alexandrine couplet, itself intended to echo the classical hexameter. In almost everything Pope wrote after the 1717 *Works* it mutates into the unheroic or antiheroic couplet. Parallelism and alliteration persist, but usually to stress ironic disparity rather than to assert the concord of things: "Now trips a lady, and now struts a Lord" (*To Arbuthnot* 329); "Gross as her sire, and as her mother grave" (*Dunciad* I.14); "With thunder rumbling from the mustard bowl" (II.226); "As verse, or prose, infuse the drowsy God" (II.396). It is not surprising that Pope was amused by Isaac Hawkins Browne's *Imitation of Mr. Pope's Style*, a paean to tobacco in resolutely structured couplets:

52. *Essay on . . . Pope*, I, 10.

> Blest leaf, whose aromatic gales dispense
> To templars modesty; to parsons, sense.
> (So raptured priests, at famed Dodona's shrine,
> Drink inspiration from the steam divine). . . .
> Rest to the weary, to the hungry, food;
> The last kind refuge of the wise and good.[53]

Pope's modern admirers are much likelier than he was to celebrate the couplet as an ontological statement rather than as a rhetorical device.

Just as the couplet no longer claims (if it ever did) to mirror the harmony of things, so Pope's poems grow directly from his personal preoccupations instead of asserting a unity beyond themselves. The seams between the separate parts are more obvious now, because the shifts of mood and indeed of conviction are so often drastic.[54] *Windsor-Forest* speaks throughout with elevated dignity, whereas in the satires, as Warton says, "Every species of sarcasm and mode of style are here alternately employed; ridicule, reasoning, irony, mirth, seriousness, lamentation, laughter, familiar imagery, and highly poetical painting."[55] What might once have been a drawback now becomes a strength: the blank verse of Milton or Wordsworth compels steady forward movement, but Pope's disjunct couplets hold incommensurable elements in uneasy suspension.

Even Pope's rhymes contribute to this effect. Wimsatt has shown how often they create an alogical contrast that plays off against the similarity of sound, and Kenner brilliantly argues that this is felt to be a falling away from "normal" rhymes that confirm meaning instead of contradicting it.[56]

53. *Of Smoking: Four Poems* (1736), pp. 7–8. Spence reports Pope's approval: *Observations, Anecdotes, and Characters of Books and Men,* ed. James M. Osborn (Oxford: Clarendon, 1966), I, 172, 214.

54. See Thomas R. Edwards, "Visible Poetry: Pope and Modern Criticism," in *Twentieth-Century Literature in Retrospect,* ed. Reuben A. Brower (Cambridge, Mass.: Harvard University Press, 1971), pp. 299–321.

55. Warton's edition of Pope's *Works* (1797), I, lx, referring to the *Epilogue to the Satires.*

56. W. K. Wimsatt, Jr., "One Relation of Rhyme to Reason," in *The Verbal Icon: Studies in the Meaning of Poetry* (New York: Noonday, 1962), pp. 153–66;

One of Pope's favorite rhymes in his later work is *hurled, world,* which he probably picked up from Creech's translation of Lucretius:

> Perhaps thou soon shalt see the sinking world
> With strong convulsions to confusion hurled.[57]

The *Essay on Man* imagines the appalling consequences if prideful man were allowed to alter the system of things:

> Let ruling angels from their spheres be hurled,
> Being on being wrecked, and world on world.
> (I.253–54)

But of course it is really man, not the world, who is frighteningly unstable:

> Sole judge of truth, in endless error hurled:
> The glory, jest, and riddle of the world!
> (II.17–18)

The same rhyme returns in the apostrophe to the complacent Codrus in *To Arbuthnot:*

> Let peals of laughter, Codrus! round thee break,
> Thou unconcerned canst hear the mighty crack.
> Pit, box and gall'ry in convulsions hurled,
> Thou stand'st unshook amidst a bursting world.
> (85–88)

One could hardly stand unshaken if the world were truly bursting, but like the curtain fall at the end of the *Dunciad,* this is only the mimic world of the theater, and the "bursting" is an explosion of laughter at Codrus's expense.

The *Essay on Man* is sufficient evidence that Pope went on believing in universal order, but also that he came to doubt man's ability to grasp and understand it. For the most part

---

Hugh Kenner, "Pope's Reasonable Rhymes," *Journal of English Literary History,* 41 (1974), 74–88. Kenner sees the tension between "normal" and conflicting rhymes as beginning in *The Rape of The Lock.*

57. Book V, lines 113–14, quoted by Miriam Leranbaum, *Alexander Pope's "Opus Magnum,"* 1729–1744 (Oxford: Clarendon, 1977), p. 53.

his late poems operate very differently, using a less obtrusive kind of couplet to ponder human folly rather than to assert profound connections.

> "Odious! in woollen! 'twould a saint provoke,"
> (Were the last words that poor Narcissa spoke)
> "No, let a charming chintz, and Brussels lace
> Wrap my cold limbs, and shade my lifeless face:
> One would not, sure, be frightful when one's dead—
> And—Betty—give this cheek a little red."
>   Old politicians chew on wisdom past,
> And totter on in bus'ness to the last;
> As weak, as earnest, and as gravely out,
> As sober Lanesb'row dancing in the gout.
>   (*To Cobham* 242–51)

As usual the characters are drawn from life, and Pope elaborates their stories in footnotes. The two verse paragraphs are thrown together without connection as instances of human folly, expressed in familiar language both by the persons themselves ("odious," "charming") and by the poet ("chew on wisdom"). But beneath the sarcasm lies a vision of death more disturbingly real than any in *Eloisa to Abelard* or the *Unfortunate Lady*. We will all indeed be frightful when we're dead.

9

Literature and Culture

Pope was unquestionably the major poet of his century, both in the quality of his verse and in the range of his achievement. Nonetheless, as I have tried to show, his position was in many ways embattled rather than triumphant, uneasily confronting problems that have proved endemic in the modern world. In the last two chapters we have considered the local implications of stooping to truth; I want to conclude by speculating more largely about a notable fact of Pope's literary generation, its inability to salvage the much-admired classical genres. A younger critic like Samuel Johnson could simply dismiss genre as irrelevant to the complexity of life,[1] but Pope was not prepared to do that. For him it was a painful discovery that the great literary forms had ceased to be effective.

As is well known, Pope had Virgil, Spenser, and Milton in mind when he began his career with pastorals, moved in *Windsor-Forest* to a longer form with political implications, and aspired to attempt in due course a great national epic. This progression was explicitly recommended by Wycherley at the end of *To Mr. Pope on His Pastorals*, printed in the first volume of Pope's 1717 *Works*. Wycherley compares Pope with Virgil,

> Whose muse did once, like thine, in plains delight;
> Thine shall, like his, soon take a higher flight;
> So larks, which first from lowly fields arise,
> Mount by degrees, and reach at last the skies.

---

1. I examine Johnson's skepticism about pastoral and epic in *The Uses of Johnson's Criticism* (Charlottesville: University Press of Virginia, 1976), ch. 4.

The 1717 book already contained an immortal mock-epic, *The Rape of the Lock*, and Pope would later write a much larger and stranger one in *The Dunciad*. He was soon to immerse himself in a decade's labor translating the Homeric epics into English. But his own epic never came into existence, even though epic was still widely regarded as the highest of all literary kinds.

We shall return presently to the mystery of the missing epic. First, the whole question of genre deserves reflection. Part of the difficulty was that the famous genres were simply too well known, too heavily encrusted with rules and precedents. This can happen even to so various and open ended a form as the novel, for as Alastair Fowler says, "The older 'appropriate forms' of the novel can now be handled with so much consciousness of their conventions that they may have suffered the death of definition."[2] In Pope's time this normal exhaustion of forms was exacerbated by piety toward the immortal classics:

> Still green with bays each ancient altar stands,
> Above the reach of sacrilegious hands.
>   (*Essay on Criticism* 181–82)

Any attempt to outgo them might seem futile as well as presumptuous.

In addition, people were beginning to suspect that modern social conditions were hostile to the old genres. The three main forms in the medieval "wheel of Virgil" were pastoral, georgic, and heroic, all of which had appealed to Renaissance poets but now seemed bookish and artificial (Pope never wrote pastorals after his teens). Hobbes, with his interest in social determinants, developed a six-part schema based on the "three regions of mankind," which he identified as "court, city and country," terms that were still in use in Pope's time. Each of the three regions has a narrative and a dramatic genre, making six in all: for the court, epic and tragedy; for

2. *Kinds of Literature: An Introduction to the Theory of Genres and Modes* (Cambridge, Mass.: Harvard University Press, 1982), p. 165.

the city, satire and comedy; for the country, pastoral and pastoral comedy.[3] Pope saw the "city" as swallowing up the rest of British culture, and he was largely right, whatever one may think about the Lake Poets' reaction a century later. And indeed all four of Hobbes's court and country categories withered away at just this time, or else joined absurdly in the hands of city writers who had no interest in their old meanings:

> How tragedy and comedy embrace;
> How farce and epic get a jumbled race.
> (*Dunciad* I.69–70)

In hindsight we can see the genres as intermingling,[4] new ones emerging from the union of the old. The novel was one product of the embrace of tragedy and comedy, and *The Rape of the Lock* might even be called a union of farce and epic. But from Pope's point of view the old stable boundaries were collapsing disastrously, leaving a shoreless sea of literary possibility that seemed altogether distressing. For as Fowler says, living genres are a positive support to a writer. "They offer room, as one might say, for him to write in—a habitation of mediated definiteness; a proportioned mental space; a literary matrix by which to order his experience during composition."[5] And dependence on genre has as much to do with readers as with writers, since they too are made comfortable

---

3. Thomas Hobbes, *The Answer of Mr. Hobbes to Sir William Davenant's Preface before Gondibert*, in *Critical Essays of the Seventeenth Century*, ed. Joel E. Spingarn (Oxford: Clarendon, 1909), II, 55. Fowler, *Kinds of Literature*, pp. 240–41, discusses both Hobbes and the wheel of Virgil.

4. See Ralph Cohen, "On the Interrelations of Eighteenth-Century Literary Forms," in *New Approaches to Eighteenth-Century Literature*, ed. Phillip Harth (New York: Columbia University Press, 1974), pp. 33–78. A caution is necessary against two claims Cohen makes but does not prove: that "the premise of social, political, and natural variety had as its basis God's plenitude and the implicit harmony underlying the universe" (p. 41); and that "eighteenth-century critics . . . saw the forms as hierarchical, comprehensively embodied or capable of being harmoniously embodied in the drama or epic" (p. 51). *Concordia* and hierarchy were precisely the ideals which the most interesting writers were beginning to find unrealizable.

5. *Kinds of Literature*, p. 31.

by the mediation, proportion, and matrix. Not until the Romantics were works of literature seriously proposed as heterocosms, self-enclosed worlds of private invention.[6] The older genres had been thought of as microcosms, imitations in little of the great world to which they held up their mirrors. "Such as it is," Rosalie Colie says, "the genre-system of the Renaissance offers us not a second world but an array of ways to look at the real world, offers us a special way to make of culture a *common place*."[7] The novel developed to exploit this disappearance of a common place: Fielding's playful mingling of genres in his comic prose epic *Tom Jones;* Richardson's joining of irreconcilable tragic, comic, and epic perspectives in *Clarissa;* Smollett's incommensurable viewpoints in *Humphrey Clinker;* Sterne's collapsing of reality into private consciousness in *Tristram Shandy.*

All of this lay in the future when Pope was writing, and it should not be surprising that he and Swift were consistently drawn to satire. For satire is the one form that regularly invokes—indeed, is parasitical upon—a "real" world, which writer and reader both inhabit. In Sheldon Sacks's formulation, "A satire is a work organized so that it ridicules objects external to the fictional world created in it."[8] More than that, satire openly tries to influence the world of external things, so that its existence is irrevocably grounded there and it can only partly survive into a later and different world. It is political in the deepest sense, not just commenting on particular events but also seeking to alter the social conditions that produce them. In the academic division of labor of the 1950s and 1960s, critics could celebrate the works of Swift and Pope as timeless universal wisdom, even while scholars were indus-

6. See M. H. Abrams, "The Poem as Heterocosm," in *The Mirror and the Lamp: Romantic Theory and the Critical Tradition* (New York: Norton, 1958), pp. 272–85. The whole of Abrams's magisterial *Natural Supernaturalism: Tradition and Revolution in Romantic Literature* (New York: Norton, 1971) is also relevant here.

7. *The Resources of Kind: Genre-Theory in the Renaissance* (Berkeley: University of California Press, 1973), p. 119.

8. *Fiction and the Shape of Belief* (Berkeley: University of California Press, 1967), p. 26.

triously amassing information on the hundreds of persons satirized in them. Nowadays we are in a better position to understand the time-bound nature of all literary achievement, and to see in the dilemmas of eighteenth-century writers clear adumbrations of our own.

Before we pursue the problem of genre further, we need to reflect upon the symbols and metaphors upon which poetry is built. As Mack splendidly demonstrates in "Wit and Poetry and Pope," there is surprisingly little metaphor in Pope, but rather a dazzling array of syntactic and aural effects that take its place.[9] "Like a green field reflected in a calm and perfectly transparent lake," Coleridge says, "the image is distinguished from the reality only by its greater softness and lustre."[10] For Pope a reflection is always different from the thing reflected, and the observer is expected to make a conscious comparison between the two, as is stated clearly in *An Essay on Homer's Battles:*

> A comparison . . . is at once correspondent to, and differing from the subject. Those critics who fancy that the use of comparisons distracts the attention, and draws it from the first image which should most employ it (as that we lose the idea of the battle itself, while we are led by a simile to that of a deluge or a storm): those, I say, may as well imagine we lose the thought of the sun, when we see his reflection in the water; where he appears more distinctly, and is contemplated more at ease than if we gazed directly at his beams. For it is with the eye of the imagination as it is with our corporeal eye, it must sometimes be taken off from the object in order to see it the better.
>
> (*TE* VII, 254)

Even in Pope's earliest poems, it is always clear that one thing is *like* another without any occult identity being presumed:

9. Maynard Mack, "Wit and Poetry and Pope: Some Observations on His Imagery," in *Eighteenth-Century English Literature: Modern Essays in Criticism,* ed. James L. Clifford (New York: Oxford University Press, 1959), p. 25.

10. Samuel Taylor Coleridge, *Biographia Literaria,* ed. J. Shawcross (London: Oxford University Press, 1907), II, 121 (ch. 22).

> So when the nightingale to rest removes,
> The thrush may chant to the forsaken groves,
> But, charmed to silence, listens while she sings,
> And all th' aerial audience clap their wings.
>
> (*Spring* 13–16)

Pope the thrush sings while Trumbull the nightingale is silent, and the birds appreciatively clap their wings. But this is neither a metaphysical conceit (how are two lovers like a pair of compasses?) nor a Romantic symbol (the wind as breath of being). Instead the two birds are briefly allegorized, as in a fable, and then the other birds are imagined as responding; the clapping sound is surely the familiar whir of wings. I take Pope to be saying that the rustle of wings is *like* applause for Trumbull's eloquence, or that it is *as if* the birds were applauding.

Pope plumed himself on deleting wolves from his pastorals because there were no longer wolves in England. But he mingles plenty of conventional pastoral images with his references to modern persons:

> Inspire me Phoebus, in my Delia's praise,
> With Waller's strains, or Granville's moving lays!
> A milk-white bull shall at your altars stand,
> That threats a fight, and spurns the rising sand.
>
> (*Spring* 45–48)

Leslie Stephen comments with some justice, "Granville would certainly not have felt more surprised at meeting a wolf than at seeing a milk-white bull sacrificed to Phoebus on the banks of the Thames."[11] The trappings of Renaissance pastoral are rather casually displayed, and are always in danger of looking ridiculous. The whole point of using images is to explain or illuminate one thing by a different thing, and the difficulty with the wolves and bull is that they are *too* literal: wolves have really lived in England (but do not now), and bulls still do live in England (but not sacrificial ones).

One of Pope's principal complaints against Dulness, long afterward, was that it inspired metaphorical chaos.

---

11. *Alexander Pope* (New York: Harper, 1902), p. 24.

> There motley images her fancy strike,
> Figures ill-paired, and similes unlike.
> She sees a mob of metaphors advance,
> Pleased with the madness of the mazy dance.
> (*Dunciad* I.65–68)

Similes are worthless if the likeness is not obvious, and confused metaphors are like a "mob," a telling analogy to subversion of social hierarchy. The connection with bad writing is explicit in the *Dunciad*, which is pervaded by images of a riotous mob or crowd.[12] But so long as signifier and signified are kept firmly apart, invention can operate freely.

> Through Lud's famed gates, along the well-known Fleet
> Rolls the black troop, and overshades the street,
> Till show'rs of sermons, characters, essays,
> In circling fleeces whiten all the ways:
> So clouds replenished from some bog below
> Mount in dark volumes, and descend in snow.
> (*Dunciad* II.359–64)

The image of the snowing pamphlets is a pure fantasy that acknowledges itself to be fantastic, but it has an intelligible basis in the fact that snow is formed from atmospheric moisture, so that something apparently beautiful ("fleeces whiten") arises from low sources ("some bog below"). The pun on *volumes* clinches the connection. But Pope objects to a similar metaphor when it is solemn rather than playful, inadvertently diminishes what ought to be great, and goes on too long:

> The skies, whose spreading volumes scarce have room,
> Spun thin, and wove in nature's finest loom,
> The new-born world in their soft lap embraced,
> And all around their starry mantle cast.

Thus Blackmore in *Prince Arthur;* Pope comments, much as Johnson would on Cowley's conceits, "When a true genius

---

12. See Pat Rogers, *Hacks and Dunces: Pope, Swift and Grub Street* (London: Methuen, 1980), pp. 99–126. On *mob* see p. 78 above.

looks upon the sky, he immediately catches the idea of a piece of blue lutestring or a child's mantle."[13]

"The worst fault of any language," says Spence, "is ambiguity."[14] One can imagine how he would have stared at Empson's *Seven Types of Ambiguity*. What Spence wants from a metaphor is "to make language visible" (I, 38), which is accomplished by carefully controlling the range and fit of the terms compared. "To say *the god of light was driving his car, down the steep of heaven* (as Mr. Pope somewhere expresses it) is metaphorical; to say *the sun is setting*, is proper: but should one say, *The sun is setting with sloping wheels*, this would be neither metaphorical nor proper, nor could it raise any thing in the mind, but a confusion of ideas" (I, 31). On the "Oft in her glass" lines in *Windsor-Forest*, Wakefield comments approvingly, "The description is at once physically correct and poetically rich."[15] A famous instance of a simile with perfect fit is Pope's exemplification of "A little learning is a dang'rous thing" (*Essay on Criticism* 215):

> Fired at first sight with what the muse imparts,
> In fearless youth we tempt the heights of arts,
> While from the bounded level of our mind
> Short views we take, nor see the lengths behind,
> But more advanced, behold with strange surprise
> New, distant scenes of endless science rise!
> So pleased at first, the tow'ring Alps we try,
> Mount o'er the vales, and seem to tread the sky;
> Th' eternal snows appear already past,
> And the first clouds and mountains seem the last:
> But those attained, we tremble to survey
> The growing labours of the lengthened way,
> Th' increasing prospect tires our wand'ring eyes,
> Hills peep o'er hills, and Alps on Alps arise!
>
> (219–32)

13. *Peri Bathous: Of the Art of Sinking in Poetry* (1728), in *Literary Criticism of Alexander Pope*, ed. Bertrand A. Goldgar (Lincoln: University of Nebraska Press, 1965), p. 50.

14. Joseph Spence, *An Essay on Pope's Odyssey* (1726), II, 26.

15. Gilbert Wakefield, *Observations on Pope* (1796), p. 31, commenting on *Windsor-Forest* 211 ff.

Johnson calls this simile "perhaps the best that English poetry can show," on the grounds that it both "illustrates" the subject to the understanding and "ennobles" it to the fancy. "The simile of the Alps has no useless parts, yet affords a striking picture by itself: it makes the foregoing position better understood, and enables it to take faster hold on the attention; it assists the apprehension, and elevates the fancy."[16] The connection is reinforced—to modern taste, made all too obvious—by the appearance of the analogy from the very start, in the "bounded level" from which rash youth hopes to "tempt the heights." The Alpine ascent does indeed form "a striking picture by itself," simply developing the point more fully and richly. Its success must lie in the energy with which it conjures up the process of mountain climbing, encouraging the reader to recognize how wearying the pursuit of knowledge likewise is.

The principle of accurate correspondence holds true for metaphor just as much as for simile. In *Windsor-Forest* hunting is represented as a "sylvan war" (148) because aggressive passions motivate both hunting and war; it is not so much an analogy as two versions of the same thing. The phrase *sylvan war* reappears in Pope's translation of the *Iliad*, where the metaphor is subtler but still expresses a deep identity of terms:

> But now (what time in some sequestered vale
> The weary woodman spreads his sparing meal,
> When his tired arms refuse the axe to rear,
> And claim a respite from the sylvan war;
> But not till half the prostrate forests lay
> Stretched in long ruin, and exposed to day)
> Then, nor till then, the Greeks' impulsive might
> Pierced the black phalanx, and let in the light.
> (*Iliad* XI.119–26)

The metaphor is set off typographically as a long parenthesis, to emphasize its illustrative role: the Greek warriors resemble

---

16. Samuel Johnson, *Life of Pope*, in *Lives of the English Poets*, ed. G. B. Hill (Oxford: Clarendon, 1905), III, 229–30.

demonic woodcutters. Whatever this simile may have suggested to Greek readers, in Pope's version it evokes a destructiveness in human behavior that is disturbing whichever way one thinks of it: the woodcutter is like a violent warrior; or, the warriors are (chillingly) like a fatigued woodcutter who is just doing his day's work.

An example of an un-Popean metaphor is Marvell's mowers who "massacre the grass along," who may sometimes kill birds but only by accident, and whose field of battle is a happy contrast to the Civil War rather than a reflection of it:

> In whose new traverse seemeth wrought
> A camp of battle newly fought:
> Where, as the meads with hay, the plain
> Lies quilted o'er with bodies slain:
> The women that with forks it fling
> Do represent the pillaging.[17]

Here the analogy is systematically imperfect. Equally un-Popean in a different way is Wordsworth's *Nutting*, an extended fragment that becomes a separate poem because its revelation of aggressive passions is limitlessly mysterious:

> Then up I rose,
> And dragged to earth both branch and bough, with crash
> And merciless ravage: and the shady nook
> Of hazels, and the green and mossy bower,
> Deformed and sullied, patiently gave up
> Their quiet being.
>
> (43–48)

Marvell inverts the metaphorical correspondences to emphasize difference; Wordsworth goes beyond metaphor into symbol, which affirms that tenor and vehicle are profoundly identical.

Romantic symbolism, especially as theorized by the New Criticism, is supposed to be a matter of thinking in images; Johnson, very differently, praises *Windsor-Forest* for alternating image with message, "the art of interchanging descrip-

---

17. Andrew Marvell, *Upon Appleton House*, 394, 419–24.

tion, narrative, and morality."[18] Among the many splendid discoveries in Roger Lonsdale's anthology of eighteenth-century verse is an anonymous *On a Female Rope-Dancer:*

> Whilst in her prime and bloom of years,
>   Fair Celia trips the rope,
> Alternately she moves our fears,
>   Alternately our hope.
>
> But when she sinks, or rises higher,
>   Or graceful does advance,
> We know not which we most admire,
>   The dancer, or the dance.[19]

The last line is oddly prophetic of, but also immensely remote from, Yeats's

> O body swayed to music, O brightening glance,
> How can we know the dancer from the dance?[20]

The eighteenth-century poet is content to experience "alternate" feelings, and admires both dancer and dance in a kind of stereoscopic vision. The dancer is the woman who performs, the dance is the action performed; there is no thought of identifying the two.

Perhaps some of the eighteenth-century anxiety about metaphoric appropriateness reflects the imaginative vacancy of the disenchanted universe. Metaphors have to prove their own case; the vertical dimension is gone. In *Paradise Lost*, published two decades before Pope's birth, the world of spirits, which "can either sex assume, or both" is utterly real:

>   but in what shape they choose
> Dilated or condensed, bright or obscure,
> Can execute their airy purposes,
> And works of love or enmity fulfill.[21]

18. *Lives*, III, 225.
19. *The New Oxford Book of Eighteenth Century Verse* (Oxford: Oxford University Press, 1984), p. 282. The poem was published in 1734.
20. William Butler Yeats, *Among School Children*, final lines.
21. John Milton, *Paradise Lost* I.424, 428–31.

In *The Rape of the Lock* there is no possibility of believing in Pope's Rosicrucian sylphs and gnomes; they are allegories of psychological behavior, not visitants from a realm beyond the human. Indeed they may be physiological as much as psychological, as the Cave of Spleen suggests; one source is the barely visible "simulacra" in Creech's translation of Lucretius,

> which like thin films, from bodies rise in streams,
> Play in the air and dance upon the beams.[22]

Pope's version is more beautiful—"Waft on the breeze, or sink in clouds of gold" (II.60)—but it is also less real. The playful use of Neoplatonic spirit lore is in part a nostalgia for a more populous universe in which the sylphs could be more than allegorical analogies: "Know then, unnumbered spirits round thee fly" (I.41).

These changes are not arbitrary swervings in literary history, but reflections of a profound cultural shift in which the whole Renaissance tradition of metaphorical thinking came to seem meretricious. As Empson says in his study of the mutations of pastoral, "After what Dryden called the Deluge, the republic, one could not take the old symbolisms, even the Elizabethan poetic ones, for granted; one must go back to the simplest things and argue from them."[23] *Especially* the Elizabethan poetic ones; as would happen again with the collapse of Romanticism, nothing looks more hollow than a symbol whose ontological basis has evaporated. Symbols may survive in outward appearance because poets are accustomed to them, as Pope's florilegium of bad verse in *Peri Bathous* proves, but now they work better in parody than in serious contexts.

> Between that disgust and this, between the things
> That are on the dump (azaleas and so on)

22. *De Rerum Natura* IV.29–30, in Thomas Creech's translation (1682). See L. C. Martin, "Lucretius and *The Rape of the Lock*," *Review of English Studies,* 20 (1944), 299–303.

23. William Empson, *Some Versions of Pastoral* (New York: New Directions, 1960), p. 193.

> And those that will be (azaleas and so on),
> One feels the purifying change. One rejects
> The trash.[24]

One reason for Pope's hatred of bad writing, which to many readers has seemed excessive, is his resentment at routine reuse of exhausted modes.

> Of gentle Philips will I ever sing,
> With gentle Philips shall the valleys ring.
> My numbers too for ever will I vary,
> With gentle Budgell, and with gentle Carey.
> Or if in ranging of the names I judge ill,
> With gentle Carey and with gentle Budgell.
> (*The Three Gentle Shepherds, TE* VI, 112)

It is no exaggeration to say that during the course of Pope's career as a poet the modern world opened up before him, and if he shrank from entering it, he knew also that it was impossible to go back.

It is significant that allegory, which in the Renaissance was a key to unlock "secret truth,"[25] became in the eighteenth century a device for simple exposition, as in the *Spectator* and *Rambler,* or else of satiric mockery, as in the *Tale of a Tub.* From the point of view of criticism, allegory was nothing more than an overdose of metaphors, as Spence summons Quintilian to confirm: "An excess this way is very blameable; you know the critics speak against it in a high strain, and one of them goes so far as to say this 'figure, when frequent, obscures the piece, and fatigues the reader; when continual, 'tis no longer a poem, 'tis all allegory and enigma.'"[26] The Augustan didactic message is presented openly, whether in *An Essay on Man* or *Night Thoughts* or *The Vanity of Human Wishes,* not teased by indirections out of the labyrinth of experience.

E. R. Wasserman has shown in detail, in an essay called

---

24. Wallace Stevens, *The Man on the Dump,* in *The Collected Poems of Wallace Stevens* (New York: Knopf, 1961), p. 202.

25. See Isabel G. MacCaffrey, *Spenser's Allegory: The Anatomy of Imagination* (Princeton: Princeton University Press, 1976), pp. 56–57.

26. *An Essay on Pope's Odyssey,* I, 33, citing Quintilian VIII.6.

"Nature Moralized," that thinkers in the eighteenth century stressed analogical thinking that could yield plausible connections between things without claiming to have deduced ultimate meaning. In place of the Renaissance identity of macrocosm and microcosm, in which a vast structure links together the whole of experience, analogy became a useful way of suggesting *possible* connections, a psychological habit that "served to explain only certain relationships between the material world and qualities of mind, not the relationship of the physical, moral, and spiritual."[27] But students of eighteenth-century literature have tended to forget the limited and tentative status of analogy, and to seize upon it as a comprehensive mechanism for interpreting poems. Wasserman's own practice in *The Subtler Language* has encouraged this, though Irvin Ehrenpreis has devastatingly exposed the arbitrariness of the analogies Wasserman claims to detect in *Windsor-Forest*.[28] And in any case Wasserman's aim was to contrast Augustan analogy with Romantic symbol, not to assert, as some others have done, an unbroken continuity between Renaissance poetry and Pope's.

Near the beginning of the *Essay on Man* Pope writes,

> Through worlds unnumbered though the God be known,
> 'Tis ours to trace him only in our own.
>
> (I.21–22)

On this Warburton comments, "We can *reason only from what we know,* and as we *know* no more of *Man* than what we see of his station here; so we know no more of *God* than what we see of his dispensations in this station; being able to trace him no further than to the limits of our own system."[29] This from

27. "Nature Moralized: The Divine Analogy in the Eighteenth Century," *Journal of English Literary History,* 20 (1953), 68.
28. Wasserman, *The Subtler Language: Critical Readings of Neoclassic and Romantic Poems* (Baltimore: Johns Hopkins University Press, 1959); Ehrenpreis, "Explicitness in Augustan Literature," in Ehrenpreis, *Literary Meaning and Augustan Values* (Charlottesville: University Press of Virginia, 1974), pp. 28–30.
29. Warburton's edition of Pope's *Works* (1751), III, 6.

a man who a few years later would be a bishop! In a later note Warburton performs a nimble sleight of hand in which physical disorders (such as Pope's "plagues or earthquakes," I.155) are made to explicate moral evil:

> Whether partial moral evil tend to the good of the universe, being a question which by reason of our ignorance of *many* parts of that universe, we cannot decide, but from known effects; the rules of argument require that it be proved by *analogy*, i.e. setting it by, and comparing it with, a thing *certain*; and it is a thing *certain* that partial natural evil tends to the good of our *particular system*.
>
> (p.21)

Milton, at the end of *Paradise Lost*, relies on a code of symbolism guaranteed by a God who gives "many a sign" of his presence even to fallen man (XI.351), and in his goodness still reveals "of his steps the track divine" (354). Warburton relies on "the rules of argument" and on an unsubstantiated assertion ("a thing certain") that earthquakes and plagues contribute to the good of the whole. What cannot be seen is either not worth knowing about or else does not exist, and analogies will show us those things that we still need to know.

The music of the spheres is gone and reason's ear does not miss it, as Addison says in his ode *The Spacious Firmament on High:*

> What though, in solemn silence, all
> Move round the dark terrestrial ball?
> What though nor real voice nor sound
> Amid their radiant orbs be found?
> In reason's ear they all rejoice,
> And utter forth a glorious voice,
> For ever singing, as they shine,
> "The hand that made us is divine."
>
> (17–24)

At one point in the *Essay on Man* Pope pretends to be glad that man cannot hear more acutely, lest he be deafened by the music of the spheres (I.201–2). Warburton comments severely, "This instance is poetical and even sublime, but misplaced. He is arguing philosophically in a case that required him to employ the *real* objects of sense only; and, what is worse, he speaks of this as a *real* object" (pp. 25–26). In effect Pope permits an analogy to expand into a metaphor. Warburton's position is much like that of Bishop Browne in his commentary on Locke: "Metaphor has no real foundation in the nature of the things compared; analogy is founded in the very nature of the things on both sides of the comparison."[30]

If metaphor is unequal to holding a poem together, then perhaps allusion can take its place. Reuben Brower built an entire book upon tracing, often eloquently, Pope's assimilation of classical antecedents.[31] But there is a limit to what allusion can do, and it is a limit that Pope sees more clearly than some of his modern admirers do. I have argued that allusions to real people are fundamental to the understanding of his poems; conversely I want to argue that allusions to earlier poets are not fundamental in the same way. That is not to say that Pope's works do not body forth an order of words that links them with earlier poems. Any poet does that, and eighteenth-century ones borrowed more than most. This is as true of translation as of original composition, as Spence remarks: "Mr. Pope has a very great happiness in *transferring beauties*. He often guides his translation of Homer by some fine thought or good expression in any other eminent writer."[32] To borrow "beauties" from other poets is certainly to pay them a kind of tribute, but it need not, and usually does not, imply that the reader should recall the whole context of the original.[33] On the contrary, the poet expects to be judged by his new use of old materials, as Dryden says: "The employment of a poet is like that of a curious gunsmith or watchmaker: the iron or silver is not his own; but they are the least part of that which gives the value: the

30. Peter Browne, *The Procedure, Extent, and Limits of Human Understanding* (1728), pp. 141–42, quoted by Richard E. Brantley, *Locke, Wesley, and the Method of English Romanticism* (Gainesville: University of Florida Press, 1984), p. 33.

31. *Alexander Pope: The Poetry of Allusion* (Oxford: Clarendon, 1959).

32. *An Essay on Pope's Odyssey*, I, 94.

33. Ehrenpreis argues the case against allusion at length in "Explicitness in Augustan Literature."

price lies wholly in the workmanship."[34] In *Autumn* Pope writes,

> Let opening roses knotted oaks adorn,
> And liquid amber drop from ev'ry thorn.
> (37–38)

As the Twickenham footnotes show, *drop* is literally the only word Pope has supplied; every other phrase comes from other pastoral poets, particularly translators of Virgil (*TE* I, 83n). We thus discover that Pope breathed an atmosphere of earlier poetry, but we do not gain anything in particular by detecting Walsh and Ogilby and Dryden.

To put it another way, poetic echoes were certainly important in Pope's imagination (as in Gray's, who was even more allusive), but their effect on the reader is of linguistic density rather than of correspondences to be worked out. Eighteenth-century readers seem to have enjoyed participating in this process of poetic assimilation, as can be illustrated by quoting in full one of Wakefield's many elaborations, annotating a "beauty" in Pope's *Summer:*

> Ver. 83. The moving mountains hear the pow'rful call,
> And headlong streams hang list'ning in their fall.

> The seeds of this beauty he found in *Virgil*, Ecl. viii.4

> Et mutata suos requierunt flumina cursus.

> The rivers stood in heaps, and stopped the running flood.
> *Dryden*

> Hence *Congreve*, in the Tears of Amaryllis:

> And rapid rivers *listened* at their source.

> And *Andrew Marvell:*

> Hark how music then prepares
> For thy stay these charming airs;

34. John Dryden, Preface to *An Evening's Love*, in *Of Dramatic Poesy and Other Critical Essays*, ed. George Watson, Everyman's Library (London: Dent, 1962), I, 155.

> Which the posting winds recall,
> *And suspend the river's fall.*

But no man has exceeded *Milton* on this topic, Comus, ver. 494.

> Thyrsis? whose artful strains have oft delayed
> The huddling brook to hear his madrigal,
> And sweetened every musk rose of the dale:

Who probably had in view *Lucan*, vi.473 as well as *Virgil:*

> de rupe pependit
> Abscissa fixus torrens; amnisque cucurrit
> Non qua pronus erat.

> Streams have run back at murmurs of her tongue,
> And torrents from the rock suspended hung.
> *Rowe.*[35]

Wakefield moves easily—not to say affectionately—among ancient and modern poems, including English translations of Latin ones, in a way that suggests a shared culture that is apprehended in the total effect rather than in a series of "allusions" to be decoded. It's worth noting that this habit of echoing or quoting is by no means extinct today. Mack's biography of Pope is filled with it: "There is a glow about one's earliest companions during those short days when Time lets us play and be golden in the mercy of his means that is never quite recapturable."[36] It is doubtful that one is expected to summon up the whole of *Fern Hill*, much less compare Pope with Dylan Thomas.

Moreover, Peter Hughes has shown in a richly suggestive essay that referential allusion, in which a text floats on a sea of identifiable quotations, was despised as plagiarism by Pope and his friends. In Pope's poems allusion functions as repetition rather than recollection, a forward-looking sense that the past is recreated in the living world, rather than a backward-looking homage to particular texts. As against Freudian theories of writing as parricide, Hughes suggests

---

35. *Observations on Pope*, pp. 8–9.
36. Maynard Mack, *Alexander Pope: A Life* (New York: Norton, 1985), p. 344.

the model of fratricide: Pope overcomes his contemporary "brothers" by assimilating to himself, and denying to them, the still-potent life of the great fathers. Pope's gift for inventing quasi-proverbial utterances confirms his appropriation of the tradition by sounding like allusion even when it's not.[37] Even when imitating Horace directly, Pope printed his text in parallel with the Latin to make the reader notice all the ways in which he altered, departed from, or omitted aspects of the original. As Frank Stack shows in subtle detail, "'Horace' here is not so much the well-known classical figure as the intense details of his poetic language."[38]

What is true of poetic allusion is true also of religious. Pope often works within a religious context, but allusion is not the same thing as argument. The *Epistle to Bathurst*, for instance, is concerned with the Christian use of riches, but no amount of quotation from the *Patrologia Latina* can turn it into a doctrinal treatise.[39] In keeping with a general tendency in modern criticism to emphasize religious contexts,[40] much has been made of the submerged theology that is supposed to underlie Pope's works. Partly because these claims exalt the intellectual weight of his achievement, and partly because it is never wise to attack distinguished scholars, they have been allowed to stand virtually unchallenged. For that reason I think it important to address the most influential of such interpretations, Aubrey Williams's account of "the Antichrist of Wit" in *The Dunciad*.[41]

Without question Pope alludes repeatedly to *Paradise Lost*.

37. "Allusion and Expression in Eighteenth-Century Literature," in *The Author in His Work*, ed. Louis L. Martz and Aubrey Williams (New Haven: Yale University Press, 1978), 297–315.

38. *Pope and Horace: Studies in Imitation* (Cambridge: Cambridge University Press, 1985), pp. xiv–xv. Even when the imitation is very close, "we know we have heard it all before, and yet it is all fresh and alive—experienced again in a new poet and a new poetry" (p. 33).

39. As E. R. Wasserman attempts to do in *Pope's Epistle to Bathurst: A Critical Reading* (Baltimore: Johns Hopkins University Press, 1960).

40. In a related field, Jerome J. McGann mounts a spirited attack on similar tendencies in *The Romantic Ideology: A Critical Investigation* (Chicago: University of Chicago Press, 1983).

41. The final chapter of *Pope's Dunciad: A Study of Its Meaning* (London: Methuen, 1955).

What is not obvious is that whenever he does this "the *Dun-ciad* rises to another level of meaning" (p. 98). Without question the dunces often resemble Milton's devils. What is not obvious is that dulness is thereby shown to be sinful and "diabolical." Consider Pope's description, quoted by Williams (p. 133), of Bentley the classical scholar:

> Before them marched that awful Aristarch;
> Plowed was his front with many a deep remark.
> (IV.203–4)

There is certainly a reminiscence of Beelzebub, with deliberation "deep on his front engraven," and perhaps one of Satan as well, whose face "deep scars of thunder had intrencht."[42] But reminiscence is not necessarily allusion, and allusion is not necessarily argument. Let us put the "Miltonic" lines back into context, where Cambridge pedantry is in question:

> As many quit the streams that murm'ring fall
> To lull the sons of Marg'ret and Clare-hall,
> Where Bentley late tempestuous wont to sport
> In troubled waters, but now sleeps in port.
> Before them marched that awful Aristarch;
> Plowed was his front with many a deep remark:
> His hat, which never vailed to human pride,
> Walker with rev'rence took, and laid aside.
> (IV.199–206)

Bentley's endless controversies (in an otherwise sleepy Cambridge lulled by murmuring waters) and his love of wine are superbly hit off in the fourth of these lines. Then comes the glance at Milton (and also, as the Twickenham editor notes, at the *Remarks* that Bentley was fond of publishing). And finally we are introduced to Bentley's vice master at Trinity, whose servility included constant attention to the master's hat:

> "Walker! our hat"—nor more he deigned to say,
> But, stern as Ajax' spectre, strode away.
> (IV.273–74)

---

42. John Milton, *Paradise Lost* II.302 and I.601.

The allusion to the ghost of Ajax ignoring Ulysses does not imply an extended comparison with the *Odyssey* or with the Trojan story. Similarly, the allusion to Milton touches in passing on Bentley's arrogance and self-love without implying an extended comparison with *Paradise Lost* or with Christian meditations on evil. Like the Ajax allusion it works as burlesque rather than as characterization or definition. The disparity is too great between the Prince of Darkness and the Cambridge don, and if the allusion is noticed at all by a reader—it might well not be—it yields amusement rather than metaphysical horror.

Moreover, the diabolical images cut both ways. Is dulness made dreadful, or is evil made ridiculous? Commentators tend to ignore the extent to which Pope (like most of his contemporaries) does not describe the frightening potency of evil as seventeenth-century writers did. Pope satirizes freethinkers who abuse reason to "doubt of God,"

> or, at one bound o'er-leaping all his laws,
> Make God man's image, man the final cause.
> (IV.477–78)

Again, there is an undoubted allusion to *Paradise Lost*, this time to the entry into Paradise of Satan, who "at one slight bound high over leaped all bound" (IV.181). But the violation is very different. In Milton, man's implacable enemy defies God's explicit prohibition and invades the world of harmony in order to demolish it. In Pope, misguided philosophers defy a never-articulated prohibition against misdirected reasoning. Milton wrote *Paradise Lost* to counter such tendencies, which were already endemic in Western culture, by rebuilding the whole vast embattled structure of Christian myth. Theology is revitalized by casting it as narrative. Pope does nothing of the kind. He invokes, quite vaguely, a dogmatic notion of prohibited inquiry, and ignores or avoids the complex problems of myth and truth that gave energy to Milton's poem. Far from being theological, the *Dunciad* is antitheological: religious belief is relegated to the background, where it can be invoked as a hazy principle of order ("o'er-leaping all his laws") while the absurd everyday world of pedantry and bad writing can occupy the foreground. Bad art is a constant offense to the sensitive reader, but it is not really presented as "the work of evil" (Williams, p. 155), and the debasement of belles lettres does not reflect systematically the death of the universe.

Pope's many references to creation and its opposite, therefore, ending with the "uncreating word" that brings back "universal darkness" (IV.654–56), function satirically rather than metaphysically. "No other action," Williams says of the poem's ending, "could have better realized for Pope's readers the Christian concept of evil—that which is the annihilation and negation of the good" (p. 141). But in traditional theology, and certainly in *Paradise Lost,* evil is frightening because it is active malice as well as negative privation. Just as Original Sin is absent from *An Essay on Man,* so is a genuinely Satanic vision of evil absent from the *Dunciad.* A conservative Christian might wish to criticize Pope for this; others should notice its significance in the development of Western culture, without imagining that Pope would be a greater writer if his vision of reality could be merged with those of Aquinas or Milton. If Cibber is the "anointed" son of Dulness and her vapors are blue (III.1–4), one may possibly think of a caricatured madonna and child, but it does not follow that "with its extremely covert allusiveness this passage is a good example of the type of theological hide-and-seek Pope forces the reader to participate in" (Williams, p. 149). The allusiveness may resemble hide-and-seek, but it is not theological. In the eighteenth century Christianity tended to become an ethical system rather than a theology, and Pope in particular, anxious to minimize the distance between Catholicism and Anglicanism, had good reason to stay clear of theology, as we have seen in the *Essay on Man.*

Pope's art, then, finds itself obliged to create its own contexts, which prove to be located much more in contemporary life than in literary or intellectual history. These considerations help to suggest why epic—the most prestigious but also the most tradition-bound of genres—should have been so hard to achieve in the eighteenth century. The problem was made more difficult by the assumption that since epic is the most comprehensive of forms, it exhibits "nature" more adequately than other forms do. Consider again the account of Virgil in the *Essay on Criticism*:

> When first young Maro in his boundless mind
> A work t' outlast immortal Rome designed,
> Perhaps he seemed above the critic's law,
> And but from nature's fountains scorned to draw:
> But when t' examine every part he came,
> Nature and Homer were, he found, the same:
> Convinced, amazed, he checks the bold design,
> And rules as strict his laboured work confine,
> As if the Stagyrite o'erlooked each line.
>
> (130–38)

The implied equation is daunting enough in itself:

$$\text{Nature} = \text{Homer} = \text{Aristotle} = \text{Virgil}$$

To put it in historicist terms which were not available to Pope, an equation is asserted between a Bronze Age culture (the "nature" imitated by Homer) as later represented in a Greek poem of the eighth century B.C., further interpreted by a Greek philosopher of the fourth century B.C., and finally imitated by a Roman poet of the first century B.C.

It has been said that "the Restoration was the great age of the failed epic,"[43] though it did produce Dryden's translation of the *Aeneid*, and of course that anomalous metaepic *Paradise Lost*. If Homer's oral epic is primary and Virgil's literary epic is secondary, then (as Fowler says) Milton arrived at a tertiary stage by reinterpreting both of the earlier types.[44] But the Christian myth could serve only once as the basis for an epic poem, both because *Paradise Lost* asserts a totality to which nothing can be added, and because the myth rapidly lost that

43. Susan Staves, *Players' Scepters: Fictions of Authority in the Restoration* (Lincoln: University of Nebraska Press, 1979), p. 41.

44. *Kinds of Literature*, p. 162. The terms *primary* and *secondary* come from C. S. Lewis, *A Preface to Paradise Lost* (London: Oxford University Press, 1942).

central role in its culture that could sponsor an epic. The obligatory "machinery" (apart from playful versions like the sylphs in *The Rape of the Lock*) became an unsurmountable obstacle, since the Christian God conforms so imperfectly to the role of the gods in Homer and Virgil. Among Blackmore's other literary offenses was a solemn attempt to make British history a contest between Lucifer and God. Thus Paris (Lutetia) learns that to resist Britain is to derange the entire universe:

> How great this day is when, with sword in hand,
> Th' Almighty marches to destroy thy land;
> Thy lofty walls, Lutetia, to surround,
> And level thy proud turrets with the ground!
> Th' affrighted stars retreat into the sky,
> And from Heav'n's brow and outmost frontier fly. . . .
> The planets starting at the dismal sight
> Forsake their orbs, and wander far in night.[45]

Pope meditated a national-political epic on the theme of Brutus but never wrote it, and one might see his position as quaternary. In a postepic world, he settled in the end for translating the primary epics of Homer into the language and values of English Augustanism. Dryden says that Blackmore "robbed and murdered Maro's muse";[46] Pope, who venerated Virgil, was too wise to take from him more than contemporary British culture could assimilate. But this abnegation was not easy to explain, since Pope sided firmly with the Ancients against the Moderns. Lovers of the classics like Swift and Pope despised "modern" classical scholars like Bentley, who were showing the profound *otherness* of ancient values and modes of life.[47]

The standard contemporary explanation for the absence of epic was not, of course, that the culture was evolving toward

45. Richard Blackmore, *King Arthur: An Heroick Poem* (1697), Book IX, p. 253.

46. John Dryden, *To My Honoured Kinsman, John Driden, of Chesterton*, 85.

47. See Joseph M. Levine, "Ancients and Moderns Reconsidered," *Eighteenth-Century Studies*, 15 (1981), 72–89. Many of Pope's notes to Homer refer uneasily to this issue, but the translation itself repels it at every point.

new and more appropriate forms, but rather that the culture was too corrupt and degraded to deserve the permanently great forms of the past. Dryden commiserates with the painter Kneller for falling short of the Renaissance masters:

> That yet thou hast not reached their high degree
> Seems only wanting to this age, not thee:
> Thy genius bounded by the times like mine,
> Drudges on petty draughts, nor dare design
> A more exalted work, and more divine.[48]

If epic was unattainable, then modern values must be unworthy of epic. In Johnson's *Dictionary epic* is an adjective, not a noun, and means a narrative which "is usually supposed to be heroic."

Dryden's own heroic dramas are highly artful concoctions for a sophisticated audience, and very remote from anything that heroism could mean in Homer and Virgil. "The two parts of the *Conquest of Granada*," Johnson says, "are written with a seeming determination to glut the public with dramatic wonders; to exhibit in its highest elevation a theatrical meteor of incredible love and impossible valour, and to leave no room for a wilder flight to the extravagance of posterity."[49] Heroism like this borders closely on burlesque, and seems more productive of mock-heroic, from Dryden's *Mac Flecknoe* to Pope's *Dunciad*, than of the "heroic poem" proper. Writers based in the new middle-class culture—Grub Street writers, as Pope regarded them—could afford to ignore epic as irrelevant. It plays no role at all in Defoe; Richardson limits epic allusions to the aristocratic villain Lovelace. Most classically trained writers were unwilling to relinquish the heroic ideal, and yet they found themselves parodying epic rather than emulating it.

In this light Pope's Homer translations are fascinating transpositions of ancient materials into a specialized kind of contemporary style. There is no need to demonstrate how he

---

48. John Dryden, *To Sir Godfrey Kneller*, 145–49.
49. Samuel Johnson, *Life of Dryden*, in *Lives of the English Poets*, I, 348–49.

euphemizes "low" material, which was widely felt to be unacceptable for both social and rhetorical reasons. "In general," Spence says, "all vulgar terms, and all very disagreeable descriptions, are beneath the heroic style."[50] What is really interesting is the heightening of material that already seems high. In a footnote Pope summarizes a "night piece" (the painterly analogy is telling) in language of eloquent simplicity: "The stars shine, the air is serene, the world enlightened, and the moon mounted in glory" (*TE* VII, 428). Twentieth-century taste likes its poetry to resemble this kind of prose, and Robert Fitzgerald translates the passage accordingly:

> As when in heaven
> principal stars shine out around the moon
> when the night sky is limpid, with no wind,
> and all the lookout points, headlands, and mountain
> clearings are distinctly seen, as though
> pure space had broken through, downward from heaven,
> and all the stars are out. . . .[51]

Pope would have thought this prose, and would have been baffled by the randomness of the line endings ("and mountain / clearings," "as though / pure space"). For him the heroic ideal means a rhetorical heightening, with much elaboration of implication and detail, and also a strenuous display of parallelism to bind the picture together. I italicize for emphasis the expansions that are in Pope but not in Fitzgerald:

> As when the moon, *refulgent lamp of night!*
> O'er heav'ns clear *azure* spreads *her sacred* light,
> When not a breath *disturbs the deep serene;*
> And not a cloud *o'ercasts the solemn scene;*
> *Around her throne the vivid planets roll,*
> And stars unnumbered *gild the glowing pole,*
> *O'er the dark trees a yellower verdure shed,*
> *And tip with silver* ev'ry mountain's head;

---

50. *An Essay on Pope's Odyssey,* II, 134.
51. *The Iliad,* tr. Robert Fitzgerald (New York: Doubleday, Anchor, 1975), pp. 198–99.

Then *shine* the vales, the rocks *in prospect rise,*
A flood of glory bursts from all the skies.
(*Iliad* VIII.687–96)

Pope turns the volume up, and contrary to what one might expect from Augustan "generality," at every point he extends or specifies the details of the scene. His aim is to recreate the richness of the moonlit world in all its fullness, not just to mount an analogy between the stars and the Greek watch fires (which is the function of the passage in context). The rhetorical climax is clearly the line which Fitzgerald renders "as though / pure space had broken through, downward from heaven." To Pope this would probably seem a conceit, and not a very perspicuous one; he might well prefer Lattimore's version, "As endless bright air spills from the heavens,"[52] which is more beautiful and fixes the metrical stress on the central word *spills*. But in Pope the effect is more dramatic, introduced as it is by the two-part line that precedes it. "Then shine the vales [caesura], the rocks in prospect rise [the lower world is brightened and seems to rise upward, and the inevitable rhyme is prepared]; A flood of glory bursts from all the skies." Far more even than in Lattimore, the stress falls powerfully on *bursts*, which suggests a more vigorous action than *spills*.

Whether all of this is faithful to Homer, I am not competent to say, nor is that altogether relevant here. Probably no translation, three millennia later, can really be faithful to a poem in a dead language. What I want to emphasize is the rhetorical excitement that Pope considers appropriate for Homer, an excitement which his ironic and worldly culture could not possibly sustain in its own original poems.

The heroic poem had to be rhetorically grand because its actions were morally grand. According to Sidney, himself a charismatic hero, "As the image of each action stirreth and instructeth the mind, so the lofty image of such worthies most inflameth the mind with desire to be worthy, and informs

52. *The Iliad*, tr. Richmond Lattimore (Chicago: University of Chicago Press, 1961), p. 197.

with counsel how to be worthy."[53] The court of George II was no doubt inferior to that of Gloriana, but more significantly the very notion of heroism was in serious disrepute by Pope's time, just as it is in our own. Romance has come in for renewed attention lately as the foundation of the fiction-making impulse,[54] and Sidney's *Arcadia* is one of the great romances, but for Pope there can be no compromise between epic significance and romance amusement. "If the reader does not observe the morality of the *Ilias*, he loses half, and mistakes the chief aim of it, which is to instruct" (*TE* VIII, 557–58n). The action of the *Iliad* may derive from the anger of Achilles, but nothing can be allowed to diminish his heroism: "Achilles is as much a hero when he weeps, as when he fights" (*TE* VIII, 535n).

Wherever possible, Pope exploits the resources of the couplet to present the characters in postures that specify their status and significance. Thus in the moving scene when Priam pleads with Achilles for the body of Hector, and Achilles weeps for his own father and his dead friend Patroclus,

> Now each by turns indulged the gush of woe,
> And now the mingled tides together flow:
> This low on earth, that gently bending o'er,
> A father one, and one a son, deplore:
> But great Achilles diff'rent passions rend,
> And now his sire he mourns, and now his friend.
> Th' infectious softness through the heroes ran;
> One universal, solemn shower began;
> They bore as heroes, but they felt as man.
> (*Iliad* XXIV.638–46)

As we have seen in Pope's shaping of his own life, Augustan values required one to define and play out one's roles. "I sighed as a lover, I obeyed as a son," Gibbon says of the

---

53. Philip Sidney, *An Apology for Poetry,* in *English Critical Essays,* ed. Edmund D. Jones, World's Classics (London: Oxford University Press, 1947), p. 28.
54. See Northrop Frye, *The Secular Scripture: A Study of the Structure of Romance* (Cambridge, Mass.: Harvard University Press, 1976).

decision to relinquish the woman he hoped to marry.[55] Priam is a father and Achilles a son, but both are men, so they can mourn differently ("each by turns") and together ("the mingled tides"). Above all both are heroes, and that is why their mutual grief is memorably instructive. They "felt as man" as all men must, but they "bore as heroes" as few men can.

In their remoteness from ordinary life, these are very specialized heroes indeed. H. A. Mason has well said that they are "delicate creatures, creatures of Decorum; they cannot bear comparison with three things: the inherently small or insignificant, the socially degrading, and the disgusting."[56] That is to say, they cannot bear the normal subjects and techniques of Popean satire, which must be carefully repressed at every point. Moreover, these heroes cannot enter the world of political reality that so fascinated Pope, for that too was "low." Leslie Stephen remarks that one is almost scandalized when they engage in combat, as if Walpole and Bolingbroke should interrupt a parliamentary debate with a fistfight.[57] This was a world of actors pretending to be heroes: "Old Edward's armour beams on Cibber's breast" (*Epistle* II.i.319). But nobody wore armor anymore.

Not surprisingly, epic behavior and epic diction were both attracted irresistibly to parody, as in the playful Homerics of Pope's friend Parnell (translating a classical work that was itself parodic):

> Lycopinax with Borbocaetes fights,
> A blameless frog, whom humbler life delights;
> The fatal jav'lin unrelenting flies,
> And darkness seals the gentle croaker's eyes.[58]

---

55. Edward Gibbon, *Memoirs of My Life*, ed. Betty Radice (Harmondsworth: Penguin, 1984), p. 208, n. 18 (from Draft C of the *Memoirs*).

56. *To Homer through Pope: An Introduction to Homer's "Iliad" and Pope's Translation* (New York: Barnes and Noble, 1972), p. 98.

57. *Alexander Pope* (New York: Harper, 1902), p. 75.

58. Thomas Parnell, *Homer's Batrachomuomachia: or, the Battle of the Frogs and Mice*, in *Poems on Several Occasions* (1726), p. 96. Parnell's gloss identifies Lycopinax as "A Licker of Dishes" and Borbocaetes as "Who Lies in the Mud" (p. 70).

One might surmise further that the "heroic" couplet is best suited to mock seriousness, as in Welsted's *Apple-Pye: A Poem:*

> Oft let your bodkin through the lid be sent,
> To give the kind imprisoned treasure vent;
> Lest the fermenting liquors, mounting high,
> Within their brittle bounds disdain to lie,
> Insensibly, by constant fretting, waste,
> And o'er-inform the tenement of paste.[59]

The last line is a nice echo of Dryden's Shaftesbury, whose fiery soul "o'er informed the tenement of clay."[60] Once brought back to earth by parody, epic values can recover something of their life, as in Clarissa's minor-key version of Sarpedon's speech in *The Rape of the Lock.* Above all, the mock-heroic allows colloquial realism to interpenetrate heroic grandeur: "But since, alas! frail beauty must decay" (V.25), but also "Or who would learn one earthly thing of use?" (V.22). Alternatively, one could ironically romanticize the comic rogue, as Empson says of Gay's amazingly successful *Beggar's Opera:* "The only way to use the heroic convention was to turn it onto the mock-hero, the rogue, . . . and the only romance to be extracted from the Whig government was to satirise it as the rogue."[61]

At one point in the preface to the *Iliad* Pope abandons piety for a moment and describes the Trojan War as an eighteenth-century Englishman really sees it: "Who can be so prejudiced in their favour as to magnify the felicity of those ages, when a spirit of revenge and cruelty, joined with the practice of rapine and robbery, reigned through the world, when no mercy was shown but for the sake of lucre, when the greatest princes were put to the sword, and their wives and daughters made slaves and concubines?" (*TE* VII, 14). Pope is not so foolish as to think such behavior confined to ancient Greece; his meaning is that it is appalling whenever it occurs. His

---

59. Leonard Welsted, *Epistles, Odes, &c. Written on Several Subjects* (1724), p. 73.
60. John Dryden, *Absalom and Achitophel*, 158.
61. *Some Versions of Pastoral*, p. 190.

later poems are full of bitter reflections on militarism as anti-life, the "iron harvests of the field" (*Essay on Man* IV.12), and heroes tend to appear as near-psychotic personalities, from Alexander the Great to Charles XII of Sweden:

> Heroes are much the same, the point's agreed,
> From Macedonia's madman to the Swede;
> The whole strange purpose of their lives, to find
> Or make, an enemy of all mankind!
>
> (IV.219–22)

Very similarly Dryden, praising Virgil in contrast to Homer, said that Homer "forms and equips those ungodly man-killers whom we poets, when we flatter them, call heroes; a race of men who can never enjoy quiet in themselves, till they have taken it from all the world."[62] Swift's campaign against the duke of Marlborough focuses not just on the general's greed and cruelty, but also on the human consequences of war, which servile artists are always ready to disguise:

> Your hero now another Mars is,
> Makes mighty armies turn their arses. . . .
> His milk-white steed upon its haunches,
> Or pawing into dead men's paunches.[63]

Even before he began to translate Homer, Pope had written *Windsor-Forest*, a poem designed to recommend the Peace of Utrecht by which the Tory administration—against the bitter protests of the Whigs and their general Marlborough—was preparing to end the War of the Spanish Succession. We tend to think of the eighteenth century as an essentially peaceful time, but in fact war had gone on throughout most of Pope's life. William III fought a series of Continental battles in the 1690s, and the War of the Spanish Succession began in 1702, when Pope was fourteen, and lasted over a decade. A long

62. John Dryden, *To the Right Honourable My Lord Radcliffe, Prefixed to "Examen Poeticum"* (1693), in *Of Dramatic Poesy*, II, 167.

63. Jonathan Swift, *Directions for a Birthday Song*, 29–30, 35–36. See also the widows and orphans who mourned before Marlborough's death rather than after it, in *A Satirical Elegy*.

section of *Windsor-Forest* is devoted to images of hunting and fishing, each of which emphasizes the suffering of the victims and the finality of their death:

> Oft as the mounting larks their notes prepare,
> They fall, and leave their little lives in air.
>
> (133–34)

One remarkable passage describes servile hunting dogs flushing partridges into nets, and then draws the analogy explicitly:

> Before his lord the ready spaniel bounds,
> Panting with hope, he tries the furrowed grounds,
> But when the tainted gales the game betray,
> Couched close he lies, and meditates the prey;
> Secure they trust th' unfaithful field, beset,
> Till hov'ring o'er 'em sweeps the swelling net.
> Thus (if small things we may with great compare)
> When Albion sends her eager sons to war,
> Some thoughtless town, with ease and plenty blest,
> Near, and more near, the closing lines invest;
> Sudden they seize th' amazed, defenceless prize,
> And high in air Britannia's standard flies.
>
> (99–110)

It is notable that Wasserman, intent upon developing a political allegory of *concordia discors*, has nothing to say about the shocking betrayal of the "thoughtless" town by "eager" soldiers who creep up like stalking hounds. But surely Pope cannot mean that the high spirits of hunters, which themselves produce such grim results, are a justification for the horrors of warfare.[64] He had written eloquently against cruelty in hunting, incidentally, in *Guardian* 61.

Since the problem of heroism, not to mention of heroic poetry, is deeply implicated here, it is worth looking at earlier

---

64. "The hunt is both proper and necessary for those in whom the essential energy is superabundant. . . . There is at this point no condemnation of war, as we might be led to expect from the account of William; rather, considerable pride invests the description of war when 'high in air Britannia's standard flies'" (*The Subtler Language*, p. 131).

attempts to make epic capital out of Marlborough's wars, which according to Blackmore were so successful that the poets hardly knew how to sustain their flattery:

> The muse exhausted pants, and hangs the wing,
> Has no more strength to rise, and no more breath to sing.
> He danger seeks, he asks unequal fight,
> He conquers faster than our bards can write.[65]

Gory battlefields were understood to be Homeric, as Oldham declared in a poem praising Homer—

> And limbs of mangled chiefs his passage strow,
> And floods of reeking gore the field o'erflow.[66]

It seems fair to say that the extravagant diction obscures what is actually being described; floods of gore are more poetical than piles of dead bodies.

This sort of bloodthirsty patriotic verse became highly conventional. Thus John Hughes (at the age of twenty-two) celebrates the explosive cannonballs of William III at Namur:

> The kindled region glows; with deaf'ning sound
> They burst; their iron entrails, hurled around,
> Strow with thick-scattered deaths the crimson ground.
> See, where the genius of the war appears,
> Nor shuns the labour, nor the danger fears. . . .
> At length the widened gates a conquest own,
> And to his arms resign the yielding town.[67]

---

65. [Richard Blackmore], *Advice to the Poets: A Poem, Occasion'd by the Wonderful Success of Her Majesty's Arms, under the Conduct of the Duke of Marlborough, in Flanders* (1706), p. 3. A review of Marlborough's triumphs, of course, revives the sagging poet:

> The inspiration comes, my bosom glows,
> I strive with strong enthusiastic throes.
> Oh! I am all in rapture, all on fire,
> Give me, to ease the muse's pangs, the lyre. (p. 26)

66. John Oldham, *The Praise of Homer*, in *Some New Pieces Never Before Publisht* (1681), p. 65; quoted by Mason, *To Homer through Pope*, p. 158.

67. *The Court of Neptune: On King William's Return from Holland, 1699*, in *Poems on Several Occasions* (1735), I, 34.

A passage like this cries out for the debunking clarity of the king of Brobdingnag: cannonballs have "entrails" but the people they kill are generalized as "thick-scattered deaths," and the "yielding" town welcomes William's "arms" like a lover. (In *Windsor-Forest* William III, thinly disguised as the Norman William I, is represented as a sadistic tyrant.)

Like Hughes, Joseph Addison at twenty-four hymned William III, sent by heaven "to curb the proud oppressors of mankind":

> Namur's late terrors and destruction show
> What WILLIAM, warmed with just revenge, can do:
> Where once a thousand turrets raised on high
> Their gilded spires, and glittered in the sky,
> An undistinguished heap of dust is found,
> And all the pile lies smoking on the ground.[68]

All sufferings are ascribed to Louis XIV, and as for brave William, "nations bless the labours of his sword" (p. 12). That Addison hoped to advance his own career in concert with Marlborough's is plainly stated by Eusden (long afterward Pope's "parson much bemused in beer") in a poem prefixed to *Cato:*

> Then, the delightful theme of every tongue,
> Th' immortal Marlb'rough was your daring song;
> From clime to clime the mighty victor flew,
> From clime to clime as swiftly you pursue;
> Still with the hero's glowed the poet's flame,
> Still with his conquests you enlarged your fame.[69]

In his most famous political poem, *The Campaign*, Addison did not fail to invoke Homeric gore:

> Rivers of blood I see, and hills of slain,
> An Iliad rising out of one campaign.[70]

---

68. *A Poem to His Majesty* (1695), in *The Works of . . . Joseph Addison* (1721), I, 11.

69. Laurence Eusden, "'Tis nobly done thus to enrich the stage," printed among the Commendatory Poems to *Cato;* in *Five Restoration Tragedies*, ed. Bonamy Dobrée, World's Classics (London: Oxford University Press, 1928), p. 376.

70. Joseph Addison, *The Campaign*, in Addison's *Works* (1721), I, 65.

This poem is clearly Pope's source for the hunting metaphors in *Windsor-Forest*, but Addison uses them without irony. When "Britannia's graceful sons" approach the enemy,

> Doubling their speed they march with fresh delight,
> Eager for glory, and require the fight.
> So the staunch hound the trembling deer pursues,
> And smells his footsteps in the tainted dews,
> The tedious track unrav'ling by degrees:
> But when the scent comes warm in ev'ry breeze,
> Fired at the near approach, he shoots away
> On his full stretch, and bears upon his prey.
> (pp. 69–70)

The terrors of the "trembling deer" are barely glanced at, and the dog is treated as an independent hunter seizing what is rightfully his. Pope, very differently, stresses the dog's subservient role in a cruel ambush, and "tainted" takes on a moral connotation in his version: "when the tainted gales the game betray" (*Windsor-Forest*, 101).

> Beasts, urged by us, their fellow beasts pursue,
> And learn of man each other to undo.
> (123–24)

As dogs are to their masters, so are soldiers to their generals.

Addison turns next to a massed army of reinforcements that delights Marlborough, "charmed with the glorious sight," and describes it with epic grandeur:

> Rows of hollow brass,
> Tube behind tube, the dreadful entrance keep,
> Whilst in their wombs ten thousand thunders sleep.
> (p. 70)

Pope brilliantly transforms Addison's language by reducing the action to a single crack of "thunder" from a single "tube":

> With slaught'ring guns th' unwearied fowler roves,
> When frosts have whitened all the naked groves. . . .
> He lifts the tube, and levels with his eye;
> Strait a short thunder breaks the frozen sky.
> (125–30)

Addison's strategy is to make war seem alternately majestic (by epic inflation) and jolly (by metaphors from hunting). Pope, as always, insists upon the reality that the diction and metaphors conceal. Hunting and heroic war betray the same aggressive impulses, and calling them by their right name is an indictment of human behavior, not an affirmation of *concordia*.

Addison's poem ends in a kind of antipastoral nightmare, all the more horrible because the poet keeps insisting on its rightness.

> Troops of bold youths, born on the distant Soane,
> Or sounding borders of the rapid Rhône,
> Or where the Seine her flow'ry fields divides,
> Or where the Loire through winding vineyards glides;
> In heaps the rolling billows sweep away,
> And into Scythian seas their bloated corpse convey.
> (p. 77)

Addison's final message is that Britain is defined by Marlborough's exploits, and is somehow freed from the normal constraints of nature:

> Such are th' effects of ANNA's royal cares:
> By her, Britannia, great in foreign wars,
> Ranges through nations, wheresoe'er disjoined,
> Without the wonted aid of sea and wind.
> (p. 81)

Pope's reply is the famous couplet

> At length great ANNA said—Let discord cease!
> She said, the world obeyed, and all was peace!
> (327–28)

Windsor-Forest is a plea to return man to nature, above all to his own best nature. So the poem does, in the end, assert an ideal of peace and harmony. But it does not do so by elaborating a system of metaphors on the Renaissance model; on the contrary, it implies the bankruptcy of the old metaphors, and of the rhetoric that sustained them, in the face of the realities of the contemporary world. Addison was of course a Whig and Pope a Tory, but to say only that is to diminish the seriousness of the issues Pope is trying to raise. At the bottom of *Windsor-Forest* lies a rejection, probably not fully conscious, of the old heroic ideal. And surely this is the deepest explanation for Pope's inability to write a heroic poem.

Conclusion

The Rape of the Lock, written at the same period as *Windsor-Forest,* is a good-humored mock-epic; the *Dunciad* is not really mock-epic at all, but rather an anti-epic that rejects the prevailing attitudes of a whole civilization.[1] In such a culture, pastoral harmony is utterly defeated by urban squalor. The mirror passage in *Windsor-Forest* ends with energetic lines that modulate from the emblematic river to the real one:

> Through the fair scene roll slow the ling'ring streams,
> Then foaming pour along, and rush into the Thames.
> (217–18)

In the *Dunciad* the same rhyme is expressive of wretchedness:

> To where Fleet-ditch with disemboguing streams
> Rolls the large tribute of dead dogs to Thames.
> (II.271–72)

The lofty term *disemboguing* is dragged down from its heroic origins,[2] and instead of the shepherd-poet musing on images of nature, we now have Grub Street hacks frolicking in urban nastiness:

> Who flings most filth, and wide pollutes around
> The stream, be his the Weekly Journals bound.
> (279–80)

1. See John E. Sitter, *The Poetry of Pope's Dunciad* (Minneapolis: University of Minnesota Press, 1971), ch. 2.
2. Pope twice used this word in the *Odyssey.* See Max Byrd, *London Transformed: Images of the City in the Eighteenth Century* (New Haven: Yale University Press, 1978), pp. 54–55.

All is not lost, of course. At many points in the *Dunciad* Pope laughs at the impotence of the ephemeral city poets:

> Now night descending, the proud scene was o'er,
> But lived, in Settle's numbers, one day more.
> Now may'rs and shrieves all hushed and satiate lay,
> Yet eat, in dreams, the custard of the day;
> While pensive poets painful vigils keep,
> Sleepless themselves, to give their readers sleep.
>
> (I.89–94)

These writers are absurd weaklings, not Satanic monsters, and in themselves they are no threat to Pope. The burden of his lament is not that bad writing exists, but that bad wit is parasitical upon good and is rewarded by a culture that can no longer tell the difference. The *Dunciad* has rightly been called an exploration "not of meaninglessness but of the partial subversion of meaning."[3] Meaning was disturbingly rootless in this period, and Pope, just as much as the Grub Street writers, had to piece it together as best he could. Milton despised the godless culture of the Restoration, but it is inconceivable that Milton would have written a *Dunciad*.

"Earless on high, stood unabashed Defoe" (*Dunciad* II.147). Socially, politically, and culturally these two writers had virtually nothing in common. What would Pope have made of modern literary histories that give Defoe equal space with himself? Defoe's apparently artless narratives did mark one of the main paths into the future, and as Sitter has shown, so did a mode of private lyric whose maternal muse has curious affinities with Pope's goddess of Dulness.[4] If one thinks of the three major kinds into which literature was traditionally divided—narrative, dramatic, and lyric—then it has to be said that Pope (like Johnson after him) was hostile to the

3. Fredric V. Bogel, "Dulness Unbound: Rhetoric and Pope's *Dunciad*," *PMLA*, 97 (1982), 847. I am not convinced, however, by Bogel's claim that Dulness is the "anterior" chaos (p. 852) from which meaning and order arise.
4. John E. Sitter, "Mother, Memory, Muse and Poetry after Pope," *Journal of English Literary History*, 44 (1977), 312–36; and see also Sitter's *Literary Loneliness in Mid Eighteenth-Century England* (Ithaca: Cornell University Press, 1982).

direction all three were taking. But it should also be said that all three ran into deep trouble in the later eighteenth century, precisely because the relation between art and reality, with which Pope was so steadily preoccupied, continued to pose serious difficulties. The lyric in that period, as I have argued elsewhere, was compromised by fear of overt subjectivity.[5] The best plays were preoccupied with the duplicities of acting and unmasking. The greatest narratives were in what a librarian would call nonfiction: Hume's *History of England*, Gibbon's *Decline and Fall of the Roman Empire*, Johnson's *Lives of the Poets*, Boswell's *Life of Johnson*. The massiveness of these works deserves remark, reflecting a need to get it all in; details supply the life and justification of the narrative. These developments clearly flow from the problems that Pope faced, but he himself needed to retain more authorial control than such modes of writing would permit. Atossa, Sporus, and the rest are presented by the poet, not imagined in themselves. Fielding's *Tom Jones*, which asserts a classical ideal of the probable and glories in artifice, is the last Augustan narrative. But *Tom Jones* too is remote from Pope, for he is deeply resistant to narrativity, preferring dynamic stasis to development.

In thinking about Pope's cultural situation, the ideas of Mikhail Bakhtin are particularly suggestive. In *The Dialogic Imagination* Bakhtin distinguishes between the unitary language to which poems aspire, and the "heteroglossia" of mingled languages in the novel. Poetic language tends to seek "correctness" (perceived differently in different times and places) and is "ideologically saturated" in that it embodies a single ideology, rather than establishing tensions among disparate ideologies as the novel does.[6] In the terms of Bakhtin's theory, one can say that the novelistic impulse in the eighteenth century extends very widely, not only in the multiple

5. "Burns, Blake, and the Recovery of Lyric," *Studies in Romanticism*, 21 (1982), 637–60.
6. *The Dialogic Imagination: Four Essays*, ed. and tr. by Michael Holquist and Carol Emerson (Austin: University of Texas Press, 1981), pp. 270–71.

ideologies of epistolary novels like *Clarissa* and *Humphry Clinker*, but also in "factual" works that juxtapose competing versions of experience.[7]

Faced with a novelistic world, many eighteenth-century poets walled themselves off in a realm of poetic diction, whose status as poetry depended on its willed evasion of ordinary speech. Richard Rorty speaks of "poetic" moments as occurring at times when a culture ceases to converse in terms that are mutually agreed upon and begins to be conscious of neologisms or stylistic innovations that are explicitly contrasted with an older mode.[8] "Gray thought his language more poetical," Johnson said, "as it was more remote from common use."[9] In his youth, Pope certainly aspired to a style of high correctness, and poetic diction was certainly prominent:

> To thee, bright goddess, oft a lamb shall bleed,
> If teeming ewes increase my fleecy breed.
> *(Winter*, 81–82)

Similarly, Pope's Homer is not so much a translation into eighteenth-century speech as transubstantiation into an exalted "literary" language. But in his later poems it would be impossible to say that the high style suppresses the babel of contrary voices that rise from below. In Bakhtin's account of the ideal poetic style, "Each word must express the poet's *meaning* directly and without mediation; there must be no distance between the poet and his word. . . . Everything that enters the work must immerse itself in Lethe, and forget its previous life in any other contexts" (p. 297). In the novel, on the contrary, "all words have the 'taste' of a profession, a

---

7. Bakhtin's list of stylistic types in the novel applies precisely, for instance, to Boswell's *Life of Johnson:* direct narration by the author; stylized versions of ordinary oral narration and of semiliterary forms such as diaries and letters; extraliterary forms such as oratory, topographical descriptions, and memoranda; and finally, speeches by individual characters (*The Dialogic Imagination*, p. 262).

8. "Deconstruction and Circumvention," *Critical Inquiry*, 11 (1984), 4.

9. Samuel Johnson, *Life of Gray*, in *Lives of the English Poets*, ed. G. B. Hill (Oxford: Clarendon, 1905), III, 435.

genre, a tendency, a party, a particular work, a particular person, a generation, an age group, the day and hour" (p. 293). Heteroglossia comes to the fore in times of cultural breakup, when a standard language loses its stable support in religious, political, and ideological authority (pp. 370–71). Pope is a poet of just such an age, and unlike Gray he confronts the challenge instead of evading or escaping it: he imposes a poetic style upon a novelistic imagination, and tries to colonize the novelistic world with the authority of poetry.

As early as *The Rape of the Lock*, Pope uses comic dialogue to reproduce the slang, expletives, and inflections of particular types, "placing" his speakers with authorial irony much as Fielding or Dickens would place them.

> (Sir Plume, of amber snuff-box justly vain,
> And the nice conduct of a clouded cane)
> With earnest eyes, and round unthinking face,
> He first the snuff-box opened, then the case,
> And thus broke out— "My Lord, why, what the devil?
> Zounds! damn the lock! 'fore Gad, you must be civil!
> Plague on't! 'tis past a jest—nay prithee, pox!
> Give her the hair"—he spoke, and rapped his box.
>   (IV.123–30)

To this inept splutter, the Baron responds with a cool irony that both invokes the "high" mode and pokes fun at it:

> It grieves me much (replied the peer again)
> Who speaks so well should ever speak in vain.
> But by this lock, this sacred lock I swear,
> (Which never more shall join its parted hair,
> Which never more its honours shall renew,
> Clipt from the lovely head where late it grew).
>   (131–36)

Pope's later poems are filled with brilliant recreations of particular modes of speech, which (as Bakhtin says) can be embodied in narration as well as in direct dialogue.

> Sir Balaam now, he lives like other folks,
> He takes his chirping pint, and cracks his jokes:

"Live like yourself," was soon my lady's word;
And lo! two puddings smoked upon the board.
(To Bathurst, 357–60)

Papillia, wedded to her doting spark,
Sighs for the shades—"How charming is a park!"
A park is purchased, but the fair he sees
All bathed in tears—"Oh odious, odious trees!"
(To a Lady, 37–40)

"Lives like other folks," "cracks his jokes," and "live like yourself" are phrases from a bourgeois world that Pope satirizes by mimicking it; "doting spark," "charming," and "odious" are expressions from fashionable society.[10]

But it is not a trivial observation to say that in actual life Sir Plume and Sir Balaam's wife and Papillia would not speak in rhyme, let alone in the inexhaustibly supple rhythms of Pope's verse. Rhythm, indeed, according to Bakhtin, is precisely the means by which a poet gains control of his materials, destroying in embryo "those social worlds of speech and of persons that are potentially embedded in the word" (p. 298). And his conclusion from this observation reads like an analysis of Pope's satires: "We experience a profound and conscious tension through which the unitary poetic language of a work rises from the heteroglot and language-diverse chaos of the literary language contemporary to it" (p. 298). Ruskin's description of "sententious pentametre" exactly catches the way in which Pope, whom Arnold depreciated as a classic of prose, concentrates and adjusts prose into richer meaning:

> In this kind of verse, the structure and rhyme (if rhyme be admitted) are used merely to give precision and weight to a prose sentence, otherwise sifted, abstracted, and corrected into extremest possible value. Such verse professes always to be the result of the writer's utmost wisdom and utmost care;

10. When Mirabell mentions the child that may result from "our endeavours," Millamant retorts, "Odious endeavours!" and a little later exclaims, "I toast fellows, odious men! I hate your odious provisos" (William Congreve, *The Way of the World*, IV.i). Johnson makes a female correspondent refer to "this odious fashion" of card playing in *Rambler* 15.

it admits therefore of no careless or imperfect construction, but allows any intelligible degree of inversion; because it has been considered to the end, before a word is written, and the placing of the words may afterwards be adjusted according to their importance. Thus, "Sir Plume, of amber snuff-box justly vain," is not only more rhythmic, but more elegant and accurate than "Sir Plume, justly vain of his amber snuff-box": first, because the emphasis of rhyme is laid on his vanity, not his box; secondly, because the "his," seen on full consideration to be unnecessary, is omitted, to concentrate the sentence; and with a farther and more subtle reason . . . that a coxcomb cannot, properly speaking, *possess* anything, but is possessed by everything, so that in the next line Pope does not say, "And the nice conduct of *his* clouded cane," but of *a* clouded cane.[11]

Swift parodies his satiric victims with a kind of ventriloquizing, so that he himself disappears from view, the skillful counterfeiter of whom Kenner has written so provocatively.[12] Where is the real narrator of *A Tale of a Tub*? When does Gulliver speak for himself and when for Swift? How are Swift's positive religious views expressed in these works, which notoriously offended many contemporary readers? In the Rabelaisian tradition, Bakhtin says, "Truth is restored by reducing the lie to an absurdity, but truth itself does not seek words; she is afraid to entangle herself in the word, to soil herself in verbal pathos" (p. 309). Thus Swift can mimic the rattling colloquialisms of a servant in *The Humble Petition of Mrs. Frances Harris*, and minor poets can similarly catch the tone of casual speech in a wholly un-Popean way:

—"Oh, Madam, I must beg your pardon there,"
The General cried, "for—'twas in the year ten—
No, let me recollect, it was not then;
'Twas in the year eight, I think, for then we lay
Encamped with all the army, near Cambray—

11. John Ruskin, "The Pentametre," *Elements of English Prosody* (1880), in *The Literary Criticism of John Ruskin*, ed. Harold Bloom (New York: Doubleday, Anchor, 1965), p. 351.

12. Hugh Kenner, *The Counterfeiters: An Historical Comedy* (New York: Doubleday, Anchor, 1973).

> Yes, yes, I'm sure I'm right by one event,
> We supped together in Cadogan's tent."[13]

The unobtrusive rhymes are the poet's, but the words are the character's, in an altogether novelistic way. In Pope's poems, even when he adopts one or another "persona," we can always see behind the mask, and truth always seeks words. The words it seeks, in contrast to the slang and jargon of the debased "dunces," are inherited verities that are supposed to retain their immemorial cultural authority. Even while he brilliantly deploys the idioms of his culture, Pope strives to raise them to a level of civilized harmony, in the spirit of the modern saying "My language is the universal whore whom I have to make into a virgin."[14]

It hasn't been sufficiently noted that when the *Essay on Man* was published anonymously, contemporary readers failed to recognize it as Pope's. Anonymity was in part a defensive maneuver to forestall hostile criticism,[15] but it was also an assertion of universality: the poem was meant to speak for the ages as well as for Pope. But as Johnson comments sarcastically, "The reader feels his mind full, though he learns nothing; and when he meets it in its new array no longer knows the talk of his mother and his nurse."[16] It would be wrong to say that Pope has bungled his task; rather, he has attempted a task that is no longer possible. For as Bakhtin says,

> The authoritative word is located in a distanced zone, organically connected with a past that is felt to be hierarchically

---

13. Charles Hanbury Williams, *Isabella: Or, The Morning*, in *The New Oxford Book of Eighteenth Century Verse*, ed. Roger Lonsdale (Oxford: Oxford University Press, 1984), p. 330. In the *Gentleman's Magazine*, where the poem first appeared, it is said to be printed "from the MS. written many years ago," and has an epigraph adapted from Pope, "In serious talk th' instructive hours they passed" (*Gentleman's Magazine*, 35 [1765], 38; *Rape of the Lock* III.11).

14. Karl Kraus, quoted by W. H. Auden, *The Dyer's Hand and Other Essays* (New York: Vintage, 1968), p. 23.

15. Maynard Mack describes the embarrassment of Pope's enemies who were tricked into praising the *Essay on Man* before they knew who wrote it (*Alexander Pope: A Life* [New York: Norton, 1985], pp. 522–53).

16. *Lives*, III, 243.

higher. It is, so to speak, the word of the fathers. . . . It is a *prior* discourse. It is therefore not a question of choosing it from among other possible discourses that are its equal. . . . It can be profaned. It is akin to taboo, i.e., a name that must not be taken in vain.

(p. 342)

All of this is true of *Paradise Lost*, which is deeply aware of competing ideologies but makes a virtue of the tension that they create, defining tension indeed as the fruit of sin. The *Essay on Man* constantly tries to harness tension and to make it productive, not to say domestic, and represents a sustained effort to put the cultural lid back on.

Much of the interest in Pope's poems arises, however, from the irrepressibility of the languages and ideologies that refuse to stay suppressed, and the thin-skinned anxiety of Pope the man as opposed to the equanimity of Pope the oracle. To quote Bakhtin once more,

We can go so far as to say that in real life people talk most of all about what others talk about—they transmit, recall, weigh and pass judgment on other people's words, opinions, assertions, information; people are upset by others' words, or agree with them, contest them, refer to them and so forth. . . . One must also consider the psychological importance in our lives of what others say about us, and the importance, for us, of understanding and interpreting these words of others ("living hermeneutics").

(p. 338)

Pope's later poems are a medley of voices and modes, of attacks and counterattacks, immersed in a changing literary culture that reflects a changing world. He never stopped trying to control his rivals through language, embedding them like grubs in amber. But the obsessiveness with which he did so confirms the power of living hermeneutics, "what others say about us." As Johnson magisterially observes, Pope's pose of Olympian detachment was only a pose:

He pretends insensibility to censure and criticism, though it was observed by all who knew him that every pamphlet disturbed his quiet, and his extreme irritability laid him open to perpetual vexation. . . . He very frequently professes contempt of the world, and represents himself as looking on mankind, sometimes with gay indifference, as on emmets of a hillock below his serious attention; and sometimes with gloomy indignation, as on monsters more worthy of hatred than of pity. These were dispositions apparently counterfeited. . . . He passed through common life, sometimes vexed and sometimes pleased, with the natural emotions of common men.[17]

Pope's world of truth was empiricist, not Platonic, and try as he might, he could not compel language to reassume the authority it possessed during the Renaissance. Apart from the brief episode of high Romanticism, indeed, it has never succeeded in doing so again. Sidney said that nature gives us a brazen world and poetry a golden; in the eighteenth century it becomes obvious that poetry henceforth will be brazen too.

At the outset of his career Pope adapted Addison's prose description of St. Peter's (*TE* I, 268n) as a model for poetic achievement:

> Thus when we view some well-proportioned dome,
> (The world's just wonder, and ev'n thine O Rome!)
> No single parts unequally surprise;
> All comes united to th' admiring eyes;
> No monstrous height, or breadth, or length appear;
> The whole at once is bold, and regular.
> (*Essay on Criticism* 247–52)

Pope's later poems reluctantly abandon this dream of perfect integration, or rather they confine it to the local perfection of the couplet. Single parts often surprise, the *Dunciad* grows to monstrous length, and if "the whole" appears bold it seldom seems regular.

There is an emblematic appropriateness in the "Gothic" analogy as used by Pope and later by Wordsworth. Pope ends his preface to *The Works of Shakespeare* with praise that is not so much ambiguous as perplexed:

> I will conclude by saying of Shakespeare, that with all his faults and with all the irregularity of his drama, one may look

17. Ibid., 209–10.

upon his works, in comparison of those that are more finished and regular, as upon an ancient majestic piece of Gothic architecture, compared with a neat modern building. The latter is more elegant and glaring, but the former is more strong and more solemn. It must be allowed that in one of these there are materials enough to make many of the other. It has much the greater variety and much the nobler apartments, though we are often conducted to them by dark, odd, and uncouth passages. Nor does the whole fail to strike us with greater reverence, though many of the parts are childish, ill-placed, and unequal to its grandeur.[18]

Puzzlement at Shakespeare's "irregular" greatness was of course usual throughout the century, but it is interesting to see the Gothic analogy start to turn positive, remembering that "Goth" still had the pejorative connotations that "Vandal" does today:

A second deluge learning thus o'er-run,
And the monks finished what the Goths begun.
(*Essay on Criticism* 691–92)

The Augustan ideal of luminous simplicity is breaking down, and Gothic strength begins to seem superior to Greek (or Georgian) elegance even if it entails darkness, oddness, and inequality.

Wordsworth too uses the Gothic analogy. *The Excursion*, he says, should be seen as subordinate to a larger whole:

The two works have the same kind of relation to each other, if [the author] may so express himself, as the ante-chapel has to the body of a gothic church. Continuing this allusion, he may be permitted to add, that his minor pieces, which have been long before the public, when they shall be properly arranged, will be found by the attentive reader to have such connection with the main work as may give them claim to be likened to the little cells, oratories, and sepulchral recesses, ordinarily included in those edifices.[19]

18. *Literary Criticism of Alexander Pope*, ed. Bertrand A. Goldgar (Lincoln: University of Nebraska Press, 1965), p. 175.

19. William Wordsworth, Preface to *The Excursion* (1814), in *Wordsworth, Selected Poems and Prefaces*, ed. Jack Stillinger (Boston: Houghton Mifflin, 1965), pp. 469–70.

Smallness and incompleteness are no longer drawbacks, as Pope had believed them to be. Fragments can have their own kind of adequacy. Yet Wordsworth too longed for a larger structure to which the fragments might be subordinated; but like Pope's *Opus Magnum*, the mighty Wordsworthian cathedral was never completed. Looking into an uncongenial future, Pope sought to accept his deposition with Horatian equanimity.

> Learn to live well, or fairly make your will;
> You've played, and loved, and ate, and drank your fill:
> Walk sober off, before a sprightlier age
> Comes titt'ring on, and shoves you from the stage.
> (*Epistle* II.ii.322–25)

If in nothing else, Pope is at one with pedantic Bentley in his unsuitability to the frivolous world of the future:

> In flowed at once a gay embroidered race,
> And titt'ring pushed the pedants off the place.
> (*Dunciad* IV.275–76)

But this vision turned out to be wrong. The future was more solemn than tittering, and a decade after Pope's death Warton, one of the lyric poets of the next generation, was regretting the absence of *poésie pure* in Pope's poems:

> We do not, it should seem, sufficiently attend to the difference there is betwixt a MAN OF WIT, a MAN OF SENSE, and a TRUE POET. Donne and Swift were undoubtedly men of wit and men of sense: but what traces have they left of PURE POETRY?[20]

Warton dismisses the "Alps on Alps" analogy in the *Essay on Criticism*, which Johnson was to find so exact,[21] as "too general and indistinct" and prefers a prose passage of rapturous sublimity from Shaftesbury (p. 142). "Poetry" begins to mean a heightened mode of language that purports to embody a

20. Joseph Warton, *An Essay on the Writings and Genius of Pope* (1756), I, iv.
21. See p. 253 above.

heightened mode of experience. One realizes how much "Alps on Alps" is a metaphor of limitation, and how much deeper Warton's dislike runs than an objection to "indistinct" description. Whereas a Romantic poet would rejoice that there are always higher peaks to aspire to—Wordsworth suffers a kind of despair in the *Prelude* when crossing the Alps proves anticlimactic—Pope expresses weariness at a journey that never ends.

By the 1750s Edward Young, formerly the author of pallid *Characteristical Satires*, was proclaiming the new poetic ideal in terms that would have astounded Pope: "In the fairyland of fancy, genius may wander wild; there it has a creative power, and may reign arbitrarily over its own empire of chimeras." [22] Fancy, whose ambiguous relation to reality had so preoccupied Pope and his contemporaries, is now hailed as absolute master of its own creations, though perhaps of nothing else. Young's formulation is well on the way to Romantic notions of the poem as imaginary heterocosm and as revelation of its author's soul. Expressivism replaces mimesis as the basis of composition, and unconscious sources of imagery are suddenly of interest:

> Few authors of distinction but have experienced something of this nature at the first beamings of their yet unsuspected genius on their hitherto dark composition: the writer starts at it as at a lucid meteor in the night; is much surprised; can scarce believe it true. During his happy confusion it may be said to him, as to Eve at the lake,
>
> > What there thou seest, fair creature, is thyself.
> >
> > (p. 288)

Pope's goal was a public self and a public poetry, expressed in Horatian verse bordering closely on prose; he would have found Young's allusion to Eve's narcissism all too apt.

Pope's career is a sustained acceptance of limits, which produces results very different from the post-Romantic crisis

---

22. *Conjectures on Original Composition* (1759), in *English Critical Essays*, ed. Edmund D. Jones, World's Classics (London: Oxford University Press, 1947), p. 283.

poem with its fear of losing one's visionary imagination. (Collins's *Poetical Character*, which seemed a very minor poem to his friend Johnson, becomes a seminal poem in the system of Harold Bloom.) Stooping to truth means accepting mundane subjects, diminished though they may be, and thereby achieving something of permanent value:

> Truth guards the poet, sanctifies the line,
> And makes immortal, verse as mean as mine.
>   (*Epilogue* II.246–47)

To compare Pope with the Romantics is to realize that if their aspirations were more exalted than his, their failures were more crushing. Pope left the Renaissance behind and knew he was doing so; it is really Romanticism, with its passionate longing for adequate symbols, that represents the last nostalgic echo of the Renaissance. But the Romantic project was fatally compromised by the simultaneous recognition that all "truth" is imprisoned in consciousness, a function of one's private world of imagination.

Platonic images of living unity are so pervasive in Western culture that one can quote phrases from the *Essay on Man* that sound exactly like Wordsworth: "blossoms in the trees . . . lives through all life . . . one nature . . . one common blessing" (I.272–73, III.117, IV.62). The crucial difference between the two poets is that Wordsworth has to ground his vision in subjective experience.

> From Nature overflowing in my soul,
> I had received so much, that all my thoughts
> Were steeped in feeling. . . . [23]

Pope speaks of "our soul" (I.275), not "my soul." His aim is to utter universal truths, not to trace them up from his own inner life, and with his balanced parallelisms he stresses the correspondence of parts as well as the whole which they comprise:

23. William Wordsworth, *The Prelude* (1850 version), II.397–99.

> All are but parts of one stupendous whole,
> Whose body nature is, and God the soul;
> That, changed through all, and yet in all the same,
> Great in the earth, as in th' aethereal frame,
> Warms in the sun, refreshes in the breeze,
> Glows in the stars, and blossoms in the trees . . .
>
> (I. 267–72)

The difference lies in the greater ontological security that Pope enjoys. He grounds his Platonic vision in a received religion, deistically diluted though it may be, for which God is the soul of the universal body:

> Heav'n breathes through ev'ry member of the whole
> One common blessing, as one common soul.
>
> (IV.61–62)

Since religious truth lies deeper than any metaphor, the poet can celebrate God in all things without fearing that he has deified the created world. Wordsworth, on the other hand, is constantly haunted by the threat of irreligious pantheism. In the 1805 *Prelude* he wrote, "I saw one life, and felt that it was joy" (II.430). In a late revision this line disappeared and was replaced by orthodox pieties about "the Uncreated," whom all created things must adore (1850 *Prelude*, II.413). Pope knows that one life flows through all things, and is free to feel it ("refreshes in the breeze"); Wordsworth feels that one life flows through all things, but fears that he does not know it.

Northrop Frye has remarked that the Bible has become fabulous just as, in early Christian times, the classical myths became fabulous.[24] Wordsworth's hope is that fiction can be rescued from fictionality by being psychologized:

> Paradise, and groves
> Elysian, Fortunate Fields—like those of old
> Sought in the Atlantic Main—why should they be

24. *The Secular Scripture: A Study of the Structure of Romance* (Cambridge, Mass.: Harvard University Press, 1976), p. 14.

A history only of departed things,
Or a mere fiction of what never was?[25]

But the Romantic solution turned out to be a very temporary one, whether one admires it as natural supernaturalism or dismisses it as split religion. The second half of the eighteenth century might best be seen not as a prologue to Wordsworth and Blake, but rather as an anticipation of our own time. Its history of departed things was founded on observation and investigation rather than on doctrine and myth. And its most memorable achievement—to invert Wordsworth's formulation—was an imaginative nonfiction of what really was.

Pope's poems are full of telling, and increasingly he tries to make us believe that they are inseparable from life as experienced, translated into rhetoric and form but not otherwise changed. "Unlike writing, life never finishes," Lowell wrote,[26] meaning perhaps that poems can have definitive endings whereas life stops but does not finish. But as Pope's veering and ever-surprising career reminds us, writing never finishes either, and Lowell's own career was much more like Pope's than like Spenser's or Milton's or even Yeats's. In his honesty and receptiveness to the events of his time, we can surely admire Pope, particularly now that idealizing modes of eighteenth-century scholarship are falling out of fashion. His critique of militarist rhetoric depends not only on a sense of the folly of Marlborough's wars, but also on an expectation that his readers will confirm his attitude from their own experience. The converse ought to hold when, in his late Patriot phase, Pope allowed himself to abuse Walpole for pacifism:

Lo! at the wheels of her triumphal car,
Old England's genius, rough with many a scar,
Dragged in the dust! his arms hang idly round,
His flag inverted trails along the ground!
(*Epilogue* I.151–54)

25. William Wordsworth, *Prospectus to "The Recluse,"* 47–51.

26. Robert Lowell, *History*, in Lowell, *Selected Poems* (New York: Farrar, Straus and Giroux, 1977), p. 159.

Keener's comment is admirable, in both its severity and its generosity: "Pope was bidding beyond his means, and we have bought whatever sensitivity we have on the subject at too dear a price ourselves."[27]

If much in Pope seems to anticipate our own moment, cultural experience is always historically specific, and it is well to end by recognizing that his preoccupying themes were rooted in an age that was rapidly coming to an end. In his celebrated *Speech for Conciliation* of 1775, Edmund Burke reviewed the economic importance of America and then ascended a historical pinnacle to survey its deeper significance. Searching for a contemporary figure whose life might link the old Britain to the new, Burke singled out Pope's friend Bathurst. His celebratory rhetoric needs to be heard in its full amplitude:

> We stand where we have an immense view of what is, and what is past. Clouds indeed, and darkness, rest upon the future. Let us, however, before we descend from this noble eminence, reflect that this growth of our national prosperity has happened within the short period of the life of man. It has happened within sixty-eight years. There are those alive whose memory might touch the two extremities. For instance, my Lord Bathurst might remember all the stages of the progress. He was in 1704 of an age at least to be made to comprehend such things. . . . Suppose, Sir, that the angel of this auspicious youth . . . should point out to him a little speck, scarce visible in the mass of the national interest, a small seminal principle rather than a formed body, and should tell him,— "Young man, there is America—which at this day serves for little more than to amuse you with stories of savage men, and uncouth manners; yet shall, before you taste of death, show itself equal to the whole of that commerce which now attracts the envy of the world. Whatever England has been growing to by a progressive increase of improvement, brought in by varieties of people, by succession of civilizing conquests and civilizing settlements in a series of seventeen hundred years,

---

27. Frederick M. Keener, *An Essay on Pope* (New York: Columbia University Press, 1974), p. 155. Keener quotes Burke in the *Letters on a Regicide Peace:* "For the war Pope sang his dying notes."